Disordered Thinking
and Communication
in Children

Disordered Thinking and Communication in Children

Mahin Hassibi

New York Medical College
New York, New York

and

Harry Breuer, Jr.

New York University Medical School
New York, New York

Plenum Press · New York and London

Library of Congress Cataloging in Publication Data

Hassibi, Mahin.
  Disordered thinking and communication in children.

  Includes index.
  1. Cognition disorders in children. 2. Communicative disorders in children.
I. Breuer, Harry Jr., joint author. II. Title.
RJ506.C63H37   618.92'89   80-22086
ISBN 0-306-40490-7

© 1980 Plenum Press, New York
A Division of Plenum Publishing Corporation
227 West 17th Street, New York, N.Y. 10011

Printed in the United States of America

Contents

Chapter 1
Introduction: Disease, Disability, and Psychodiagnostic
Concepts in Childhood   1

Chapter 2
Childhood Psychosis: A Historical Review   7

Chapter 3
Specific Language Dysfunctioning in Children:
A Historical Overview   28

Chapter 4
Deviant and Normal Social Development   59

Chapter 5
Normal Social Development   76

Chapter 6
Psycholinguistic Development: Functioning
and Dysfunctioning   86

Chapter 7
Disordered Thinking   118

Chapter 8
Diagnosis and Evaluation of Disordered Thought
and Language   137

Chapter 9
The Psychological Testing of Dysphasic
and Psychotic Children   163

Epilogue   189

References and Bibliography   195

Index   205

1

Introduction: Disease, Disability, and Psychodiagnostic Concepts in Childhood

Webster's Dictionary defines disease as "an aberration of a living body that impairs its function." By this definition, the concept of disease is easily applicable to physical illnesses where the optimal functioning of an organ or a system is known, and direct links can be traced between a damaged or pathological organ and various symptomatic manifestations of its deviant functioning. Thus, one can speak with relatively high levels of assurance about physical disease-entities, their distinguishing characteristics and, in most instances, their defined etiologies. When one enters the realm of aberrant psychological states and behaviors, however, the disease-concept is applied problematically at best. Behavioral abnormalities and psychiatric conditions do not have simple linear relationships with the brain and its malfunctioning. Furthermore, even though the state of physical well-being is almost universally recognizable, behavioral or psychological normalcy is a value-laden concept, varying broadly in its application from community to community and subject to changes in interpretation in different times. Psychological disorders are more aptly defined and better understood when they are conceptualized as disabilities rather than diseases. By disability, we mean failure to perform as expected in a psychological task or function that is considered essential at a given point in life by a particular cultural community.

Since the human organism is not a finished product at birth, it requires both continuing organic maturation and accumulating social experience for the attainment of the psychological functions expected in its cultural milieu. Thus, for behavior to be ascertained as deficient or deviant, it must be evaluated within the developmental dimension in terms of maturational and environmental norms. On the maturational side, the order of events is fairly clearly established, and while there are normal fluctuations in chronology, behaviors related predominantly to central nervous system development can be quite reliably assessed according to existing norms. Taking into account the lags and spurts that normally vary from child to child, one can judge fairly certainly whether specific perceptual-motor behaviors deviate from the usual range of variance at different ages. On the environmental side, matters are not nearly as clear. What a child *should* be doing at any given point is determined not only by what is expected in his community, but also according to the nature, quality and quantity of the environmental experiences to which he has been exposed. These two factors—expectation and input—do not necessarily coincide. Even when one broadly applies the somewhat ambiguous concept of the "average expectable environment," all of the elements necessary for growth in each instance may not be present, or their combinations and sequential orderings may not be so arranged that each child receives the kinds of experiences suited to his or her needs at the most opportune moments. Moreover, children differ, both developmentally and individually, in their interpretations of what is demanded and given by their environments. In short, expectations vary, experiential input varies, and individual needs vary, and not always congruently. While the great majority of children manage to acquire the skills necessary for expected functioning, not all receive what they require for *optimal* functioning. These distinctions are particularly crucial for children who are developmentally disabled.

It is within the social context that essential and optimal performances for every individual at every point in his or her life are defined, and successes are rewarded or failures are punished, tolerated, or rectified. The negative consequences of failure for disabled children range from the extreme of virtual abandonment to more subtle social isolation and stigmatization. The resultant distortions in interactional patterns and truncation of corrective opportunities, in turn, place further obstacles in the way of development. Therefore, the source of ongoing difficulty for a disabled child is to be looked for in the interaction between the social environment and the psychoneurological state of the child.

There has been a lingering tendency in the theory and clinical conceptualization of developmental psychopathology to dichotomize deviant behaviors according to presumed organic or environmental etiologies. Because of this conceptual dichotomy, the focus of clinical evaluation typically has been upon the child's anomalies on the one hand, and the environment's expectations and reactions on the other, and rarely upon the reciprocal interrelationships between them. Studies of developmental disabilities have traditionally begun with the assessment of the disabled individual's deficient or deviant behavior in relation to broad statistical and clinical norms of functioning on tasks dictated by standardized test construction and clinical interview techniques. Assessment of the individual's social milieu, its imperatives, and the way in which the child's failure to meet them affects the learning experiences presented to him and vice versa, have received relatively little attention. Any meaningful discussion of developmental psychology and delineation of factors involved in developmental psychopathology necessitates in-depth understanding of the multidimensional character of individual children's assets and deficiencies, and of the interlocking aspects of their psychoneurological and social behaviors, in reciprocity with immediate environmental forces.

The ambiguity of diagnostic norms and the need for an interactive and individualized approach to assessment is exemplified in the area of disorders of language and thought in children. Although cognition, language, and social responsiveness are inextricably intertwined in the normal course of development, the deleterious consequences of lags and anomalies in any one of these areas upon the others has been given little more than passing notice in the literature. This state of affairs has resulted in a profusion of diagnostic concepts and labels, more often than not overlapping or unclear in their criteria and providing little valid basis for studies of etiology and prognosis. Furthermore, because the distinction between what is essential task performance and what is the optimal level of functioning in every area is frequently not made, erroneous conclusions are drawn from clinical examination, and diagnostic labels are misapplied. For these reasons, in addition to the varying conceptual orientations, and personalities and competencies among clinicians, an abysmal lack of reliability exists in childhood psychodiagnosis, and intervention is often poorly or erroneously planned.

Historically, the evolution of psychodiagnostic concepts about deviant children has proceeded from the global to the increasingly differentiated. Before childhood was regarded as a unique period of life, with its own special hazards and potentials, the behavioral deviations of children, their causes and their implications for later functioning, remained unexplored. When children did not learn what they were taught, they were assumed to be forever intellectual idiots. When they misbehaved in spite of immediate punishment or promises of dire consequences, they were considered moral idiots. Behavioral concepts changed with changing social demands and philosophical notions, but generally, children were presumed to be either linear heirs to their parents' proclivities or open receptacles for possession by sinister or benign influences. After the serious study of dementia became widespread, investigators began turning to the idea that such disorder can exist prematurely in children (Maudsely, 1867; De Sanctis, 1906). In the late nineteenth and early twentieth centuries there was increasing notice that some children who were classified as total imbeciles, actually suffered from circumscribed anomalies of spoken language (Worster-Drought and Allen, 1930), and when seemingly bright pupils did not learn to read, the status and development of particular central-nervous-system functions came into question (Orton, 1937).

Over the past three or four decades, as more refined observation and careful recording of behavior have revealed the inadequacies of earlier global categorizations, it has become increasingly evident that psychological development represents a synergistic phenomenon, in which each element and progression affects, and is affected simultaneously by others, in the overall system. The functioning of a child at any point must be viewed in terms of the sum total of all interacting factors and movements up to that time, and each area of functioning must be studied in its reciprocal relationships with other relevant areas. Whether one holds that the predominant impetus for development comes from the maturation of inborn potentials or from the accumulation of environmental conditioning and instruction, truly meaningful study and clinical evaluation occurs only when the growing organism is seen in the totality of its internal and external givens.

It is against this background that we have undertaken to review the ambiguities and contradictions in psychodiagnostic thinking regarding deviations in children's communicative behavior and thought. With the awareness that we would only add to the explicit and implicit disagreement already existing in the field should we attempt to redefine current diagnostic classifications, we have elected to focus on the multidimensional and interactive nature of the anomalies involved in two major and frequently confusing areas of childhood communicative difficulties—psychosis and central language dysfunctioning. Our purpose is diagnostic, in the sense that we are seeking to distinguish between those situations in which the primary difficulty is with the content of a child's communication and those in which the form of communication is primarily defective. Our direction, however, is neither categorical nor etiological, but rather functionally analytical. What we hope to do is impart a sense of the intricate difficulties involved in making such distinctions, and of the need for stringent delineation of all the facets involved in every individual case.

In order to define categories of behavior as generally deviant in one way or another, one must assume a broad range of equivalencies in the conceptualization and communication of children at different ages, across cultural and familial, as well as individual lines. Once one makes such an assumption, it is a relatively easy matter to match any child's behavioral repertoire to one's notion of categorical criteria, and so apply a diagnostic label. However, the issue of what to call a particular patient, which seems to dominate so many clinical case conferences, does not necessarily coincide with the question of what is wrong with him or her. The former usually entails fitting the observed behaviors to the diagnostic concept and relying upon the concept to explain the behavior. The latter requires a painstaking process of delineating primary and secondary reasons in the child's functioning itself, for behaviors that are multiple and interactively determined.

In the areas of language and thought, the ambiguities of diagnosis are frequently great. On the surface, deviant behaviors that are incongruous within their contexts are most apt to be taken as indicative of disordered or bizarre conceptualization. Yet, in many instances, they may be primarily the result of linguistic disability. Unless adequate linguistic comprehension is established, one cannot be sure that the form of instructions, demands, and explanations given to the child have been perceived and assimilated accurately, and as long as he does not or cannot express himself verbally, his behavioral intentions and justifications remain largely uncertain or unknown to others. Further, because of the central role played by language in the organization of thinking, defective linguistic form may be accompanied by varying degrees of difficulty with conceptualization. On the other hand, when thinking *per se* is disordered, the meaning of linguistic communications to and from the child may be distorted. Whether transactions with the environment are aberrant by reason of extreme peculiarities in the conceptualization of reality or of defects in the processing of verbal communication, the resulting behavioral incongruities are more than occasionally similar.

Precise identification of the primary and secondary anomalies in a child's communicative disability is, of course, vital to appropriate planning and treatment. Of equal import is the fact that misidentification can and frequently does have ruinous social effects. Psychiatric diagnoses are not value-free designations. Beyond the behavioral criteria that they connote, they carry significant social consequences for the individual to whom they are authoritatively applied. In the case of children, such designations determine the sort of living experiences that will be made available to them or placed beyond their reach. In order to avoid the self-fulfilling prophesies that can follow upon misdiagnosis, clinical impressions must be studied in depth. Since there are no nonbehavioral parameters by which to verify the primary causes of developmental communicative disabilities, the burden of proof commonly falls upon subtle and not always readily determined differences in individual clinical pictures.

2

Childhood Psychosis: A Historical Review

The official glossary of the American Psychiatric Association defines psychosis as "a major mental disorder of organic or emotional origin in which the individual's ability to think, respond emotionally, remember, communicate, interpret reality and behave appropriately is sufficiently impaired so as to interfere grossly with his capacity to meet the ordinary demands of life." According to this definition, the severity and pervasiveness of the impairment are the two key features of the clinical diagnosis. However, it must be noted that in order to designate any function as deviant or impaired the range and fluctuation of its normal operation must be clearly defined. Also, "the ordinary demands of life," against which the individual's shortcomings are to be judged, need to have identifiable criteria. The official classificatory scheme is silent on both of these accounts. Diagnosticians differ in their assessment of the degree of impairment due to their sociocultural expectations of the normative behavior, professional training, philosophical bent or their personal life history.

The identification of abnormal behavior in a child is further complicated by the fact that normative behavior must be defined in terms not only of age and developmental stage, but also of the inevitable influence of particular norms and expectations established for the child within his family. Lorna Wing (1978) has tried to address the question of age and development by stating "a psychotic child is one whose behavior is in all or most areas continuously strange and unpredictable for his mental age." In this definition, pervasiveness is stressed along with the requirement that the particular behavioral anomaly be of more than transient nature. How-

7

ever, the two key adjectives, "strange" and "unpredictable," remain vague. Furthermore, even if one somewhat optimistically assumes that the "age" of a child's mentality can be ascertained by quantifying intellectual performance on a given psychological test, the normal, predictable behavior of a child of a certain mental age is by no means better defined than "the capacity to meet the ordinary demands of life."

Such lack of clarity in definition is only one among the many problems which confront a reviewer attempting to summarize and interpret the vast psychiatric literature related to psychosis in children and adults. Descriptions of behavioral manifestations are not always separable from the interpreted meanings that the observers and reporters have assigned to them. The effects of the observer on the observed behavior have received scanty attention from psychiatrists. Helzer *et al.* (1977) question the validity of the free form psychiatric interview as an instrument by which psychiatric diagnosis is made. Weitzel *et al.* (1973) point out the need for operational definition of symptoms before their significance and implication can be ascertained for the individual's psychological state or functional adequacy. The authors believe that "the specialty of psychiatry has developed neither a basic language, nor common definitions related to patient evaluation which are accepted across various schools and regions of the country." Earlier researchers had reported difficulties in achieving diagnostic agreement among psychiatrists due to differences in interviewing techniques, weighing of symptoms, interpretation of the same symptoms, and finally the unclear diagnostic criteria. Vagueness of diagnostic criteria was found to be responsible for 25% of diagnostic disagreement among psychiatrists regarding presence or absence of psychosis (Ward *et al.*, 1962).

These unresolved issues have far reaching implications for psychiatry and psychology as investigative and clinical disciplines as well as for the health and social policies based on the observations and explanatory theories that emerge from them. Research findings (whether social, epidemiological, or biochemical) are dependable only to the degree that basic questions are clearly formulated and the results of one study can be compared with other studies on the same subject. The questions take on added significance when applied to behavioral deviations of childhood. Educational policies and decisions regarding health-care resources are influenced by the manner in which a child's behavior is viewed and by the number of children who are variously labeled. Furthermore, the consequences of categorization and labeling by experts can be of lifelong significance to the affected individuals.

In the following discussion, the evolution of the concept of childhood psychosis, more specifically, childhood schizophrenia, is reviewed as it is reflected in psychiatric literature.

The earliest attempts at definition and classification by psychiatrists working with children were focused on the identification of similarities between the patterns of behavioral abnormalities of adults and those displayed by young patients. Kraeplin (1918) expressed the opinion that *dementia praecox* is a disease of the second decade of life, even though some patients had been considered deviant during their childhood. De Sanctis (1906/1973) reported some childhood cases of what he called *dementia praecocissma*, asserting that differences in symptomatology with *dementia praecox* can be accounted for by the young age of the patients.

In 1911, Bleuler published his monograph entitled, *Dementia Praecox or the Group of Schizophrenias*. Although the book was not translated into English until 1950, the formulations set forth by him became, and have remained, the foundation of psychiatric thinking about a class of deviant behaviors in adult life. Furthermore, with some refinements, alterations and minor twists, the Bleulerian concepts have been applied to certain types of behavioral anomalies in childhood. Bleuler defined schizophrenia as a group of psychoses whose course is at times chronic, at times marked by intermittent attacks. It can stop or retrograde at any stage but does not permit a full *restuto ad integrum*. Throughout his long monograph, he repeatedly restated his initial assertion that schizophrenia is a lifelong infirmity which may cease in its course but is nevertheless incurable—even though no symptoms may be exhibited by the patient during clinical examination. This notion of schizophrenia without the classical symptoms of the disease has fostered the more recent concept of a *schizophrenia spectrum*, utilized in theoretical accounts of the genetic etiology of schizophrenia (Kety *et al.*, 1968).

Another of Bleuler's important legacies to psychiatry is his description of the illness. In his thinking, "the fundamental symptoms consist of disturbances of association and affectivity, the predilection for fantasy against reality, and the inclination to divorce oneself from reality (autism)." "Fundamental symptoms" refers to those symptoms whose presence are necessary and sufficient for the diagnosis. Later, however, while discussing the significance of individual symptoms, one symptom is singled out as the most crucial one: "definite schizophrenic disturbances of association alone are sufficient for diagnosis." Interestingly, Bleuler insisted that such symptoms as "primary disturbances of perception, orientation and memory" are incompatible with the diagnosis of schizophrenia.

The profound influence of Bleuler's thinking on psychiatrists, at least in English-speaking countries, is attested to by the fact that not only the term *schizophrenia* came to be universally accepted, but also Bleuler's description of the symptomatology of the disease became the guiding principle in diagnosis. Potter (1933) delivered a paper at the 88th Annual Meeting of The American Psychiatric Association in which six cases of schizophrenia in children under 12 years of age were discussed. The criteria for "typical schizophrenia in children" were reported as:

> General withdrawal of interest from the environment.
> Dereistic thinking, feeling and behavior.
> Disturbances of thought, such as incoherence of speech, blocking, symbolization, perseveration and at times total mutism.
> Deficiency of emotional rapport.
> Distortion and deviation of affect.
> Increase or decrease of motor activities, bizarre and stereotyped movements and mannerisms. (p. 1264)

Although Potter's criteria are similar to those Bleuler reported for adults, a cautionary note is added by Potter. "Children are essentially beings of feeling and behavior. Consequently their psychopathology may be expected to be expressed largely through distorted affective responses and altered behavior reactions." Thus the most fundamental of Bleuler's symptoms, namely, disturbance of thinking, is replaced by "distorted affective responses and altered behavior reactions." However, neither symptom nor class of symptoms is operationally defined. Potter also asserted that the disorder is a malignant lifelong process and refractory to all the known treatment methods of the time.

The relative rarity of the condition in childhood as opposed to its higher incidence in adulthood was explained by Potter as due to "superficial resemblance to certain so-called unstable mental defectives" and the possibility that a great number of young schizophrenics may have been misdiagnosed and classified as mental defectives and housed in institutions for retardates. Even before this tentative hypothesis could be tested, the question of differentiation between retarded children and children with schizophrenia, or deficient cognition and "distorted affectivity," acquired crucial importance.

A report concerning a larger group of children appeared in the literature in 1938 by Despert who attributed the behavioral abnormalities of her 29 child patients to "a disease process in which the loss of affective contact with reality is coincident with or determined by the appearance of autistic thinking and accompanied by specific phenomena of regression and dissociation." Neither regression nor dissociation were operationally defined, although both concepts seem to have been taken from psychoanalytic theory and thus were more interpretive than descriptive. Furthermore, Despert reported that in 19 of the 29 families observed, mothers were "aggressive, oversolicitous" while fathers "play a very subdued role." Although the author did not attempt to relate this interactional pattern of the family to the disorder identified in children, the role of family in precipitating, causing, or affecting the particular symptomatology became the subject of much speculation in subsequent literature.

The book by Bradley in 1941 entitled *Schizophrenia in Childhood* was a summation of earlier literature on the subject and contained a list of criteria on which most child psychiatrists had based their diagnoses of the condition. According to Bradley, diminished interest in the environment, defined as "an active tendency toward seclusiveness," is the most essential symptom of schizophrenia in children. Other symptoms include: (a) Emotional disturbance, appearing as "coldness" and blunting of affect in some and as negativism, irritability, and anxiety in others; and (b) disorders of motor behavior, perception, and the vegetative system, which are mentioned by some authors and ignored by others. On the issue of disturbances in thinking, the author states: "due to uncertain status of investigating children's mental content by introspective means, discussions of schizophrenic thinking during childhood are more speculative than is the case regarding other symptoms of the disorder." Bradley does not attempt to reconcile the differences of opinion among the experts but sets forth his own criteria for diagnosis as follows:

- The child must be psychotic.
- The mental disorder must follow a period of normal development.
- Evidence of regression or deterioration of functions.
- Severe disturbance in social contact.
- A variety of symptoms resembling adult schizophrenia.
- Characteristic performance on psychological testing.

Because for Bradley the disturbance of social contact occupies a central position in schizophrenia of childhood, a variety of other symptoms and clinical phenomena are said to stem from this with-drawal. Another interesting point in Bradley's discussion is his emphasis upon "hereditary taint" which to him is more significant than the interactional pattern within the family. Obviously dissatis-fied with the state of knowledge reflected in the literature, Bradley states: "The concepts of dementia praecox and schizophrenia origi-nally resulted from the study of adult patients. They may eventually prove to be concepts unsuited to children."

Two years after the publication of Bradley's book, Leo Kanner published his first paper on what came to be called early infantile autism. According to Kanner's (1943) observation among the eleven children who were the subjects of his report, "the inability to relate themselves in the ordinary way to people and situation" was pre-sent from the beginning of life. The children were all psychotic and manifested peculiarities in their behavior, language, and emotional responsiveness. They were remarkably free of signs of physical and neurological damage, appeared intelligent, and showed special abilities in certain areas of cognitive functioning, such as memory for details and deftness in manipulation of objects. Although there was little evidence of mental illness in the family and thus "hereditary taint" could not be proved, another peculiarity was noted in that the parents were predominantly educated, ambitious, and emotionally aloof. Kanner believed that the children represented examples of "inborn autistic disturbances of affective contact," constituting a distinct diagnostic category which may or may not belong to schizo-phrenia in childhood. For some child psychiatrists, the symptoms reported by Kanner were not enough to warrant a new name. Others, particularly in Europe, felt that differentiating early infantile autism from mental retardation was not a simple task.

In quest of a unitary conceptual framework, within which the varied symptomatologies presented by diverse authors could be explained, Bender (1942) formulated a new definition. According to her, schizophrenia in childhood "reveals pathology in every area of integration or patterning within the functioning of the central ner-vous system, be it vegetative, motor, perceptual, intellectual, emo-tional or social." This new formulation, while stressing the perva-siveness of impairment beyond Bleuler's concept, leaves out the dimension of severity altogether. The distinction between funda-mental, or sufficient and accessary symptoms, and secondary man-ifestation is obliterated. No single symptom is weighed more than others in making or ruling out the diagnosis. Another subtle, but significant, change occurs in Bender's conceptualization of the problem—instead of *schizophrenia in childhood*, a new conceptual entity called *childhood schizophrenia* became the subject of her investigation. The first consequence of this loosening of criteria and establishment of a new entity, not necessarily characterized by adultlike symptoms, was the rapidity with which the disorder, considered rare up to this point, became relatively easy to find. Bender, who in 1942 had conceded the rarity of the disease, five years later gave a report on one hundred cases of childhood schizophrenia (Bender, 1947).

Mahler, Ross, and DeFries (1949) made an effort at synthesizing the psychoanalytic theory and Bleulerian phenomenology into a system applicable to childhood psychosis. In a report on sixteen "benign and malignant cases of childhood psychosis," the authors described the primary symptoms as:

- Psychotic panic reaction.
- Inappropriate affect appearing as "unpredictable outbursts of hilarity and giggling alternating with violent destructiveness."
- Confusion about self-identity, "fusion of the orbit of the self with non-self."
- Difficulty in differentiating between animate and inanimate objects.
- Nondiscriminating, nonspecific attachment to adults.
- "Direct manifestations of the primary process, the *id*, appearing on the surface of behavior," clinically described as disordered thought and disordered language.

According to Mahler and her co-workers, these primary symptoms are most prominent during infancy and early childhood, and encompass most of the symptomatology described by Kanner in early infantile autism, as well as other less distinct cases of early childhood psychosis. Other symptoms designated as "secondary" are more often seen in psychosis of middle childhood and may be associated with a deteriorating course of illness. These symptoms are:

- Diminished interest in the surroundings
- Mechanical identification
- Violent temper tantrums
- Discrepant and disharmonious development
- Autistic manifestations
- "Endowing parts of the body with concentrated libido"
- Whirling

In late childhood, the disease is described as arising in an insidious fashion with symptoms that may appear as "neurotic manifestations."

Although Mahler considered the presence of psychosis as the first condition for diagnosis and further theorizing, the introduction of interpretive terminology from psychoanalysis could not help but introduce more ambiguity to an area already fraught with unclear criteria.

The effort to relate the personality structure of the child with the symptomatology of childhood schizophrenia is also apparent in Bender's grouping of patients in three categories of pseudodefective, pseudoneurotic and pseudopsycopathic. In this, Bender not only dispensed with the requirement that the patient be psychotic, but she also neglected to discuss the criteria by which these "pseudo-" entities may be differentiated from the established psychiatric entities of the same names.

The general confusion and ambiguity in the area are reflected in a series of papers published in 1956 in the *American Journal of Orthopsychiatry* under the title, "A Symposium on Childhood Schizophrenia." Bender's contribution is a paper called, "Schizophrenia in Childhood, Its Recognition, Description and Treatment." Her report begins with an abstract statement regarding the presumptive etiology of the disorder: "Childhood schizophrenia involves a maturational lag at embryonic level characterized by a primitive plasticity in all areas from which subsequent behavior develops. It is genetically determined and activated by a physiological crisis such as birth." She also now asserts that the disorder is identical to the entity of the same name in adults and, thus, represents a lifelong problem beginning at birth. Further, while frank psychosis may appear at some point in life, its absence need not exclude the diagnosis.

On the question of differential diagnosis, Bender's guidelines are not as clear as one might wish them to be. For example, the pseudodefectives are described as "regressed, inhibited, withdrawn, often mute and incapable of adequate object relationships." Pseudoneurotics are said to have "disturbed thought processes, disturbed speech, sensory distortions, exaggerated or unusual introjection and projection." However, it is also reported somewhat paradoxically that these children may show "an exaggerated capacity to relate." Thus, while some of the symptoms appear to be similar to those in adult schizophrenia, other symptoms of the adult are not mentioned, or their opposite may be true for children. The major difficulty with Bender's classification appears when nonpsychotic children (i.e., those without the traditional symptoms such as hallucination, disordered thinking, and bizarre ideation) are to be identified.

In another paragraph of the same paper, Bender asserts:

> The schizophrenic infant organism responds to stress, sometimes by regression, sometimes by spurts of growth, sometimes by disorganization into unpatterned behavior, sometimes by over organization as with compulsive rhythmic motility, sometimes by precocious neurotic mechanisms, sometimes by psychosomatic illness.

Schizophrenia, even in adults, so far has been diagnosable only as a particular cluster of clinical symptoms without the benefit of corroborative biochemical or pathophysiological findings. The generalized and varied clinical picture described by Bender, on the other hand, presupposes that the disease process has been identified on grounds other than the clinical symptomatology. The confusion in the field is articulated by another investigator in the same symposium. Szurek (1956) sums up the situation by stating:

> We are beginning to consider it clinically (that is, prognostically) fruitless and even unnecessary, to draw any sharp dividing lines between a condition that one could consider psychoneurotic and another one could call psychosis, autism, atypical development or schizophrenia.

Meanwhile, the clinical picture described by Kanner in 1943 had attracted the attention of child psychiatrists, and Kanner's numerous papers and discussions on the subject had opened another new avenue of investigation and theoretical speculation. By 1949, Kanner had already collected 50 cases of early infantile autism, and by 1954 his group reached the one hundred mark. Characteristics of the patients were described as:

- Early onset—"the first signs are noticed sometime during the first two years of life." Boys outnumber girls four to one.
- "Aloneness," rather than active withdrawal, characterizes the child's relationship with people.
- Desire for the preservation of the environment. The child "struggles to live in a static world."
- "Aloneness and obsessive insistence on sameness are the two principal diagnostic criteria." All other symptoms are derivative so that children are mute because "there is no felt need for communication."
- Mental retardation which is more apparent than real. Even those patients "who functioned on idiot or imbecile level in preschool age, achieved intelligence quotients of well over 100 in their early teens."

As to the relationship between early infantile autism and childhood schizophrenia, while in 1949 Kanner had stated: "I do not believe that there is any likelihood that early infantile autism will at any future time have to be separated from the schizophrenias," by 1954 he was of a different opinion. He then stated that "developmental and symptomatic peculiarities" of the syndrome were important enough to justify the separation of the two entities.

The followup study of 42 children was reported by Kanner and Eisenberg in 1955. Language development by age 5 seemed to have a significant prognostic value in that, of the 23 speaking patients, 13 had achieved some degree of independent functioning, while only one of the 19 who were mute had made social and academic recovery. Contrary to Kanner's expectation, a sizable number of children had not shown a rise in their intellectual quotients and were either in state schools for the retarded or at home "in a state of biologic helplessness."

The psychiatric literature of the sixties reflects the intense interest of the researchers and clinicians in the subject of childhood psychosis. Even though the existence and relative frequency of the problem is no longer debated, the questions of which symptom, or constellation of symptoms, ought to be viewed as diagnostically sufficient or necessary and how to classify this heterogenous group of children into subgroups have remained unsettled. Furthermore, investigations are confronted with the problem of differentiating between the clinical entities which had been established earlier and the newly developed, but often divergent, concepts of childhood schizophrenia and autism.

In the following discussion, symptoms which are frequently associated with the diagnosis of childhood psychosis will be considered in detail.

DISTURBANCES OF HUMAN RELATEDNESS

Impairment, inadequacy, and distortion in human relationship seems to be the most widely accepted symptom of psychosis. However, in spite of the crucial importance of the symptom, it remains inadequately studied and only impressionistically defined. Some authors stress impaired peer interaction (Bender, 1956). Others describe a more global deficiency (Creak, 1964). Description of children with early infantile autism leads one to believe that disinterest in and disregard of people is so generalized as to include the child's immediate caretakers, and at least for months or even years this disinterest remains unmodified. On the other hand, Goldfarb (1964) points out that such behavioral anomalies are subject to fluctuations which are "linked to specific temporal and spatial circumstances." Lorna Wing (1978) considers this lack of contact to range from mild to quite severe forms. In the mildest form, the child initiates contact, but lack of necessary social skills hampers his further success, and he is consequently left friendless. O'Gorman (1971), although considering the withdrawal from human interaction to be the most important feature of the "schizophrenic syndrome" in childhood, hastens to add that in many cases the withdrawal is partial or selective; the patient may be disinterested in all human interactions except for one or two familiar figures. Other authors find the child's relationships to be qualitatively (as opposed to quantitatively) deviant. Mahler *et al.* (1949), commenting about the psychotic children of their sample, state: ". . . quality of attachment to adults, although it was strong, it was spurious and the clinging was never specific." According to Bender (1947), the withdrawal sets in only after "the child's problems have plagued him for some time." She indeed goes so far as to say "in contrast with adults one can often make an unusually good contact with schizophrenic children." And still further: "Their charm results in a strong reciprocal relationship. The most dearly beloved of the problem children on the ward in the past ten years have usually been schizophrenic children."

The ambiguity of definition and the discrepancies in the opinions of various authors regarding the quality and quantity of relationships of psychotic children, are also reflected in the paucity of objective studies and lack of systemized attempts at constructing theoretical formulations regarding this symptom. Kanner's description of early infantile autism seems to suggest the inability to form attachment as one of the most significant symptoms of the condition. It is further hypothesized that this particular deficiency may be at the root of the noncommunicativeness of these children's language.

Lack of visual contact or the very fleeting nature of it has come to signify the autistic child's difficulty in relating to people. However, in a study of looking behavior of children, Churchill and Bryson (1967) failed to find any difference between the amount of time that normal children and children diagnosed as autistic or schizophrenic spent in looking at a preoccupied adult. From another series of investigations, Churchill (1970) concluded that looking behavior shows vast variation among different children as well as in one child under various conditions. On the other hand, another group of investigators (Hutt *et al.*, 1965) analyzed the videotape records of free play activities of a group of normal children and another group diagnosed as autistic. They found that the autistic group showed fewer instances of behavior directed at adults or other children present on the playground as compared with their normal agemates. These types of studies have not been repeated by other workers in the field, and the reports of deviations and disturbances in human relatedness in various groups have all been impressionistic. Furthermore, followup studies of autistic children have shown that while avoidance of eye contact and disinterest in people decreases with age, no increment in communicative abilities can be ascribed to this improvement.

Although a close reading of the voluminous literature reveals that both the quality and quantity of human relationships are impaired in psychosis of childhood, such impairments are not limited to psychotic states (Rutter *et al.*, 1964). Furthermore, at this stage, no acceptable manner has been found to define the specific nature of this deficiency and to differentiate it from the adverse effects of factors other than psychosis on the establishment and maintenance of human interactions in their multiplicity of forms and intensity. Although the presence of severe and identifiable impairment in the quality or quantity of relationships has been used to argue in favor of the diagnosis, the absence of such deficits has not been invariably used to rule out the designation of schizophrenia. Another point of special interest is that even though the importance of human attachment and interaction in the development and maintenance of psychological equilibrium is uncontested, the centrality of it as the organizing factor of personality remains unverified. Indeed, one may just as convincingly argue that impairment in human relatedness results from cognitive, perceptual, and emotional problems as that it causes them, or that all symptoms of disorganization are the effects of whatever psychological factor is responsible for the appearance of psychosis.

DISTORTIONS AND DEVIATIONS OF EMOTIONAL REACTIONS AND AFFECT

Reports on childhood psychoses are so unanimous in their assertions regarding the disordered emotions of these children that the term *emotionally disturbed* has come to be used as synonymous with psychotic. In his book, *Schizophrenia in Childhood*, Bradley (1941) concludes that there is no agreement among various authors as to the kind of disturbed emotion which characterizes schizophrenia. Some of the earlier writers describe "coldness and blunting of affects." Others report on negativism, irritability, and extreme anxiety bordering on panic episodes. Despert (1938) states "with regard to the affective rapport with the environment, either it is completely severed or it is in the form of impulsive and apparently unmotivated demonstration." Outbursts of temper and destructiveness, unpredictable bouts of hilarity and giggling, apathy and anhedonia, and chronic unrelieved anxiety have all been noted. Speculations regarding the source or the implication of various emotional reactions have been limited usually to chronic anxiety and panic states. Despert (1938) considers high anxiety as a poor prognostic sign. Kanner (1954) believes panic reactions of autistic children to be caused by changes in the environment and a threat to the maintenance of sameness so desired by an autistic child. A dim awareness of the disintegration of the core of the personality is what Bender (1947) postulates as the cause of chronic anxiety, and, indeed, she advises clinicians to consider schizophrenia as a possible diagnosis whenever chronic anxiety in a child cannot be otherwise accounted for. Deviations are observed in emotional expression and substituted for experience of emotions since, particularly in noncommunicative children, experience of emotion can only be inferred from overt behavior.

Overreactivity, which may appear as intense response to minor provocations or prolong reaction unmitigated by changes in situations, outbursts of temper, rage reactions, or sustained fear, despite reassurances are conditions most frequently reported.

Unpredictable, unmotivated episodes of strong emotional display such as hilarity, anger, or crying spells are also common reactions. These episodes seem to be independent of external stimuli and resemble an outpouring of internal tension. At times the unpredictability and the unexpected nature of the outburst is underscored by the suddenness with which it is terminated.

Underreactivity or lack of response and interest is described as manifested in some children by joyless demeanor, indifference, apathy, and restricted capacity to derive pleasure from their interactions with the environment, even when such interaction is self-initiated.

In verbal children, the disturbed emotional state is said to be revealed in talks of violence and destruction and frank statements about death wishes and lack of pleasure. Fantasies and graphic productions are imbued with the sense of impending disaster and the threat of disruptive forces unleashed on the whole world.

Because subjective distress and its concomitant behavioral expression are the integral part of all interactional failures, emotional disturbances are not limited to the most severe forms of psychiatric disorders in this age group. Furthermore, maturational factors involved in development of emotional experience and regulation and expression of affectivity are not delineated. Consequently, while various authors seem to indicate that a regression in functioning is at the root of the disordered emotionality of psychotic children, others have refrained from any speculation in this regard. It is worthy of notice that no systematic study has been conducted to chart the course of emotional symptoms in childhood psychosis, nor has there been any attempt to relate the severity of psychotic state to emotional and affective disturbances.

DISORDERS OF LANGUAGE AND THOUGHT

Anomalies and deviations of verbal behavior in schizophrenic adults were considered as diagnostically significant by the originators of the notion of the schizophrenic syndrome. However, Bleuler (1911/1950) asserted that "the abnormality does not lie in language itself, but rather in its content." More recently, Brown (1973) has made similar observation. On the other hand, disordered thought manifested in loose or idiosyncratic association, thought withdrawal, or, conversely, thought insertion, have always been viewed as an indication of schizophrenia.

Early writers on schizophrenia in childhood transposed the adult symptomatology to childhood so that Potter (1933) reported "blocking, symbolization, perseveration, incoherence" and "diminution sometimes to the extent of mutism" as characteristic of patients' speech and thinking. A cautionary note was sounded by Schilder (1954) who pointed out that because of the children's tendency to generalize and use words for their emotional rather than intellectual connotations, the investigators may be misled, identifying the end product as abnormal. A similar view was expressed by Bradley (1941) regarding disorders of thought and such other symptoms of adult schizophrenia as hallucinations, fantasies, and delusions.

A different set of observations was reported by Kanner in 1943.

Of the 11 children observed, 3 were "mute" and 8 had speech. According to Kanner, both groups lacked "intent to communicate." The mute children were reported to have used full sentences in emergency situations, but those with language formed irrelevant and incoherent sentences because of their delayed echolalia, reversal of personal pronouns, and use of private metaphors and repetitious verbal negation as "magic protection against unpleasant occurrences." At some point, the disinclination to use "I" in referring to oneself had come to be viewed as almost pathognomonic for infantile autism. Some authors had inferred an absence of sense of self or lack of differentiation between self and non-self based on this verbal peculiarity. In Kanner's view, on the other hand, lack of communicative intent is what sets the language of autistic children apart, otherwise "the linguistic processes through which the transfers of experience into symbols are achieved do not as such differ essentially from poetical and ordinary phraseological metaphors."

Research studies have shown that a sizable percentage of young children who are psychotic either do not develop speech at all, or their vocabulary remains limited to very few words. In those who speak, immediate and delayed echolalia make up a substantial part of their speech production. Although pronominal reversals have been identified as possibly pathognomonic of early infantile autism, it seems to be a characteristic found only in about a quarter of those with echolalic speech. Children with more advanced language development, as measured by the length of their sentences, display a proportionally smaller amount of echolalia than those with more severe speech lag. Since echolalic speech is not limited to psychotic children, a number of investigators have tried to map out the differences between developmental and pathological echolalia. Most authors suggest that imitative speech is more rigid (Shapiro *et al.*, 1970) and articulation of phrases thus imitated is of higher level of clarity than the spontaneous production of the nonpsychotic child (Ruttenberg and Wolf, 1967). Aug (1971) considered the difference between autistic echolalia and normal echolalia to be the lack of modification of the original utterance, and concluded that the normal echolalia response is "more selective according to meaning . . . [showing] more independence from the original 'stimulus' situation."

Another pertinent subject is the psychotic child's comprehension of the speech of others and his own overall communicative skills. Even though the level of language development is intimately related to communicative function of speech, such nonlinguistic variables as attentiveness to others and the ease with which the child initiates and remains within an interpersonal situation are important considerations. As a two-way process, communication presupposes the ability to send out and receive messages about the emotions, percepts, concepts, and needs and desires of the two parties. In addition to such nonvocal clues as bodily gesture and facial expressions, the rhythm, pitch, volume, and degree of stress on parts of the sentence or words are of immense communicative value.

Studies of communicative skills in psychotic children with different levels of language development have shown deficiencies and inadequacies in nonvocal parameters of communication. Most researchers have indicated that mute psychotics and those whose speech is mainly echolalic are equally deficient in communication (Kanner, 1968). However, others have reported that at times echolalic phrases are used for entreaties, expression of desires, or tentative questions. For example, a child may repeat the sentence, "Do you want some juice?" to indicate a positive response to the speaker's question at that moment, or he may do so after he has finished the first glass in order to request an additional one.

In a study of the speech characteristics of a group of speaking psychotic children, Goldfarb *et al.* (1956) concluded that deficiencies of communicative skills are also present in the modulation of pitch, rhythm, and the volume of speaking voice, so that one detects "a flat unfinished quality . . . commonly called monotonous speech." Gestures and facial expressions are not in harmony with the intent and meaning of the spoken words, and incorrect syllables or words are stressed. Consequently, the most meaningful part of the message is not necessarily the part which is stressed. Mood and emotional reactions are not conveyed with the help of differentiation and modulation of the voice, and the common range of pitch is not employed.

In addition to difficulties in communication, poorly developed and deficient language in psychotic children is also related to the overall cognitive status and severity of the clinical picture of psychosis (Fish *et al.*, 1968; Gittleman and Birch, 1967; Wolff and Chess, 1964). Furthermore, it has been noted that development of communicative speech in children who are mute or echolalic is associated with a better prognosis. Follow-up studies have failed to show an increment in the level of language development resulting from a decrease in psychotic behavior which indicates that linguistic deficits are of primary nature, even though communicative skills

may improve as the result of improvement in interpersonal relationships or better organized behavior. It is fairly well established that
language defect in autism is a more global disability than poor
speech comprehension or limited production. An array of nonlinguistic behaviors, which are used to convey or decode messages, is
also deficient. In addition, certain peculiarities in cognitive strategies
result in seriously limited conceptualization and intellectual disability. Hermelin (1978) states that the autistic child is not able to
process the incoming informations through the sensory system
which is best equipped to do so. For example, normal children will
transfer spatial information to the visual system and temporal information to the auditory-vocal system even though they may have
received these informations via tactile or visual stimulation. Autistic
children do not have such "mental mobility" and according to
Hermelin, they are "operationally deaf and blind," meaning that
their cognitive strategies for handling both temporal and spatial data
are deficient.

INTELLIGENCE

Although early clinicians had not made specific comments about
the intelligence, or more accurately, the performance of schizophrenic children on psychological tests, impaired functioning in this area
had been alluded to in various statements regarding the possible
inclusion of these children among the mentally defectives. Attempts
at differentiation between the retarded children and those whose
psychotic states were held responsible for their poor performance on
tests centered around finding differential patterns of responses between the two groups. Bradley (1941) considered such specific
patterns as "evidence for or against diagnosis" in schizophrenia.
According to him, the diagnosis of schizophrenia would be
strengthened

> if a severely maladjusted child shows a progressive lowering of in-
> telligence quotient, and yet does better on tests of speed rather than
> those of accuracy, better on verbal than on performance material, tends
> to improve his performance on immediate retesting but does not re-
> spond to urging and praise.

Although these were viewed as preliminary findings, the notion of
discrepancies and "scatter" (characteristic variations) among the
results of various subtests gained acceptance. Kanner (1943) em-

phasized "good cognitive potentialities" of children with early infantile autism by asserting that

> the astounding vocabulary of the speaking children, the excellent memory for events of several years before, the phenomenal rote memory for poems and names, and the precise recollection of complex patterns and sequences, bespeak good intelligence in the sense in which this word is commonly used.

Subsequent case reports and follow-up studies failed to substantiate the optimistic view of these children's intellectual potentials. However, the assertion about the uneven pattern of performance on tests of intelligence remained unchallenged. By the early sixties, when the British Working Party (Creak, 1964) proposed its criteria for diagnosis of psychosis in childhood, one of the six criteria was "serious intellectual retardation with islets of normal, near normal or exceptional function or skills."

From various reports in the literature, it appears that at least in psychotic preschoolers, more than half of the children are untestable or their functioning on psychological tests falls within the severely retarded range (Hingtgen and Bryson, 1972). These results have been obtained through the use of various tests, some standardized and others specifically designed to take advantage of those limited abilities that can be tapped in these children. Although verbal scores of psychotic preschoolers may be depressed due to underproductivity, nondevelopment or other deficiences in language, both the verbal and performance results are also lowered by such factors as disorganized behavior, short attention span, or lack of motivation and unresponsiveness to human interactions. Furthermore, at least in some reports, the results of tests and retests have remained consistent over time and have been shown to correlate with the outcome and amount of schooling that these children receive (Rutter, 1964). However, it must be noted that some psychotic children score within, or well above, the average on standardized tests (Gittleman and Birch, 1967).

The frequently cited scatter patterns among subtest scores is more difficult to interpret. Experiments have failed to support the superior rote memory (Hermelin and O'Connor, 1967). When psychotic and nonpsychotic children were matched for mental age, no significant difference was detected on tests of the visual motor skills between the two groups. Nor has it been shown that these children have higher visual discrimination (Ottinger *et al.*, 1965). Furthermore, various studies have shown that auditory discrimination as well as processing and sequencing of words are deficient (Hingtgen and Coutler, 1967). The evidence from the literature so far does not support a consistent pattern of "normal, above normal or exceptional abilities" in young psychotics. However, the contention that there exists a pattern of variability in cognition which sets the autistic children apart from mentally retarded remains unrefuted (Rutter, 1974).

COURSE AND OUTCOME

In describing the 18 cases in whom the psychotic process had been identified before age 7, Despert (1937) reported three types of onset: acute, insidious, and insidious with acute exacerbation. Of the 7 cases with acute onset, 6 deteriorated rapidly. Other clinicians followed Despert's example, attempting to map out the age and manner by which the problematic behavior became clinically manifested, to characterize the course and outcome as related to the age and type of onset. Bender (1947) reported that children who were diagnosed as psychotic before age 5, with marked regression in their fundamental habits, had the poorest outcome, particularly if they did not exhibit a considerable degree of anxiety as a part of the clinical picture. Eisenberg (1957) repeated the statement regarding the poor outcome and speedy deterioration of cases with acute onset, and concluded from the extant clinical observations, "if there be any characteristic of childhood schizophrenic which is manifest in all clinical accounts, that characteristic lies in its long and fluctuating course." Most follow-up studies of children with early onset psychosis have failed to reveal an intermittent course (DeMyer *et al.*, 1973; Rutter, Greenfield, and Lockyer, 1967). Furthermore, the relationship between the type of onset and the severity of outcome has not been established. What is more universally agreed upon is the poor prognosis of more than half of the children diagnosed as psychotic before ages 5 or 6. A large portion of the severely afflicted children are diagnosed as mentally retarded in later life; another significant group presents a picture resembling adult schizophrenia. Among those with better outcome, a considerable percentage remain handicapped in social relations and emotional growth. Although it has been fairly well established that the severity of the clinical picture, the extent of language deficiency, and the low level of intellectual scores on tests and subsequent limited educational opportunities are all related to the poor outcome, factors responsible for future normal or near-normal adjustment are not fully understood. Furthermore, although it appears that groups of children treated with differing modalities do equally well or poorly on the average and therefore no treatment regimen is shown to be statistically superior to others, the possible harmful effects of various intervention on any particular individual have not been studied. Although such extreme measures as lobotomy and ECT are no longer used, or at least are not reported, the effects of various psychopharmacological agents on the status of patients are scrutinized only in terms of their beneficial results rather than their possible disadvantages.

DIFFERENTIAL DIAGNOSIS

Early descriptions of psychoses in childhood reflect the clinicians' concern with differential diagnosis between psychotic states and other identifiable problems of this age group. However, whereas the earlier researchers believed that childhood schizophrenia and autism were underdiagnosed, more recently the possibility of excessive diagnosis has been entertained. As befits an entity whose manifestations are dependent on the ever changing picture of developmental status in a growing child, the type and severity of deviations are a source of misinterpretation and puzzlement. Kanner (1969) summarized this fundamental dilemma by stating, "we are still confronted with many child patients whose profiles cannot be easily matched with those for which a joint heading already exists. This is true especially of the more severe disturbances in the first year of life." However, for each age group and each diagnostic entity, various clinicians have tended to use a different combination of necessary and sufficient symptoms. Consequently, even for diagnosis of early infantile autism, which is viewed as the more distinguishable type of childhood psychosis, a variety of essential symptom pictures appears in the literature. For instance, DeMyer (1975) describes the necessary symptoms as extreme withdrawal, uncommunicativeness, or muteness, and nonfunctional use of objects. On the other hand, Bartok (1975) considers "ritualistic or compulsive phenomena" in addition to withdrawal and delayed language as differentiating characteristics of the syndrome. Further complexity is introduced when Sahlman (1969) asserts that about 26% of the nonverbal children who had been referred to her school as autistic proved instead to be aphasic, and Cohen *et al.* (1976) report a cluster of behavioral abnormality in aphasic children resembling autism or early childhood schizophrenia. Some clinicians have reported changes in their own initial diagnoses of autism or schizophrenia to psychotic brain syndrome (Menolascino and Eatons, 1967) or central language disorder (Piggot and Simson, 1975).

Diagnostic certainty is by no means easier to achieve among the older age group. Potter (1933) reports a "superficial resemblance" between schizophrenic children and "unstable mental defectives." Mahler *et al.* (1949) believe that cases with insidious onset may have been mistakenly classified and

> only prolonged clinical observation and the reactions occurring during psychotherapy can usually clarify the differential diagnosis in the case of severe obsessive-compulsion neurosis, anxiety hysteria, psychopathic and conduct disturbances, organic and schizophrenic pictures, post-encephalitic "driveness," impulse neurosis and epileptoid conditions.

It thus appears that from the early stages of conceptualization of the entity of childhood schizophrenia, the overlaps between this new entity and other classes of behavioral deviations has plagued the clinicians. No less authoritative a personage than Bender (1947) found it necessary to stress that children with "diffuse developmental deviations" or "diffuse encephalopathy" may present schizophrenic features due to their reactive anxiety and frustration, or that children with "a deep anxiety in interpersonal relationships may react with profound biological disturbance and regressive behavior akin to the schizophrenics."

In the final analysis, it appears that the most important reason for designating a constellation of symptoms as schizophrenia in childhood is the hope that research will provide us with more information about the natural history, course, and possible etiology of the group of mental disorders called schizophrenias in adults. This information will be particularly useful if the etiological search results in identifying psychobiological factors which can be modified and corrected, or if the disease process could be prevented before it begins.

3

Specific Language Dysfunctioning in Children: A Historical Overview

The origins and growth of awareness of specific impairments in the linguistic functioning of children may be looked at in terms of three roughly chronological but overlapping and ongoing aspects: clinical recognition, conceptualization, and classification. The first aspect is characterized by the discovery, mainly during the first third of this century, that a population of children existed in facilities for the mentally deficient or the deaf who were neither imbecilic nor hard of hearing. Rather, these children displayed what appeared as circumscribed aberrations in the development and use of their native language, but they were relatively normal in other respects. On the basis of the paucity of published studies, the occurrence of such cases was thought to be something of a rarity. Gradually, an increasing number of writers reported such cases, and detailed accounts of directly observable symptoms grew. As more probing questions were posed, more thorough examinations appeared in the literature, and inferences were made regarding the specific nature of the linguistic defects and their etiology. Thus emerged the second aspect—theoretical conceptualization.

When childhood language impairment was receiving its initial recognition, acquired aphasia in adults had been for some time a widely studied and argued topic so the observers of children's impairments simply adopted the adult diagnostic reference. Therefore, the concept of a congenital form of aphasia was introduced, with the implication that the observed linguistic anomalies in the developing child were comparable to those in an adult who suffered language impairment through brain injury of one form or another.

However, the notion of an aphasia present from birth was not without its opponents. The fundamental argument posed against the theory was that one cannot lose what one has not yet developed, and the nature of a loss of matured linguistic functions, resulting from injury to their presumably related cerebral structures, is categorically different from a deficiency in the development of language arising from a defect or failure in the early growth of the central nervous system. In this view, there are essentially no parallels to be drawn between the acquired aphasic behaviors of the adult and the developmental anomalies of language exhibited by the child. Somewhat surprisingly, although the issue of congenital aphasia vis-à-vis adult aphasia was discussed, that of traumatically acquired aphasia in children was paid scant and fleeting attention in the literature. To date, the writing on this topic remains sparse, and no comparative investigation of congenital and acquired defects of language in children has been undertaken.

The third aspect, that of classification, evolved concurrently with the other two. In attempting to construct more articulate behavioral pictures and conceptual suppositions, the writers set boundaries around their notions of specific language dysfunctioning in childhood, marking it off from other taxonomic entities that involve deficiencies in the development of language. Further, some grouped particular behavioral symptoms together according to the functional defects they seemed to represent, thus subdividing the overall classification. The breadth of the diagnostic category and the sharpness of its boundaries (and, therefore, the incidence of the dysfunctioning it described) depended in large part upon the conceptual bent of the writer. Likewise, its unity or subdivision depended upon varying theoretical views of the underlying impaired linguistic functions.

Initially, the emphasis in diagnosis lay upon distinguishing anomalies of *congenital aphasia* from those associated with general mental retardation or deafness. While over the years the existence of congenital disability specific to language has become generally recognized, the matter of whether it represents a form of retarded development or a distinctly aphasialike dysfunction is still open to argument. Most recently, with the widespread acceptance of psychodiagnoses emanating from Kanner's and Bender's conceptual formulations of infantile autism and childhood schizophrenia, a few workers have begun to examine the distinctions or relationships between these illnesses and what has now come to be called *developmental* aphasia or dysphasia. In the following review of the literature, we will focus on the evolution of concepts regarding both acquired and developmental language dysfunctioning in children, first presenting a synopsis of recent thinking on adult aphasia by way of reference. We have not attempted to cover comprehensively all of the published material, but rather to present the observations and positions of writers who represent predominant trends.

ACQUIRED APHASIA IN ADULTHOOD

From the viewpoints of both the observer and the afflicted individual, a loss of the highly developed capacity of linguistic communication, which has become second nature in adulthood, is a much more dramatic and discernable phenomenon than a delay or defect in the early learning of language, or even an acute interruption in its development during childhood. The attention-commanding quality of language impairment in adults is attested to by the antiquity and volume of the published accounts. The known documentation of language impairment following upon cerebral insult in adults dates back to a report on papyrus by Egyptian surgeons (circa 3000 to 2500 B.C.), who attributed their patients' difficulties with speaking to "the breath of an outside god or death" (Jenkins et al., 1975). Over the centuries, from the era of Hippocrates to the present, the literature on adult aphasia has proliferated to immense proportions, including self-reports of the traumatic aphasic experience by patients of such fame as Samuel Johnson (Benton and Joynt, 1960; Benton, 1965).

The inception of the modern era of clinical work in adult aphasia is commonly credited to Broca. In 1861, he announced a relationship between the symptoms of expressive, or motor, aphasia and lesions of the third frontal convolution of the left cerebral hemisphere. The two patients, who were the focus of Broca's finding, had shown severe loss of vocal expression, ostensibly without any concomitant loss of understanding or intelligence. Broca coined the term *aphemia* to describe their impaired language, and, after autopsy, attributed this condition to the cerebral area that came to bear his name. In 1864, Trousseau substituted the label "aphasia" for aphemia (Meyer, 1974). Subsequently, "Broca's aphasia" became the designation for those patients whose aberrant linguistic characteristics are dominated by "awkward articulation, restricted vocabulary, restriction of grammar to the simplest, most overlearned forms, and relative preservation of auditory comprehension" (Goodglass and Kaplan, 1972). In short, they are marked by a hindrance in the production of vocal language.

At the time of Broca, the notion that an acquired language impairment might be predominantly receptive in origin was not yet widely entertained. Although a number of writers in the 1860s did implicate receptive functions in some cases of aphasia, their observations had relatively little impact in the field (Meyer, 1974; Jenkins *et al.*, 1975). After Broca's historical announcement, the emphasis in the formulation of diagnostic syndromes in aphasia was placed on anatomical evidence of localization in the brain, and most of the observers of deficient auditory comprehension presented none. Thus, as late as 1929, Bonvencini would make light of the concepts of receptive aphasia before Wernicke because they were " 'theoretical' and not based on autopsy findings." Wernicke's contribution in 1874 was to present postmortem evidence of localized temporal-lobe damage in conjunction with apparent anomalies of auditory reception or comprehension, and he, too, came to see his name associated with an aphasic syndrome. Patients who receive the designation, "Wernicke's" or "sensory" aphasia, present a picture of

> impaired auditory comprehension and fluently articulated but paraphasic speech . . . word finding difficulty . . . neologisms . . . irrelevant insertions . . . [and] a press of speech, often at a greater rate than normal, while the patient is unaware of anything wrong with his speech. (Goodglass and Kaplan, 1972)

Wernicke is credited also with the early postulation of another major subclassification of adult aphasia, based on an "interruption of fiber tracts connecting the auditory areas and the motor-speech area" of the brain (Jenkins *et al.*, 1975). This presumed disconnection gave rise to the term *conduction aphasia* or *central aphasia* (Goldstein, 1948), used to describe patients whose major problem lies in the inability to repeat spoken language accurately, with less difficulty in speaking spontaneously, and good comprehension of what is said. These patients are portrayed as also displaying paraphasia of the *literal* variety, in which there is a misselection and missequencing of sounds within syllables and words, as opposed to *verbal* paraphasia, in which there is a misselection of whole words or phrases. *Anomia*, a disability in naming things and the loss of individual words in running speech, is usually present as well. Since auditory comprehension is relatively intact, the conduction aphasic is said to be distinguishable from the Wernicke's aphasic because he is "acutely aware of his inaccuracy and rejects his incorrect efforts" to find the words he intends to use (Goodglass and Kaplan, 1972).

The prominence of anomia in some patients, and their marked forgetfulness of words, led to the delineation of another adult syndrome, variously called *amnesic aphasia* (Weisenberg & McBride,

1935), *nominal aphasia* (Head, 1926), and *semantic aphasia* (Wepman and Jones, 1961). In this instance, the patient is literally at a loss for words. He speaks quite fluently and spontaneously with intact grammatical construction, and comprehends what he hears in running conversation. Yet he is prone to circumlocute in the attempt to compensate for the missing words. Thus, his expression may have a disordered or ambiguous quality to it (Goodglass and Kaplan, 1972). Frequently, too, one will find such a patient seemingly groping for words, with many "umm's" and "uh's" and torturous pauses in his expression. However, somewhat paradoxically, there may be little difficulty naming common objects when they are pointed out, and words that are lost on one occasion may be present on another.

The trend, then, in the clinical literature on adult aphasia has been not in differentiating specific language dysfunctioning from other abnormal states in which language is affected, but in articulating the anomalies involved, relating them to particular anatomical areas or processes, and grouping them into diagnostic subcategories. Within the major syndromes mentioned above, one finds all of the generally recognized aphasic symptoms (with the exception of the often-accompanying, parallel difficulties with reading and writing). There is little disagreement on their nature, but substantial disagreement regarding their multidimensional grouping according to the presumed localization of cerebral damage and characteristic differences in impairment across language modalities (auditory-vocal, visual-graphic). Some have claimed that adult aphasia is a more uniform than multiform entity, citing both clinical and research findings to support their arguments (Schuell, 1969; Smith, 1972; Duffy and Ulrich, 1976). The proponents of the locationist standpoint have done the same (Goodglass and Kaplan, 1972).

CLINICAL RECOGNITION AND CONCEPTUALIZATION

Acquired Aphasia in Childhood

In his clinical study of aphasia in children, Guttmann (1942) noted that in the literature up to that time "many contradictory statements are encountered. Some doubt has even been expressed as to whether such a condition exists." MacDonald Critchley (1970), writing on true acquired aphasia occurring in childhood, described the accumulated accounts of such disability as "meagre in the extreme and far from adequate." The cause for this meagerness or the effect of it, depending on one's point of view, was stated by Alajounine and Lhermitte (1965). "It is common belief that it [children's acquired aphasia] is a rare disorder and moreover is remarkably transitory so that sequelae are very few or absent." Guttmann explained the low incidence of reported cases and, at the same time, provided a cogent description of the clinical conditons which often obscure its diagnosis:

> . . . it is surprising that the rarity of aphasia in children is so often emphasized, and I think this can be accounted for only by the lack of understanding of the clinical picture of aphasia in children. Aphasia in the adult is mostly diagnosed or sought for when the patient complains of difficulty in his speech—which children do not—or if he uses wrong names for objects; in other words, apart from cases of complete motor aphasia, the early diagnosis of aphasia is commonly based on subjective or objective word-amnesia. The clinical appearance in children is different, and the signs of aphasia in a sick, apathetic, shy and often morose child are easily overlooked unless specially sought. (1942, p. 208)

As to the incidence of the condition, Guttmann presented more than suggestive evidence from his review of 30 cases of "primary hemisphere affection in children of 14 years and under," that it is far from a rare occurrence. As to the symptoms he detected, they varied in generality or specificity according to chronological age, and the relationship was relatively straightforward.

The presence of aphasic symptomatology of one form or another was noted in 14 out of 16 cases of left-hemisphere damage and in two out of 14 right-hemisphere cases, leading Guttmann to conclude that "aphasia in left-hemisphere lesions in childhood is not at all rare, and examination of the few exceptions proves that it is just as regular a symptom in children as in adults." Then, of the 16 aphasic patients, he noted that the most common symptom under age 10 was a "reduction of spontaneous speech, varying in degree from complete mutism to what was described in case records as 'reluctance to speak' or 'unwillingness to speak.' " This hypoproductivity in language was invariable under the age of 6, and appeared to become less dominant with increased age. Over age 10, the picture was mixed, with some showing the general reduction and others producing "the picture generally seen in the adults."

Guttmann did not define what he meant by "the picture generally seen in the adult," and one must peruse the three case records presented for some indication of what he meant. Two (ages 10.6 and 11.6) were described as displaying "nominal aphasia" (anomia), and the 11-year-old was said also to be "paraphasic and paragrammatic." (Paragrammia is usually used to designate a loss or defect in the syntactical ability to construct phrases and sentences.) The 10-year-old showed "marked dyslexia and some difficulty in writing" (a-graphia), but there was no mention of reading and writing being checked in the other. The third case (age 12) showed "complete motor aphasia and gross disturbances on the receptive side," and was thus so severe as to preclude well-differentiated, adultlike symptoms.

Despite the relatively undifferentiated reduction in speech in many of the children, even to the point of mutism in some, Guttmann states unequivocally that "one can clearly distinguish those in which the understanding of spoken language is affected from those where only speech production is impaired." Among the same cases he presented, the distinction could be seen in the patients' incapacity or capacity to echo adequately (though with some distortion), to respond to questions appropriately in limited speech, or to respond nonverbally to commands. Guttmann made no reference to the incidence of receptive problems, nor to the ages of patients so afflicted. Alajouanine and Lhermitte (1965), in their study of 32 children suffering from acquired aphasia, stated that auditory-perception problems were "rare." However, "rare" to the authors meant 10 out of 32 cases or 31%, with 4 cases, or 12.5%, described as marked. They also noted that 8 of these receptively dysfunctioning cases were under age 10.

With regard to the reduction in spontaneous speech (hypo-productivity) observed by Guttmann, Alajounine and Lhermitte concurred in its predominance in aphasic children. However, they found hypoproductivity in *all* cases, regardless of age, and it was accompanied by a similar reduction in communication by gesture and in writing. This generally hypocommunicative phenomenon was referred to as a "peculiar behavior of psychomotor inhibition . . . [that] bears no relationship with the existence of dysarthria." (*Dysarthria*, or anarthria in total cases, refers to an impairment in the production of speech sounds due to dyscoordination in the vocal musculature.) Moreover, not only was spontaneous speech reportedly affected, but there was a hindrance or resistance to responding verbally when directed. Children needed repeated encouragements to speak or answer questions. The only indication of a relationship between age and linguistic hypoproductivity was the authors' notation that in the 9 children from 5 to 9 years of age, "the reduction of verbal expression was severe," while no qualifying reference was made to the hypoproductivity of the 23 children in the age range of 10 to 15 years.

As to the adult symptomatology in their child patients, Alajouanine and Lhermitte place primary emphasis on what they did not see or what was infrequent and only secondarily noted what was present. In agreement with the general consensus of writers on the subject, they affirmed that logorrhea (a loss of control over the flow of speech and subsequent flood of verbiage often seen in adult Wernicke's aphasics) is not characteristic of aphasic children. Then they mentioned a number of other specific anomalies that were not observed or were uncommon in their patients, including verbal stereotypes, word intoxication or perseveration, and verbal or literal paraphasia. Again, however, the authors' choice of adjectives is to be questioned, since the "very rare" incidence of verbal paraphasia amounted to 7 cases or 22% of the total group. Among the younger children (5 to 9 years), they saw a 100% incidence of dysarthria and "phonetic disintegration." In the older children, they noted a lower incidence of dysarthria (60%), and "phonetic disintegration" (43%), about a 40% rate of dyslexia and dysgraphia, and 4 cases of jargonaphasia. Also, it was in the older group that all the instances of verbal paraphasia appeared. On the whole, the trend was apprently from general linguistic hypoproductivity to more differentiated adultlike symptoms with the advance of chronological age.

This same general trend is explicitly or implicitly apparent in other writings on childhood acquired aphasia, though there is significant disagreement regarding the ages at which well-defined adult symptomatology makes its appearance. Discussing children who acquire unilateral lesions after having established some degree of language development, Lenneberg (1967) stated: "The aphasic symptoms seen in the adult traumatized patient may also be observed in children with comparable lesions," excepting logorrhea (increased flow of speech). Thus, he avers, "in patients between four and ten years of age, the symptoms are similar to adult symptomatology. . . ." The major distinction between the acquired aphasia of children and adults, according to Lenneberg, lies in the prognosis. Children are markedly faster in recovery and much less prone to show any residue in later life than adults.

In a more recent compilation of clinical data, Hecaen (1976) found language problems in 19 of 26 cases involving children treated for cortical lesions due to cranial trauma, tumor, or abscess over a 14 year period. The ages at the time of treatment ranged from 3.5 to 15 years. Since the focus of his investigation was on hemispheric functional specialization, the author paid only general attention to the linguistic anomalies and offered no information as to specific variations related to age. On the whole, the observations of Hecaen were similar to those presented by Alajouanine and Lhermitte, stressing "the frequency of mutism, of loss of initiation of speech or more generally of the ability to communicate, and . . . the fact that paraphasias are exceptional and there is a complete absence of logorrhea." Auditory imperception was found to occur in more than a third of the children, but this finding was qualified by the observation that the symptom disappeared after the acute stage had subsided. Dysarthria was relatively frequent, and in mild or severe form, it was noted either from the outset or following a period of mutism.

Unlike previous writers, Hecaen noted a relatively high frequency of "disturbances of naming" (anomia), listing 7 instances out of 15 cases of left-hemisphere damage. He also found that this anomaly tends to be persistent, "lexical poverty being noted at later stages and even mentioned explicitly in the school reports" (i.e., after the children were well enough to return to school). Dyslexia was also frequent, but only in the acute period and then it tended to clear up rapidly. Agraphic defects, on the other hand, "are the most frequent and the most variable of all the symptoms in the acute period, and tend to persist the longest, at times even permanently." Acalculia (impairment in mental and sometimes written arithmetic computation) was also a high-frequency symptom which sometimes lasted well beyond the period of general recovery.

The writings on acquired aphasia in children discussed so far have dealt with cases where there is clearcut insult to the brain, in many instances confirmed by surgery. There have been, however, a number of notable cases reported in the literature, in which the aphasia appears in a child of normal linguistic development, without any apparent precipitating trauma or illness, and often without established signs of neurologic dysfunction other than the aphasia itself. Cohen and his colleagues (1976) have dubbed such cases, "idiopathic acquired aphasia." In 1971, Worster-Drought documented 14 such cases, with receptive aphasia as the predominant aberration. Shoumaker *et al.* (1974) reported on three, and Cohen described three. In all instances, the aphasia appeared before age 6, and in many, after age 4. All patients seemed receptively impaired, and the dysfunction was of the general language loss or hypoproductive variety. There were reported "epileptiform attacks" which were few in number, usually occurring *after* the onset of aphasia and disappearing totally without medication (Worster-Drought, 1971). The EEGs were sometimes bilaterally abnormal (Shoumaker *et al.*,

1974), but otherwise, the neurologic findings were negative, and etiology has been a matter of pure speculation. Generally, recovery was markedly slow, and there were frequent residual deficits ranging from severe to mild.

One point of unanimous concurrence among observers of children's acquired aphasia is the rapid and complete recovery of the great majority of patients. With the exception of the idiopathic cases described above, most children with diagnosis of acquired aphasia are reported to regain their normal use of language fairly quickly and continue the course of development without long-term residual effects. This finding stands in contrast to the overall picture in adult aphasia, where recovery is a more prolonged affair on the average, and permanent residual anomalies are more the rule than the exception. In making such generalized prognostic statement, though, one must call to attention the fact that recovery is related to the extent and severity of the underlying structural damage as well as to the period of onset, and that in a significant minority of aphasic children the aberrant language functioning is not temporary.

Guttmann (1942) noted that the prognostic rule for "purely motor aphasia" in children was recovery within four weeks, but he made no predictions about those with receptive defects. Alajouanine and Lhermitte (1965), following up on their group one year after onset, found two-thirds fully recovered, and could see no significant difference between those below 10 years of age and those above, other than an earlier initiation of the recovery process in the younger children. They concluded that the rapid and full improvement of language is characteristic of children and that this fact is not related to the "reversability of the cerebral lesions as 16 of the 23 [recovered] children were keeping severe motor sequelae and EEG disturbances."

Lenneberg's (1967) summary of 25 cases (18 involving patients up to 10 years old, and 7 involving 10- to 18-year-olds), all with apparent unilateral left-hemisphere involvement, led him to conclude that "aphasia runs a different course before the end of the first decade than after it." He set the age of initial language acquisition at about 20 months, and observed that the occurrence of simple aphasia between 20 and 36 months results in a total loss of early progress in development, after which the child begins again, proceeding through all the normal landmarks at a sometimes faster rate than normal. When the aphasia occurs between ages 3 and 4, there is more apparent difficulty with established language than with developmental regression, but the child also suffers partial developmental loss which is rapidly recovered. From ages 4 through 9, the usual course is "that of a typical aphasia which gradually subsides," and seemingly language-learning continues without loss from the point of premorbid development *during* the recovery period. When aphasia is acquired at puberty, or has not cleared up fully by then, Lenneberg states that the linguistic impairments "commonly leave some trace behind which the patient cannot overcome . . . and by the middle teens the prognosis for recovery rapidly becomes the same as that for the adult patient."

Hecaen's conclusions regarding prognosis were on the whole in consensus with previous writers in emphasizing the relative quickness of recovery. Unlike the others, he offered no observations as to apparent relationship between age of onset within the period of childhood and rate of recovery. Also, he did add the caution that at times some verbal deficit may remain permanently, especially in writing. Further, he noted that the maturational period during which the nondominant hemisphere is able to support verbal learning (and, by extension, fully compensate for a lesion on the dominant side) is "of a briefer duration than suggested by Lenneberg." He implicated the size of the lesion as a complicating factor, but offered no specific estimate of that "very limited time period" when the nondominant hemisphere can take over the verbal function.

There is one further aspect of childhood acquired aphasia which is of interest in theoretical conceptualizations of language dysfunctioning in children. Guttmann (1942) had observed that "among the aphasic patients with unilateral damage, there was nothing to suggest any general intellectual backwardness," deriving from the aphasia itself. By way of contrast, some patients with bilateral involvement did show evidence of retardation upon follow-up two to three years later. Guttmann surmised that this observation, "if confirmed by a wider survey, would point to the brain damage rather than to the aphasia as the factor responsible for the disturbance of intelligence." Alajouanine and Lhermitte (1965) provided one such wider survey by following 14 of their patients after resumption of schooling for periods ranging from three to twelve years. In addition to estimates of academic progress, they obtained evidence from psychological testing. Their results, too, indicated that when there is general cognitive retardation after cerebral damage, "aphasia is not directly responsible for the intellectual impairment. It is only one of the consequences of the cerebral lesions which disturb cerebral mechanisms sub-serving many other activities than language."

Developmental Dysphasia[1]

The earliest reported reference to specific language dysfunctioning in children that dates from birth, or at least is present before the appearance of intelligible speech, was made by Gall in 1828 (see McCready, 1926). According to McCready, Gall had discussed "faulty speech memory in children giving a clear clinical picture of that form of what we now call congenital aphasia . . . [and] differentiated those who were feeble-minded from those with otherwise normal intelligence." Thus, Gall anticipated by nearly a century the clinical recognition of congenitally dysphasic children and their segregation from the generally mentally retarded. Burr exemplified this later trend, somewhat irately, in 1912:

> So widespread indeed is the belief that all children who hear but do not speak are imbecile and speechless because of imbecility, that but relatively few men have made any careful study of the congenital cerebral defects of speech . . . if he [the congenital dysphasic] becomes mentally weak, it is because of an avoidable accident of environment and not a necessary result of his disease . . . [the child] may be backward in development and finally feeble-minded but it is from the same cause that neglected deaf and blind children are, or rather become, mentally feeble and not from weakness of the cerebral cortex that has to do with thought. (p. 138)

The significance of Burr's paper lay in the insistence upon the basic cognitive intactness of young dysphasic patients, and in the affirmation that, incorrectly diagnosed, they eventually became retarded through neglect. A number of nineteenth-century writers had recognized aphasic symptoms in children, but regarded them as defects of generally retarded minds. Thus, Wilbur, in 1867 (see Worster-Drought and Allen, 1930), classified the speech anomalies of 443 mental subnormals and noted what he referred to as "aphasia" in some, but considered the patients thus afflicted to be "idiotic aphasics."

The early clinicians emphasized the aberrations of the expressive language due to congenital defects. Later on, the impairment in the receptive processing of language as a contributing factor to the expressive anomalies gained significance. In a series of now-classic articles, Worster-Drought and Allen (1929a,b; 1930) reviewed the literature up to that time, and, from their own observation, they

---

[1]In an attempt to lessen the confusion of terms used by various authors, we will refer to the congenital or developmental variety of linguistic dysfunctioning in children as *dysphasia*, reserving the term *aphasia* for references to the acquired variety.

drew up diagnostic parameters for a syndrome which they named "congenital auditory imperception." This category of impairment is one in which "the speech defect is often the most prominent feature, but the fundamental defect is the inability to appreciate the significance of words (word meaning deafness) and sometimes even cruder sounds" (1930).

They described nine clinical characteristics of the syndrome as follows:

1. Impairment from birth
2. Normal hearing
3. Misunderstanding or lack of understanding of speech when the speaker is out of sight
4. Inability to reproduce correctly long series of words and sounds even when individual words are repeated accurately
5. Occasional failure of patients to appreciate musical sounds or understand the significance of crude noises
6. Defective or total absence of expressive speech
7. Deficient understanding of printed symbols and words
8. Similar defects in writing
9. Difficulty in writing from dictation when the speaker's lips cannot be seen

The syndrome was said to be due to congenital auditory imperception and the incapacity to appreciate the significance of linguistic sounds or "word-deafness." However, the presence of some degree of reading and writing deficiencies led the authors to postulate a "complicating verbal aphasia" in these children. In essence, what could not be explained directly by the misperception and miscomprehension of spoken words, was explained on the basis of a generic language dysfunction that may be manifested in diverse degrees across modalities.

The differentiation drawn in the early literature between the incapacity to appreciate the significance of linguistic sounds, described as "word-deafness," and true deafness to the sensation of sound, was based on the assumption that the receptive anomalies displayed by the patients neither derived from, nor at all involved, a defective hearing apparatus. Clinically, hearing loss was ruled out by means of relatively gross and unsophisticated tests and examinations. Working contemporaneously with Worster-Drought and Allen, Ewing (1930) utilized more refined audiometric techniques to test hearing at varying levels of the audible frequency range. In an effort to investigate the issue of perceptual defect versus hearing loss in dysphasic children, Ewing applied his methods to ten presumed cases of childhood aphasia. Six of them were found to be suffering from a significant binaural insensitivity to high-frequency tones within the range of speech (512 cps and up). According to Ewing, this selective impairment resulted in a debilitating loss of "the characteristics of the sounds of speech and most noises," which in turn retarded linguistic development and rendered the children's condition indistinguishable from that of the dysphasic with fully normal hearing.

Ewing pursued his clinical investigation of the ten children longitudinally and in some depth during remedial training, and compared their functioning with that of two aphasic adults who also had been referred to him for training. Looking at the functioning of the high-frequency deaf children across four modalities of language (hearing–speaking, reading–writing), a fairly consistent picture emerged. Most significantly, in all instances the comprehension of spoken words was found to depend primarily upon "a constant factor—their [the children's] distance from the source of sound and its intensity." Further, there was no variability in the comprehension of the language they had learned. The appearance of expressive language was seriously delayed in all, but once appropriate remedial training was begun, "the development of speech appears to pass through the same stages as that of the normal child." Given time and remediation, they all learned to comprehend speech auditorily and displayed no evidence of the anomalies that characterized the adult aphasics.

The next major writer on congenital language dysfunctioning considered the symptomatology from exactly the opposite viewpoint as Ewing. In his *Reading, Writing and Speech Problems in Children*, Orton (1937) drew parallels between adult aphasias and developmental language dysfunctions according to a theoretical model of the receptive and expressive functions involved in the four linguistic modalities. He categorized the predominantly auditory-vocal anomalies as "developmental word deafness" (akin to adult auditory aphasia), and "developmental motor aphasias" or "motor speech delay" (akin to adult motor aphasia). Analogous to these in the visual-motor realm are "developmental word blindness" or "strephosymbolia," and "developmental apraxia" or "abnormal clumsiness."

As to the clinical features of developmental word-deafness, the primary characteristic was said to be "a difficulty in the recognition of the spoken word" with one of the underlying defects frequently being slowness of the processing of auditory intake. The patients exhibited better understanding of what was being said when the speaker was slow and deliberate in enunciation than when speech was produced at a normal conversational rate. Therefore, they could be distinguished from children suffering high-frequency deafness,[2] since neither the proximity of the speaker nor loudness affected comprehension.

Considering common factors in the evolving but defective language-functions of the children that he trained, Orton observed that, in addition to the frequent slow rate of auditory intake, an impairment in auditory memory was invariably involved in the difficulties of word-deaf children. As a result, words previously heard are not recalled and cannot be used for speech or recognized when heard again. In turn, he saw this lack of recall as related to observed problems with sequencing, so that "the trouble lay in the recall of sequences of word sounds in the correct time order, comparable to the difficulty in the recall of spatial sequences in developmental word blindness." However, it was noted that some patients could echo accurately many of the words that they could not recall in spontaneous expression.

Orton also noted a frequently marked delay in the development of expressive language. Speech does develop in the word-deaf child, but more slowly than in a normal child, and with quite definite, characteristic distortions. However, the basic dysfunction ranges in severity, and thus the developmental delay and subsequent anomalies show significant variation from case to case. On the whole, as linguistic expression makes its appearance, there is a "tendency to a prolonged period of echolalia and a prolix use of the small and often defective vocabulary which is available." The latter, according to Orton, is analogous to the paraphasic fluency of adult sensory aphasics. The child, then, like the adult, may go on and on in a flow of difficult-to-understand speech, seemingly without perceiving his own unintelligibility. With growth, he does gain some degree of speech comprehension, but even though individual words may be grasped and learned, there is often an added lack of

[2]Orton qualified Ewing's findings by suggesting that hearing loss in the high frequencies is not the only selective hearing impairment that interferes with language development. Although less common, "lessened acuity may be found for only the lower pitches," equally affecting the acquisition of language. Therefore, he suggested the term "regional deafness" to describe all nondysphasic language impairment that arises from selective dysacuity.

comprehension when they are combined syntactically in phrases and sentences.

The specific distortions that Orton observed as development proceeded included elisions and inappropriate substitutions of sounds within words, and a tendency to elide whole words in sentences, together with uncommonly defective grammar. Among those children he saw with mild degrees of word-deafness, there was a "tendency to misuse words through confusion with those of somewhat similar sound. . . ." Difficulty in reading was encountered by those children who tried to learn to read.

Orton drew a fairly sharp distinction between patients with developmental word-deafness and developmental motor-aphasia. Both show lags in the appearance of expressive language and distortions in the speech that does evolve, but although the word-deaf exhibit little if any appreciation of the significance of what is spoken to them, the motor-aphasics "appear capable of comprehending the speech of others." The latter did not show the inattentiveness to auditory stimuli characteristic of children with word-deafness, and were distinguishable from the deaf. Further, once verbal expression has developed, such children can recognize their own inability to produce the correct pronunciation of the word which they have heard.

The fundamental defect that Orton attributed to developmental motor-aphasia again involved sequencing, but in this instance the difficulty was said to lie in the encoding rather than the decoding or recalling of linguistic sound-sequences in the correct temporal order. The motor-aphasic patients were able to accurately reproduce isolated sounds which they could not then use to construct syllables or words. Some could echo correctly all the sounds of the alphabet, but were unable to combine them into words. Therefore, from Orton's viewpoint, "it is this sequential blending which seems to constitute the greater part of their difficulty in acquiring propositional speech." Unlike the developmentally word-deaf, the motor-aphasic child's problem is relatively easily compensated and improvement is spontaneous. Often, however, there are noticeable sequelae in the form of stuttering, lisps, or other immaturities of speech that persist after the child has begun to speak intelligibly. In many instances, a degree of difficulty with blending sounds may persist even when the child can repeat words without errors immediately upon hearing them or from memory.

Although Orton recognized that "combined or mixed syndromes" exist among the developmental impairments (including dyslexia and apraxia), he stated that linguistic dysfunctions in children seem to be more highly selective and, thus, "more nearly approach the abstraction of a pure condition than do those which follow a lesion of the brain in the adult."

Other researchers have taken strong exception to Orton's views regarding the pure condition. For example, Myklebust (1952) states that mixed cases are the norm rather than the exception, and the matter of whether to call a child either expressively or receptively impaired depends upon which aspect seems most defective. Further, since inner language is composed of both receptive and expressive processes, its impairment can be viewed as *central aphasia*. The more severe the expressive and/or receptive defects, the more central the condition becomes. "From this point of view, [pure] central aphasia is a lack of symbolic behavior; there is no facility either expressively or receptively."

In spite of this deemphasis of pure conditions, Myklebust (1954) rather sharply differentiated the characteristics of expressive dysphasia from those of the receptive, mixed, and central categories. He described the expressive symptomatology as "peculiarly limited to the lack of speech." A child thus afflicted rarely will vocalize, even in jargon or by echoing. He is less apt than other dysphasics to be seen as brain-injured, because he is more likely to be intact both emotionally and motorically. The condition is rather rare and considerably variable in severity from case to case:

> Some are lacking in ability to speak, while others have minimal disability which is not readily determinable. Intermittent ability to use words, phrases, or sentences is common and frequently symptomatic. (p. 149)

As to the receptively impaired child, Myklebust reflected the thinking of previous writers in stating that the essential anomaly consists of a lack of comprehension of speech that is adequately heard. The accompanying expressive defects are seen as directly related to this. In the more common mixed cases, the expressive defects are not only a function of faulty reception, but rather "a superimposed deficiency of an expressive type is present." While Myklebust stressed the importance of delineating the expressive versus the receptive components in such cases, he also stated that the "behavioral symptomatology of children with mixed receptive-expressive aphasia cannot be differentiated from those with predominantly receptive aphasia."

Myklebust's description differed in some notable ways from those of other writers. In general, he discounted the importance of delayed speech development as a diagnostic feature, noting that a lag in linguistic development is characteristic of a variety of conditions, of which dysphasia is only one. The basic symbolic disorder, or impairment in the decoding (and encoding) of meaning, results in incapacity to communicate with others and with oneself, which is reflected in a quite specific symptom picture. The speech attempts of the very young patient consist mainly of meaningless, purely random jargon. When recognizable words do appear, they are used indiscriminately to refer to a variety of objects. In moderate conditions, words may be used correctly but with little consistency. For example, the child may correctly identify an object by its name but be unable to do so again a moment later. Echolalia is commonly observed, but Myklebust defined it as *involuntary* verbal imitation. In other words, the child may appear to be imitating or using words accurately on occasion, but he cannot do so intentionally or upon demand. In fact, the sporadic meaningful use of words, seemingly by chance and without conscious intention, was seen as "indicative of receptive aphasia . . . and a good prognostic sign." Furthermore, the symbolic impairment is not limited to auditory-vocal language, and unlike the deaf child, the receptively dysphasic child is greatly deficient in the use of gesturing as a means of communication.

According to Myklebust, because of the general meaninglessness of auditory stimuli for the child, the auditory experience is confused and fragmented, and the patient's responses are exceptionally erratic. Moreover, due to the generalized incapacity to relate perceptually or symbolically to the environment, compensatory uses of other senses are also defective.

In 1964, Benton summarized the trends in clinical observation and thought regarding developmental dysphasia. Among the array of reported expressive anomalies, he described muteness, idioglossia, "telegraphic speech," defective spontaneous and imitative speech (or spontaneous, but not imitative speech), and syntactical poverty. All of these anomalies he presented as representing differences in the severity of "articulatory disturbance." In addition, he noted the frequent contribution of varying "symbolic and praxic factors." The latter ranged from "the child who is apparently unable to formulate his intentions or ideas in verbal terms and who seems to be suffering from true 'central aphasia,' " to the child who displays "an apraxia or dyspraxia of speech with central language processes being more or less intact." He also observed that some partially deaf children fail to learn language in spite of a degree of sensitivity to sounds that ought to have made such acquisition possible.

Gordon (1966) approached the problems involved in categorizing the child who does not talk predominantly from the point of view of reception. The issue of expressive dysphasia he quickly dismissed as a question of severity, by noting that mild disorders of language affect expression while more severe difficulties impair reception and comprehension. From there, he went on to distinguish between peripheral and central deafness. He defined "congenital peripheral deafness" as impaired sensory reception due to "faults in the outer, middle and inner ear, and in the auditory nerve and its nucleus in the brain stem." "Congenital central deafness," on the other hand, was generally concordant with other workers' notions of auditory imperception, and developmental word-deafness. At its most profound level, central deafness is an incapacity to associate meaning with any environmental sounds, but in less severe forms only language sounds are affected. The author noted the lack of attention or "orienting reflex" to sound in early childhood, but added that there is often a progressive factor involved. In early life, the child might alert normally to sound, but then, mystifyingly, lose this reflex as he grows older. This finding was corroborated by a piece of research (Mark and Hardy, 1958), showing that disturbances of the "orienting" reflex in a significant portion of children with "congenital CNS pathology" emerges as late as the third or fourth year of life.

In 1968, Worster-Drought returned to the literature with a summation of his observation of childhood language dysfunctioning over the years. The concept of congenital auditory imperception remained largely unchanged excepting that he now accorded "defective auditory word memory" a more prominent, though not essential, role in among the characteristic defects. Four grades of auditory imperception were delineated:

1. Pure word-deafness only
2. Word or language deafness with inability to distinguish between cruder sounds
3. . . . some actual hearing loss although insufficient to account for the child not learning spoken language to some extent
4. . . . more profound auditory imperception . . . [in which] electro-encephalogram responses may constitute the only evidence that they possess hearing. It appears quite clear that they cannot distinguish between different sounds and it is probable that to them all sounds seem alike. (p. 434)

Another line of thinking regarding language-impaired children has been presented by Eisenson (1963; 1968). According to him, the majority of children he determined to be "developmentally aphasic" presented evidence of central nervous system involvement, and he considered the presence of auditory imperception in itself an indication of organic dysfunction. When his book, *Aphasia in Children*, appeared in 1972, his observation was that "about one child in two or three" in whom he saw congenital aphasic features, displayed hard evidence of neurologic impairment. At least another third gave the soft indications of "minimal brain damage," apparently leaving room for a sizable group who showed neither hard nor soft signs.

With regard to the rarity of developmental dysphasia, for which he coined the term *dyslogia*, Eisenson declared that in his experience of the nonverbal children seen at the Stanford University Institute for Childhood Aphasia, only a comparatively small number could qualify as truly dysphasic. The great majority showed such impairment of overall intellectual functioning that with or without other signs of central nervous system damage they could be viewed as mentally retarded. The clinical features which, for Eisenson, placed children in the category of the developmentally dysphasic or "dyslogic" were as follows:

> 1. Perceptual dysfunctions are in one or more sensory modalities, but not in all modalities. Auditory perception is almost invariably involved. . . .
> 2. Auditory dysfunction is in excess of what would ordinarily be implied on the basis of conventionally determined (audiometric) hearing loss. Such dysfunction includes difficulty in speech sound (phonemic) discrimination and phonemic sequencing. . . .
> 3. Sequencing difficulties are pronounced for auditory events, but also may be present for visual events.
> 4. Intellectual inefficiency is over and above any objectively determined mental limitation. . . .
> 5. Language development may be so retarded that the child at age four or five may still be essentially non-verbal both for the comprehension and production of speech. In other instances . . . the child may have a delayed onset of speech. (1972, pp. 62-65)

Eisenson's emphasis on auditory imperception as *the* fundamental defect in developmental dysphasia eliminates children such as those described by Orton, Myklebust, Benton, Worster-Drought, and others as exhibiting seemingly normal comprehension but varying degrees of expressive difficulty. Like Lenneberg (1962), he classified such children on the basis of a purely motoric, as opposed to symbolic, defect. Thus, Eisenson (1972) referred to them as suffering an "oral" or "articulatory" apraxia, a condition that could involve specifically the muscular dynamics required to produce intelligible language:

> Oral apraxia may be defined as an inability or a severe impairment in the individual's ability to perform voluntary movements involving muscles of the larynx, pharynx, tongue, palate, and cheeks, although automatic movements of the same musculature appear to be unimpaired. (p. 190)

Instances of expressive difficulty that could not be categorized in this manner were considered to be causally related to a basic anomaly in auditory perception—all these children suffered from a defect in their capacity to process verbal intake. He described these children as being less efficient listeners than normal group and to be more dependent on visual input than auditory input. He further noted that a major problem among many diagnosed dysphasic children rests in perceiving and/or maintaining the temporal order of sounds of varying qualities other than amplitude. In addition, it was assumed that "the storage system for speech signals may be defective." In severe instances, the child might appear deaf and mute because of an inability to maintain the auditory information even for the instant it takes to immediately repeat it. When the problem is less severe, immediate imitation of speech may be possible, but longer-term recall could be defective. Other writers have indicated that defects and limitations of auditory memory are the central issues in language-impaired children (Masland and Case, 1968). These defects are of four types: (1) limited span of auditory attention; (2) decreased capacity for recall; (3) deficient memory for sequences of auditory information; and (4) faulty memory for "patterning of phonetic details" resulting in elisions and substitution.

Some research findings have tended to corroborate Eisenson's postulations; others have failed to substantiate them. Using pure tones of different pitch, Lowe and Campbell (1965) showed that a group of "aphasoid" children required significantly greater intervals between tones to distinguish which, high or low, came first in each pair than did a normal control group. However, the dysphasic children were no different from the controls in terms of the minimal intervals necessary to perceive the signals as nonsimultaneous. McReynolds (1966) demonstrated a difference between "aphasic" children and normals in learning to discriminate between speech sounds produced in a nonsense word context and in isolation. The linguistically defective group took longer and made more mistakes on the average than the controls under both conditions. Their most markedly discrepant functioning, though, lay in the slowness and inaccuracy of their attempts to distinguish between the sounds in context as opposed to those in isolation. Tallal and Piercy investigated the issue in a number of experiments (1973a; 1973b; 1974; 1975), including among their variables the interval between the speech sounds to be discriminated, the number of sounds presented, and types of speech sounds with inherently different temporal cues. In all instances, the dysphasic children as a group had more difficulty identifying the correct temporal order of sounds than the normal control children. However, Bloom and Lahey (1978) made note of the fact that a sizable minority of the dysphasic children in the groups under study did *not* exhibit notable differences from the controls in auditory sequencing. They posed the, as yet unanswered, question of how the language of such dysphasics differs from the language of those who are defective in the perception of sequential sounds.

More recently, clinicians have viewed dysphasia as one factor contributing to the overall disability of the affected children. De Hirsch (1973) identifies the fundamental linguistic defect of the child as due to difficulties in perception of the temporal sequence and patterns of verbal events resulting in serious incapacity in deducing and learning syntactical rules and structures. However, she also points to a series of related deficits:

> . . . the majority are children with a family history of language disorders, a cloudy prenatal and postnatal history, some developmental deviations, and almost always, delayed speech onset and academic difficulties. Investigation reveals a degree of hyperkinesis, hypotonia, global motility, patterning and fine motor and grapho-motor clumsiness, instability of perceptuo-motor experience, difficulty in focusing, and some social dyspraxia. More or less subtle gaps in language processing, semantic limitations, dysnomia, and a paucity of syntactical options are present in most of the youngsters. In short, they show . . . "atypicality" and, one might add, immaturity of central nervous system organization. (p. 158)

Because of the developmental nature of the condition, de Hirsch emphasized the necessity for considering it from an organismic point of view, and to approach the child's problems categorically (as arising from either the organic defects or the neurotic components), she regarded as oversimplified. Whether the emotional conflicts and cognitive anomalies are an integral part of the organic impairment or a result of it, or whether they are coexistent and mutually reinforcing, they are interactive and must be understood as a whole.

It was from this standpoint that de Ajuriaguerra and his colleagues (1976) approached their cross-sectional and longitudinal studies of developmentally dysphasic children, considering language "not as a function in itself, but rather in connection with mental and affective dynamics." In the initial cross-sectional study of 40 dysphasics, they found the most meaningful linguistic distinction among them in "restrained" versus "unrestrained" verbal behavior. Common to both was the impairment of verbal comprehension and expression, which the authors regarded as the constants of dysphasia generally. Allowing for situational variations, they described the predominant features of each group. The restrained were those whose expression was restricted and marked by the use of simple sentences and enumerative or descriptive narration, and who showed little discrepancy between comprehension and expression. The unrestrained, on the other hand, were more voluble (yet also more variable), and displayed "intermittent use of complex sentences, variant word order . . . more complex but generally incoherent narration . . . [and] showed a rather large discrepancy between comprehension and production."

De Ajuriaguerra *et al.* determined the intellectual levels of the children quantitatively on a standardized test, the Wechsler Intelligence Scale for Children (WISC), and found the majority to be normal. However, normality of intelligence was not a criterion for diagnosis. Also, contradicting Eisenson (1972) and numerous other clinicians and researchers like Morely (1972), they eschewed the exclusive use of nonverbal tests as indicators of cognitive ability in dysphasic children:

> . . . to call certain tests "non-verbal" seemed to us to constitute a kind of misrepresentation, since presenting a child with a situation not requiring an explicit verbal expression still does not indicate that language plays no role in his comprehension of meaning and in his making a response. (p. 348)

In analyzing their data from the WISC, de Ajuriaguerra *et al.* found that some subtests in the verbal portion of the test could be taken as a measure of intellectual level in spite of language problems. The consistent discrepancies they uncovered did not include the traditionally posited dichotomy of low verbal–high performance, but rather an uneven picture, with inadequate functioning in particular verbal areas (i.e., Information, Vocabulary, and Arithmetic) and markedly higher functioning on others (i.e., Comprehension and Similarities). This was linked most often with discrepancy among the performance subtests that indicated a deficit in spatial structuralization.

Describing the cognitive function of their children in Piagetian terms, the researchers came to the conclusion that, generally, dysphasics are prone to run into significant problems as they develop toward thought processes beyond the level of "concrete operations" (i.e., where conceptualization is still closely associated with the actual concrete world of objects and events, as opposed to the hypothetical world of the possible that opens up with the development of formal cognitive operations). Having observed some problems with nonverbal aspects of symbolization (i.e., representational imagery and figurative anticipation), they predicted that the children would be unable to achieve the level of formal operations: "the lack of mobility of his [the dysphasic's] thought prevents him from handling abstract concepts and from putting the appropriate distance between himself and the problem to be solved." This coincides with the impressions garnered by Inhelder (1976) from her observations of dysphasic children, to which, however, she added a cautionary note: "our present knowledge of the origin and laws that govern language development is far too rudimentary to allow us to assign a place to language deficiencies in relation to the total symbolic and linguistic structures."

Regarding the affective-social aspects of dysphasic functioning, de Ajuriaguerra and his colleagues categorized their subjects as follows:

> (1) . . . personality organization *within normal limits* except for verbal dialogue; (2) . . . developmental disequilibrium with free-floating anxiety characteristic *of an affective retardation or of a so-called pre-neurotic state;* (3) *neurotic, prepsychotic,* or psychotic organization of personality—with solidly constructed defense mechanisms and a relatively rigid, almost closed personality structure. (pp. 349–350)

Essentially, they found that while the affectively normal children were less delayed on the average in the onset of expressive language, the *severity* of the linguistic anomalies among all of the children bore no relation to their affective-social condition. What was significantly related to this condition was the *need* to communicate, either verbally or nonverbally. They further observed that the majority of well-adjusted children had a verbally restrained form of communication, whereas children with serious emotional problems belonged to the verbally unrestrained category.

After following 17 of their subjects over a two-year span, they noted that, although the children individually retained the same basic picture of specific defects, there was development in the majority of linguistic functions studied. However, on the whole, some areas of functioning showed greater development than others, and these were described as having the greatest "utilitarian" value in enabling the children to interact communicatively with others, despite their continued impairment. Further, these improvements occured, to the greatest extent, among those children who displayed the greatest need to communicate and the least affective disturbance (the verbally restrained). In a like manner, among the verbally unrestrained, progressive adjustment coincided with the appearance of inhibition and better communication skills.

Because of the compensatory nature of its development, the language of these dysphasics was said to be *different* rather than retarded. The researchers concluded that "dysphasia . . . is not reducible to an obstruction in the development of language, but it represents a particular form of language disorganization in development." In agreement with de Hirsch, de Ajuriaguerra *et al.* observed that the difficulty rested in the child's inability to acquire the structural or syntactical logic of language, hence their peculiar mode of decoding what is said to them:

> Since the internal logic of the message is not grasped, the learning of the [linguistic] operation is confused. It is in the gist of what is said, in the gray of what is transmitted, and in the fringes of the formulated or of the unformulated implied in communication that the dysphasic finds his mode of reference; it is in this way that, even if the dysphasic does not understand the exact form, he will nevertheless receive the message. (p. 367)

As evidence of this peculiarity among their children, the workers pointed to the relative lack of improvement in auditory perception coupled with clearly greater improvement in auditory comprehension over the two years. Likewise, in coming to express himself, they noted that the dysphasic stresses those aspects of verbal development that are most vital to getting the message across. Therefore, they found it relevant that their children showed little improvement in motor–speech coordination, while they did improve the phonetic organization of their expression in such a way as to render themselves intelligible.

BEHAVIORAL PROBLEMS

Over the years that developmental dysphasia has been a topic of discussion in the literature, some writers have attempted to delineate the emotional and social problems that typically arise, secondary to the linguistic impairment. Among the early researchers, a number were concerned with a tendency to delinquency among the patients who came to their attention (McCready, 1926). However, after 27 years of observing dysphasics, Orton (1937) came to emphasize the variability of emotional reactions, and added,

> As the child who carries any form of unrelieved language handicap grows older, there naturally ensues an accumulated emotional overlay which in many instances makes any effort to assign etiological significance to either the organic or the emotional factors that are then apparent in the situation as purposeless as attempting to allot preeminence to either the warp or the woof of a piece of cloth. (p. 132)

As one scans the literature on developmental dysphasia, one finds that among reported cases, the variance from child to child appears too wide to accommodate any simple characterization of the children's personalities or emotional responses. Myklebust (1954) portrayed dysphasic children as deficient in the depth and intensity of emotional reactions. He felt that defective interpretation of symbols results in failure to comprehend social cues, and although the child is not withdrawn or uninterested in interpersonal relationship, he is incapable of smooth, easy relationships. Other writers have described individual, or small numbers of children and commented on the varied outcomes (Weiner, 1974; Berg, 1961; Morely, 1972).

In 1977, Cantwell and Baker extensively reviewed the literature on emotional disorder in children with impairments of speech and language, and drew a number of tentative conclusions beyond which they noted that attempts at generalized statements remained purely in the realm of the hypothetical. First, they reported an increased prevalence of psychiatric disorders over the years in the published accounts and studies of childhood speech and language anomalies. However, they concluded that there is no particular type of psychiatric picture characteristic of language deficits. Furthermore,

> . . . it seems that children with pure speech disorders are less likely to have psychiatric problems than children with more global language disorders. Children with receptive language disorders may be more likely to have psychiatric problems than children with pure expressive disturbances. . . . It seems that children with comprehension defects are likely to demonstrate an autistic-like impairment of social relationships. . . . the data reviewed indicate that many of the effects of speech and language retardation on emotional development are indirect and due to the child's interaction with his environment. . . . (pp. 585–586)

PROGNOSIS

The issue of prognosis in developmental dysphasia also has been approached rather ambiguously by most writers. The general tenor of prognostic statements is that such children do develop in linguistic functioning regardless of the nature of their predominant anomalies. However, the degree to which they become linguistically facile depends upon a complexity of interrelated factors. Those most frequently mentioned are the severity and cross-modal breadth of the dysfunctioning, intellectual capacity, the emotional aura in which the child develops, and, reciprocally, the make-up of the child's growing personality as well as early and accurate recognition of the impairment and appropriate intervention. There also has been fairly consistent allusion to the relatively temporary nature of expressive dysphasia, versus the more persistent impairment involved in receptive or mixed dysphasia, by those writers who have made such diagnostic distinctions. Relatively little has been said specifically about the course (or courses) of dysphasia over the years, though the described anomalies in most cases appear to progress from an overall delay in the onset of language to increasingly differentiated defects as the child develops. Finally, very little has been written about the dysphasic in later life. As of 1974, Weiner noted the "almost complete lack of published data on the functioning of language delayed children beyond the pre-school and primary years."

Among the early writers, the significance of remedial training to prognosis in dysphasia was particularly stressed, largely in reaction to the fact that most cases severe enough to be brought to professional attention had been diagnosed and neglected as mentally feeble, and were regarded as having become "imbeciles from deprivation" (Burr, 1912). Worster-Drought and Allen (1930) observed the beneficial results of education in the auditorily imperceptive child. The amount of progress that could be expected from child to child was quite variable and dependent upon the severity of the overall dysfunctioning: "some can make only a few sounds, while others have a fairly large vocabulary which includes sounds and expressions for most of the objects and affective states which come within their experience." A much brighter prognosis picture was drawn by Ewing (1930). Although he averred that without special teaching the linguistically retarded child will not develop full functional and communicative use of language, he reported impressive progress for the cases under his care, to the point of normality or seeming normality for many.

Orton (1937) echoed the warnings of "feeble-mindedness by deprivation," but apparently only for those cases suffering "developmental word deafness." To the motor dysphasic, he was clear in assigning a generally good outlook. He believed that, with or without training, expressly dysphasic children will improve over the years, so that by school age very little of their deficiencies are detectable. On the other hand, without appropriate training, it was deemed likely that the word-deaf child would not attain normalcy. Cautioning that the small number of those word-deaf patients followed in training precluded definitive prognostic statements, he described their progress as "suggestively promising." However, his position on mixed cases (i.e., those involving word-deafness, dyslexia, and apraxia) was implicitly pessimistic, due to the complexity of the problem and lack of substantive knowledge and appropriate remedial techniques.

This same emphasis on training as the key factor in the eventual functional ability of dysphasic children continued among later writers. Some have offered a highly positive prognosis on the whole, while others have predicted less optimistic outcomes. Representing the positive, Silver and Hagin (1965) stated:

> The diagnosis of a developmental language disability implies a much more optimistic prognosis provided that the defect is clearly identified, the areas of perceptual deficit described, and a stimulating educational experience offered. (p. 486)

Eisenson (1963) regarded the child classified as dysphasic in his terms (i.e., with a fundamentally receptive problem) as prognostically hopeful providing that their intellectual functioning and hearing are normal. His hopefulness, however, bore the qualification that such children may remain somewhat concrete. In spite of this, he considered it quite possible for the dysphasic to acquire average levels of academic and communicative skills. The prediction of limitation in the level of abstract thought processes eventually attainable by dysphasics due to a lack of facility in the use of articulate verbal symbolization, is essentially the same made by Inhelder (1976) and by de Ajuriaguerra and his colleagues (1976). The implications for restriction in later educational and career options is evident; however, with little direct evidence to go on, these authors remained more or less tentative in their general prognostications.

Morely's (1972) prognostic statements were considerably more definite due, at least in part, to the fact that the severity and duration of the anomalies presented were factors in drawing up her original diagnostic categorizations. Receptive dysphasia was regarded holistically as a severe disability, and as such was seen to indicate poor response to treatment and serious lifelong limitation. Expressive dysphasia, on the other hand, was subcategorized according to the duration of the initial speech delay, with the vast majority of patients falling under the classification of "transient," and the remainder designated as "prolonged." The former were those patients whose speech did not make its initial appearance until age four, but developed satisfactorily after that. These patients, she noted, could be considered as representing the "terminal gradient on the slope of normal development," and thus essentially not a pathological entity. The prolonged dysphasics were those whose onset of speech was delayed six years or more. Of these patients, she stated that normal schooling is interrupted, but she considered them in an, apparently, much more optimistic light than receptive dysphasics.

One point that recurs throughout the literature is the prognostic importance of early recognition of the anomalies and initiation of treatment. Commenting on the inadequacy of remedial facilities, Myklebust (1952) declared: "if such specialized remedial programs were inaugurated during the child's early school life, there is strong suggestion that like many other handicapped children, the aphasic child could progress with the normal child during his later elementary school life." De Hirsch (1973) considered early recognition *the* most relevant factor in the efficacy of treatment, and thus in prognosis:

> . . . linguistic intervention cannot come too early. I know from many years of experience how much better the chances are for success at 30 than at 40 months. We need the earliest possible intervention because of the far greater plasticity of the brain at earlier ages and because failure to progress and use language has severe repercussions on the ego functions that are essential for learning. (p. 162)

CLASSIFICATION

Looking at the literature on specific language dysfunctioning from the standpoint of the homogeneity or heterogeneity of observation and conceptualization, a fairly sharp contrast is evident between the writing on acquired aphasia and congenital or development dysphasia in children. Though studies of acquired aphasia are few, there is a comparatively high level of agreement among the writers as to symptomatology, course, and prognosis. One could arrive at a quite specific and well-delinated concept of acquired aphasia from the literature alone, without too much straining to accommodate conflicting statements.

In the case of acquired aphasia, there is some inconsistency regarding the prevalence and timing of specific aberrations of language according to developmental stage. However, one gets a strong sense, in reading the different authors, that they have been observing essentially the same phenomena. One major reason for this is that the cases from which all have derived their descriptions have been selected on the basis of a common, straightforward, directly observable sequence of pathognomonic events. In each child, linguistic development had proceeded, as one might expect, from the child's endowment and environment up to the point of abrupt impairment, following an incident that was highly probable, if not certain, to have caused brain damage.

In the absence of recognizable precipitating events and, as is frequently the case, of unequivocal neurologic findings, most writers have presumed that the developmental dysphasia derives from central nervous system damage or defect of one form or another.

In the effort to explain more cogently the linguistic impairments they have observed and to draw more clearly bounded and logically unitary concepts of dysphasia, some writers have sought to define the underlying functional defect from which all children, so diagnosed, suffer. Others have subcategorized the impairments according to the predominant modality of dysfunction (receptive, expressive, central, etc.), and defined the underlying anomaly in each. These fundamental dysfunctions, in turn, tend to become essential criteria for applying the diagnostic label, and thus for depositing children who consequently validate the original diagnostic conceptualization into the category.

Another means of clarifying the diagnosis of dysphasia, particularly in the early literature, has been to rule out conditions that also are associated with impaired language development. So, to be sure that the dysphasic child is not to be confused with the deaf child, a finding of hearing-loss was held to be a contraindication of dysphasia. The possibility that a child might suffer an auditory dysacuity as well as dysphasic anomalies was precluded, only to be recognized as a fairly common phenomenon by later observers. Similarly, the need to distinguish dysphasia from general mental retardation led to the notion that dysphasic children must be of at least "normal" or "average" intelligence. This restriction is still seen from time to time in the literature, although it implies that retarded children are somehow immune to dysphasic impairment and vice versa. The answer for some writers has been to multiply sub-categories of dysfunction, according to predominant and secondary defects or the presence or absence of organic indications. After reviewing taxonomic confusion in the area of children's language disorders, Hardy (1965) came to the following conclusions:

> One way toward freedom from this tendency, which I suspect is common to all of us, is to agree to use the term *aphasia* in broad reference to *an individual's incapacities in language comprehension and use,* and then go on to describe and demonstrate as thoroughly as possible what these incapacities are and what residual, or possibly substitute, capacities are available. (p. 5)

At this stage, it can be safely assumed that there exist, in some children, impairments specific to the developing linguistic in-strumentalities of communication which vary widely in form, and may be met in indeterminate numbers of combinations and degrees of severity, and in association with any number of other resultant or concomitant disabilities or disorders. In the subsequent chapters, we will outline the nature of linguistic behavior and its development, and discuss the characteristics and clinical evaluation of its dys-phasic impairment. Although we will refer to them broadly as developmentally dysphasic phenomena, it is neither our intent to add yet another set of diagnostic criteria to the literature nor to typify dysphasic children. Although there are more or less evident trends to be seen among those bearing such anomalies, the unexpected seems always to make its appearance just as one is growing comfortable in one's categorical generalizations.

4

Deviant and Normal Social Development

The child's adaptation and development of various aspects of his personality are dependent upon the availability of a group of well-tested coping mechanisms and viable strategies provided in the social network. Their need for social survival makes it necessary for parents to help induct the child into the social milieu through encouragement, direct teaching, and even coercion. The innate impetus for socialization compels the child to accept what is offered, learn what is exhibited, and actively select from what is present. Gradually the child's unique personality is shaped, and a complex psychological being is created. On the other hand, incorporating each new individual into the social network confronts the system with a new challenge. As the social system shapes the child's personality, it is in turn modified by him. This reciprocal interaction prevents the fossilization of the social network, and assures the guided development of each individual's psychology.

In spite of much research effort, it cannot be confidently claimed that parental cognitive styles or their maladaptive thinking are learned or inherited by their children. However, it is fairly clear that the child's affective development and his emotional expressiveness are greatly influenced by the prolonged and intimate interactions with them. Regardless of the variety of unknown, presumptive factors responsible for development and expression of adaptive or maladaptive cognition and organized or disordered thinking, the totality of the child's adaptation to the environment is influenced by the internal symbolic frame which he has managed and been made to create for himself.

In this and the following chapter, some of the presumptive factors responsible for the development of this internal framework as well as the dim outlines of its reflection on the adaptation are under discussion.

Socialization is the process by which innate endowments of a neonate are nurtured and shaped. It is the continuous interplay between biological, maturational, and social factors through which these interlocking threads are woven into a complex tapestry of behavioral propensities, dispositional characteristics and attitudes. Deficits and peculiarities of any one factor are reflected in the imperfection of the totality and various degrees of deviations in all characteristics. Even when deficiencies are compensated for, these compensatory mechanisms may, on their own, derail the train of development revealing the weaknesses of the whole system. Various elements of the interactional system may range from nonfunctional to highly effective. Near optimal adjustment may be achieved in spite of suboptimal functions in a few areas provided that compensatory mechanisms are at work during crucial periods of development and provided that the level of deficiency is not below a critical point. Much of the work in clinical psychiatry has been directed toward describing the most deviant outcome of the continuous interaction between the individual and his environment. Questions of etiology have been addressed either in global impressionistic terms such as psychosis, or one factor has been unduly stressed as the explanatory proposition (such as organic brain syndrome). The interactionist view of pathological development must assess the contribution of several factors at the same time and determine the degree of deficit which cannot be wiped out by compensatory resources within or without the individual (Wolff 1966). The combination of several suboptimal factors may impair the coping ability as much as any major deficit. For example, it has been shown that any possible behavioral deficiency emanating from low birth weight and prematurity is exaggerated in poor families, even though premature infants of the more privileged class are often indistinguishable from their normal peers (Sameroff and Chandler, 1975). In trying to delineate disabling factors and their overall impact on development, it is unavoidable that each area be discussed separately even though the interdependence and interpenetration of various parameters are unquestionable. Admittedly, much of what can be logically hypothesized is in need of experimental verification. A reasoned exposition of the hypothetical interaction between various forces exemplified by clinical situations is all that can be provided at the present time.

The first step must be a discussion of those factors which may result in suboptimal endowment. Little is known about the specific effects of molecular and submolecular disorders on the functional capacity of the central nervous system. Chromosomal abnormalities which exhibit no identifiable damage to the structure of the central nervous system and yet markedly lower the cognitive abilities are good examples of this category. Even when structural damage to the central nervous system is suspected or verified, the type of dysfunction associated with it does not show the constancy in quality or magnitude of the malfunction which would allow for assertion of causal relationship. The same ambiguous connection exists between biochemical abnormalities and the resultant disabling psychological conditions. What is more clearly substantiated is that the capacity for recovering certain lost functions and the possibility for reversal of, or halt to, deteriorating influences of some biochemical disturbances decreases with time. The notion of a critical period or a necessary and sufficient level of functional neurologic substrate for normal development—although not illogical—has not received much clinical support. In a vast majority of disorders which begin during the intrauterine period, not only the central nervous system but other organs are also affected. It is not possible to separate the role played by these nonneurologic abnormalities from those which are related to the brain (Wynne, 1978). For example, we do not know to what degree the muscular hypotonicity of a child with Down Syndrome may impair the patient's overall adjustment. Inborn deficiencies may remain unrecognized for months or years, either because their expression requires accumulation of certain kinds of life experiences, or because the failures signifying them do not appear before certain challenges are to be met. Furthermore, it is as yet unclear whether dissimilar disturbances create similar abnormalities in the neurochemistry of the brain, or the specificity of biochemical anomalies is lost in interactional processes leading to the emergence of common behavioral pictures. Thus it is the frequent association between certain biochemical or physical events or presumptive occurrences which form the basis for etiological considerations. In present day psychiatric thinking, the notion of unitary causative agent has been replaced by the concepts of risk factors and degrees of vulnerability which allow for the multiplicity of causation and cumulative or mitigating results.

Disturbances of Arousal

Fluctuations of state of arousal may reach abnormal proportions in both directions of hyper- or hyposensitivity. Identifiable factors such as administration of painkillers and anesthetics during labor, maternal addiction to narcotics, or disturbances of metabolism may account for transient irregularities of the first few days. However, unknown factors causing chemical or structural anomalies of the central nervous system may underlie the peculiarities of the more prolonged nature (Escalona, 1962). Regardless of the cause, the newborn's state of arousal will influence the kind and intensity of stimulation directed at him. Moreover, the uncommon pattern of arousal makes it necessary for the caretakers to engage in a process of trial and error in order to understand and accommodate the infant. Although decreased reactivity on the part of the neonate may go unheeded or be a welcome situation for the parents, hypersensitivity and the concomitant excessive reaction can hardly be ignored. Even when parental expectation calls for vigor and intensity of response in the newborn, the increased reactivity of some infants may be to such an extent that general limitation of stimuli and overprotectiveness become necessary. At times cautionary measures outlive their usefulness, and the infant's search for novel stimuli runs counter to what parents are ready to allow. This may result in a continuous conflict between the child and his caretaker and retard the establishment of a good fit between the interacting pair. It may also make it more difficult for the infant to develop his own neutralizing and outscreening strategies for dealing with environmental contingencies.

Hyporeactive infants may elicit an increased degree of stimulation from parents who regard the sluggishness with alarm, or conversely, a change in their early patterns may disrupt the smooth interactional flow between them and their caretakers. Occasionally, the hyporeactivity of the neonate is the starting point in a complex picture of environmental understimulation and neglect resulting in decreased curiosity and inefficient exploration of the surroundings. At times, the high level of stimulation necessary for early interactions becomes the norm leading to a state of frenzied hyperactivity. Because an as yet unmeasured optimal level of arousal is prerequisite for exploration of the environment and for the registering of the properties of objects and characteristics of interpersonal events, irregularities of arousal and responsiveness will influence the infant's patterns of interactions, his interpersonal relationships, and his attitudes and expectations.

Excessive hyper- and hyposensitivity have been reported in the backgrounds of some young children diagnosed as psychotic or autistic (Fish, 1968). At times, the extreme hypersensitivity is limited to one class of stimuli (auditory, tactile, etc.); at other times, there is a generalized pattern of avoidance behavior exhibited by the child. Some children will preferentially limit the amount or the intensity of certain stimuli; for example, they will close their eyes or ears. Other children achieve the same result by concentrated attention to a narrow range of stimuli which make it easy to ignore the overall picture. Such selective attentiveness to one type of sensation may underlie certain stereotypic behavior resulting in the general unavailability of the child to other types of environmental influences, and finally, in restriction of the behavioral repertoire. Moreover, such defensive limitation need not be characteristic of the states of hyporeactivity, but it may be used on occasions when a low threshold for certain sensations necessitates the establishment of a protective shield. Sudden breakdown of the protective barrier, regardless of the cause, results in acute disorganization of the behavioral pattern, manifested in paralyzing panic or temper outburst. Insistence on sameness, which is inferred from the acute distress of some young autistic children confronting a change, may be due to the fact that any change in perceptual configuration will deprive the child of his customary focus for selective attentiveness and open the floodgate to all aspects of the environment. This capacity to concentrate on one kind of stimulus in order to bar entrance to unwanted ones is a property of consciousness throughout life. In older children, preoccupation with daydreams and fantastic imageries is resorted to when the environment is devoid of novelty or full of threatening stimulations. When arousal is undirected, or efforts at direction do not succeed for more than a few seconds to a few minutes, no aspect of the environment can be fully registered or comprehended. Such fleeting attention, regardless of its cause but depending on its severity and duration, may result in inadequate exploration and unsubstantial conceptualization of the objective world. Another functionally important aspect of attentiveness is its flexibility. Although characteristics of stimuli have some part in attracting attention, the more significant factor is the ease with which attention can be focused on, or released from, its subject. When this flexibility is seriously compromised, some relevant features of stimuli may receive deficient exploration and investigation while other aspects acquire exaggerated importance. The resulting picture is an imbalanced configuration which is in fundamental discord with the consensually validated image of reality.

Disturbances of Human Relatedness

Regardless of the cause or the nature, the severest form of disability in this area is inferred from lack of eye contact, social smile, or other signs revealing the infant's differentiating responses to people and inanimate objects. It has been repeatedly noted (Fantz and Nevis, 1967; Kagan, 1976) that the human face, with its distinct configuration and movement, is of significant interest to a newborn baby. This interest can be attested to by the length of time that an infant will regard a human face. Such preferential viewing of the human face is the source of a considerable amount of information simultaneously received by visual and auditory channels. Differences between human and nonhuman objects are discovered when mutual imitative behavior and reciprocal interactions are established (Call and Marschak, 1966). The good fit between the infant and the mother results from continuous, subtle accommodation and adjustment on the part of the interacting pair. Identification of the infant's rhythm of activity and his level of tolerance for intensity and duration of interaction depends on the mother's sensitivity. However, the responsiveness and flexibility of the infant to modifications initiated by the mother is of significant import in the smooth flow of the interactive pattern (Blank, 1964). Disturbed interactions and deviant patterns of interpersonal behavior may result from any combination of pathogenic factors. For example, the integrative and organizing matrix necessary for perceptual, cognitive, and emotive differentiation between people and objects may be compromised by unknown neurochemical abnormalities. Such a state of affairs will make it extremely unlikely, if not totally impossible, for any mother to identify the infant's needs and to accommodate them. When the underlying organization necessary for the regularity and predictability of response expression is missing, the behavior cannot be comprehended with any degree of certainty. On the other hand, it is conceivable that maternal insensitivity or an inadequate capacity for accommodation results in deficient feedbacks and distorted interactive patterns as well as deviant conceptualization by the infant. Such a hypothetical scenario can account not only for extremes of unrelatedness, but also for the corrective and modifying influences of the later experiences and developmental changes. Since all social influences are mediated through interpersonal relationships, extremely limited or distorted interactions, regardless of their origins, will hamper normal psychological development. This fact remains true even when it can be shown that biological maturation is the primary force behind the attainment of certain functions. As an example, we may consider development of fine motor coordination. Leaving aside the question of the role of experience in nurturance and direction of muscular growth, it is still clear that the ability to coordinate movements of the small muscles may form the basis for acquiring a variety of social skills, or it may be only exercised in isolated, nonutilitarian fashion (Safrin, 1964). Similar nonfunctional situations exist when a child's prodigious memory or good mechanical ability remains undirected by socialization. The clinical picture in these cases is baffling and strange. The observer may note indications of average or superior abilities in a markedly disabled child who does not utilize his capacities to further his own functioning.

LACK OR DIMINUTION OF SELF-AWARENESS

The process of individuation is the summation of two parallel and complementary abilities of awareness of self and others. Because the human infant is a social-obligate animal, the potential for awareness of self and others must be among the species' specific endowments. As in any other inborn propensity, the organic substrate, or the particular configuration of biological schema in any individual member of the species, may be faulty or damaged, or deviation and disturbances may occur in the course of the unfolding process due to anomalies and deficiencies of those circumstances whose contributions are of vital import for the expression of the inborn capacity.

The birth cry signals the arrival of a sentient being, and from then on, the caretakers treat the baby's cries as indications of its awareness of its own discomfort. This awareness and its expression is diffuse and vague, but some mothers claim that the character and quality of the cries become more distinct and differentiated as the infant grows older. When, within the first six months, the infant averts his gaze in certain situations or attempts to remove a cover blocking his breathing, it is clear that the rudimentary knowledge required for individuation has been gained already. However, the attainment of more complex levels of self-awareness must await growth and integration of cognitive, emotional, and interpersonal experiences. Cognitive organization of the perceptual data of the external world, sensations, and the emotional states experienced from within proceed in contemporaneous fashion. However, though the world of objects and its attributes are similar for all individuals, interpersonal experiences may confront each person with a unique combination of opportunities. Limitation of intellectual ability will also limit the extent and complexity of self-awareness. But it does not distort it. On the other hand, deficiencies and distortions in interpersonal experiences will be reflected in deviations and distortions of the sense of self.

When the ability to integrate and organize sensory data and to make lawful elaboration and generalization is impaired, the child's reactions and responses are disorganized, aimless, and incomprehensible. Under these circumstances, even the optimal social milieu can do little more than attempt to provide a loose outer structure and keep the ambiguities of interpersonal relationships to a minimum. To this end, the intensity and quantity of relationships are curtailed; the child's wants and desires are anticipated, and expectations for age-appropriate learning and task performance are lowered. The most desired result of such sensitive—though decidedly difficult—child rearing may be revealed in the establishment of a simple differentiation of self from nonself and a primitive organization of behavior on that basis. Conversely, a suboptimal social environment aggravates deficiencies of organization and integration, with the result that the totality of the child's experiences and behavior remains chaotic and unpatterned. Without a cohesive collection of internal experiences, no sense of self can emerge to act as an organizing axis for future experiences. Examples of these extreme situations can be found among children who are profoundly retarded and are kept alive in custodial institutions.

More frequently the infant's disability is not as pervasive, and some categories of experiences are organized even though the overall integration is faulty. In these children, self may be separated from nonself in certain dimensions, but the separateness is not experienced in relation to all varieties of objects, or it is of such a tenuous nature that any intense sensation will tend to obscure its boundaries. Deficiencies in human relatedness or distortions in interpersonal relationships may hamper or postpone the development of the sense of self. In the first instance, the organism is unable to receive and/or organize the experiential data which would result in the establishment of the distinct sense of humanness. In the second situation, the distorted conceptual frame is based on anomalous experiences. Such distortions may be corrected and modified in the course of development, or they may exert a detrimental influence on different aspects of it. At the same time that separateness of self and nonself is established, various aspects of self begin to acquire a more differentiated and articulate form. The child becomes aware that his own desires may run counter to the wishes of others or the unyielding-ness of physical objects. As he tests his powers, he discovers the more rigid limits placed by objects and the continuously changing boundaries imposed by others. He deploys his meager resources to affect change and develops various strategies to cope with the external barriers at the same time that he is struggling with his own reactions, triumphs, and frustrations. He gains wisdom by trying to identify those clues which signal the possibilities for successful confrontation and achieves insight by reflecting on his own internal states. His cognitive abilities are challenged by an array of problems in need of solutions, as his global emotions undergo differentiation and modulation. Events, their resolutions and his own activities and reactions associated with them, are registered, sorted out, abstracted, and stored in memory. Some segments of imageries and emotions are labeled as dreams or daydreams and distinguished from objective reality either because expected consequences do not follow, or people and objects do not participate in the unfolding drama. The ability to detect similarities and dissimilarities, to organize perceptual data and integrate the ongoing impressions with memories of past experiences, and to formulate strategies for adaptation are component parts of self-identity. Disturbances of identity may be due to deficiencies in any one component; however, the interpenetrating nature of these factors makes it impossible to assign a primary or subsidiary role to any one factor. As the child grows older, the ambiguities and uncertainties of the objective reality as well as interpersonal events are slowly clarified; this clarity helps in articulation and definition of the child's subjective experiences. By the same token, confusing inner states cast puzzling shadows over the external world.

Limitation of the quality of human relatedness will restrict the quantity and duration of each meaningful interaction. This global deficiency results in underdevelopment of self-image, or the image thus created will be fragmentary and unsubstantial. Because the child has only inadequate or inefficient experiences of himself in interpersonal exchanges, he is unable to form a concept of himself as an effective agent in the interpersonal world. The fact that he is more at ease in manipulation of inanimate objects provides him with an alternative manner of adaptation. Thus, some severely psychotic children treat people and parts of their own bodies as inanimate objects. Lack of an internal integrative core may be inferred from the observation that some of these patients disregard the pain and injury that they inflict upon themselves. Others fail to distinguish the uniqueness of human identity in spite of similarities and common attributes with nonhumans, and their behavior toward all elements of the external world is haphazard and indiscriminate. The resultant chaotic interactions cannot aid the development of a differentiated sense of inner reality.

Disturbed Emotions

The neurohormonal substrate of emotions and the fine physiologic tuning which correlates with the intensity and variety of emotional experience are as yet uncharted. Because emotions are cognitively evaluated and selectively conveyed, intellectual development as well as communicative intent and skills are parts of the observable behavior from which emotional states are inferred. Since emotions are viewed as one of the prime motivating forces behind the individual's behavior, designation and labeling of the child's behavior as signifying certain emotions begin in the early months of infancy (Dunn, 1977). This identification of the child's behavior which is made by the caretakers cannot help but influence their own responses to the child's activities, thus reinforcing, regulating, or modifying them. Viewed in this light, the child's experience of emotion is the outcome of a complex circuit of repeated reactivities shaped by the reverberations and resonances set in motion within an ongoing interpersonal context. In this complicated interactive and interdependent process, disorders and disturbances may begin from any direction. The infant may be hypo- or hypersensitive. The caretaker may ignore certain types or intensities of reactions, show extreme sensitivity to others, designate emotions in an inconsistent or chaotic manner, or respond to them in an incongruent way. These inconsistencies make the task of sorting out emotions and their cognitive abstractions and evaluations difficult, if not impossible, for a growing infant (Emde *et al.*, 1978). Because emotions are organizing elements in certain behavioral propensities, and act as motivational factors in the development of some coping strategies, disturbances and disorders of emotions will be reflected in disorganized behavior and maladaptive coping mechanisms. Moreover, since intense, undifferentiated emotions tend to invade the consciousness, problem-solving behavior, requiring a high degree of goal-directed concentration, may be impaired. Another detrimental influence on intellect is the fact that a great deal of the individual's thinking and imaginative resources are directed toward dissipating the intensity of emotions, and neutralizing their impact, through fantasies and daydreams. This inward preoccupation causes the individual to be unavailable for interaction with the environment and beyond the reach of incidental and imitative learning.

A veneer of detachment may hide a state of undifferentiated emotions erupting in an unpredictable manner without commonly identifiable provocation; or the individual may remain in a persistently highly excitable state vacillating between overpowering emotional experiences which denote emotional immaturity. Suppression of emotions may be total or selective, and consequent deficits of character will be accompanied by deficiencies in conceptualization and integration. For example, inability to experience guilt and empathy goes hand in hand with intellectual incapacity to project oneself into the future or to analyze the probable consequences of certain courses of action.

A decrease in the scope or variety of emotional experience is reflected in a shrinkage of interest and involvement in the environment. This external withdrawal is accompanied by an internal barrenness. Fantasies and daydreams are scarce, and a feeling of emptiness replaces the experience of an active, commanding self. In the absence of an emotional imperative to seek certain goals, or to avoid certain situations, the coping mechanisms necessary for psychological survival do not develop. The child not only fails to initiate exploratory behavior and invite interactions, but he also fails to respond to stimulation initiated by others. This failure may result in diminished quantity and duration of exchanges directed at the child and thus, inadvertently, strengthen the child's isolationist tendencies. Cognitive growth is severely limited and spotty because concepts derived from the interpersonal context are meager, communicative skills are neglected, and insight generated by projection of the self into situations involving others is missing.

Regulation of emotions is inseparable from their differentiation and cognitive evaluation. Modification in reactivity follows changes in context or meaning of a given situation. This is the strategy used by parents from early infancy. The child is reassured when frightened, encouraged and cheered up when unhappy, and soothed when he is angry. Verbal and nonverbal communications are differentially employed to affect changes in emotional states. Explanations are employed to reinterpret the meaning and thus modify emotional responses. The child's anger is deflated by statements regarding the ignorance or weakness of the offending agent, or clarification of the misunderstood intention. Guilt is mitigated by pointing out the unknown or unknowable factors, the absence of desire to inflict harm, or expression of regret and acts of restitution. Sadness is made bearable by recounting past happinesses or prospects for future joy. It is clear that the more differentiated the emotions, the easier it is to attempt to modify and regulate them. This is true even when the task of regulating emotions is left to the individual himself. Children learn to modify their emotions and regain their internal equilibrium with the help of reflection upon the nature of their emotional experience; the source, character, and meaning of the stimuli generating it, and its similarity or difference with retrieved memories. As a result of this process of cognitive evaluation and regulation, the emotional experience is gradually harmonized with the expression of emotions. Moreover, even though the experience of emotion and the ideational aspect of it are contemporaneous and invariably linked, the expression of emotion is controlled by the individual and may or may not be in harmony with the subjective state. As the child grows older, the expression of emotions becomes a powerful conscious tool in influencing the interpersonal milieu.

When the regulatory mechanisms are deficient or underdeveloped, the child's interpersonal skills remain in a rudimentary stage, and his internal equilibrium is both easily imbalanced and difficult to reestablish. Such an unstable state may be due to cognitive deficiencies, deviations of the interpersonal milieu, failure of socialization processes, or a combination of all these factors.

A child—overwhelmed with anxiety, anger, or depression—remains dependent upon external sources for relief because he cannot modify his own perception, his thinking is befuddled, and his judgment of the significance and import of the interpersonal factors is poor. The reality constructed on the basis of a fragile alliance of uncrystallized emotions and confused ideation is in constant danger of imminent collapse. Awareness of the self is weakened by the inability to construct and preserve the notion of an independent, active, and organizing agent, to select the type and quantity of information, and to stimulate and regulate the output of emotions, thoughts or activities. Concurrently, others are seen as wielding the irresistible power to effect changes within and without the individual. The social network thus becomes a source of fear as well as magical power. The child's relationships with people are governed by these notions. He fears them and therefore, withdraws, fights with, or clings to them indiscriminately. He expects them to know his wishes and feels ignored or maligned. Because many of his thoughts and much of his attention are absorbed by the everchanging universe of people and their relationships to him, he is unable to construct a thorough image of the inanimate world. Distinctions and differences are blurred; objects and people are equally unfathomable. No fixed boundary is discovered or drawn. He may be an object, an animal, or a person. Unifying features of classes and categories are hard to discern; people and things are equipotential and interchangeable. Rules of logic are not discovered since relationships between various categories do not seem to remain constant and lawful.

DISTURBANCES OF COMMUNICATION

Communication is a process by which meaning is extracted from, or conveyed through, an organized sequence of behavior. An intent to communicate can be said to exist only when the child develops an awareness of himself as a separate identity whose inner world is not transparent to those around him. Parents consider the neonate's total behavior as communicative and attempt to adjust their own reactions to his messages. As the infant grows older and a wider range of behavior becomes available to him, the communicative significance is assigned more discriminately. However, throughout this period, intentionally or habitually, parents' behavior toward the child is accompanied by their own highly differentiated communicative methods. The child's awareness of communicative messages is the result of his interactions within the interpersonal milieu and the recurrence of identifiable patterns of communicative behavior. Responsiveness and sensitivity to facial expressions, voice quality, and vocalization can be detected from the changes in the infant's alertness, attentiveness, and the tranquility or excitedness exhibited upon presentation of such stimuli. Language comprehension predates speech production by some months and the gap remains unfilled for the first few years of life. The discovery of the superiority and primacy of language as a means of communication is fostered by the child's own experiences as well as by the solicitous attention paid to his attempts at verbalization. Long before the communicative intent is developed, the child's half-truncated utterances are dignified with meaning and significance rather than being viewed as exercises of newly acquired functions. Thus, the utilitarian social purpose is superimposed on the innate ability from the beginning, and language development is shaped and directed toward its dual task of conceptualization and communication.

Disordered communication may result from deficiencies in the experiential and/or neurosensory components. Marked defects in the neurosensory component will hinder, and otherwise damage, the development of experiential factors since the communicative instrument is dysfunctional. On the other hand, the deleterious effects of deviant experiences on neurosensory factors is not easily discernible. Emotions, communicated through verbal or nonverbal, means will result in the objectification of a subjective state by the child—he will receive feedbacks and observe the modifying influences of his emotional forces on others. Because he is subjected to the emotions aroused in his listeners, the nature of social network, and the reciprocity of interactions become available for his comprehension. Similarly, the child's cognitive evaluation and generalization as well as his efforts in symbolization and concept formation must undergo the test of communality and validation through verbal exchanges with others. Disordered communication both reflects and complicates disordered thinking and disturbed emotions. Deprived of the clarifying role of explanation, logical connections and reasoning, emotional and conceptual domain remain undifferentiated and underdeveloped. These developmental deficiencies, although restricting the flexibility and adaptability, may not interfere with the individual's functioning within a limited range; however, signs of distress will appear when the established equilibrium is unsettled, and a new organization effort is required. The rigidity of the interactional styles of some children reveals their compensatory efforts in view of their extensive vulnerability to stress and challenges for readaptation. Unsuccessful attempts are signalled by persistent anxiety, a variety of phobic reactions, and avoidance maneuvers. When deficits of communication are not taken into consideration, the child's distress may prove refractory to usual handling and assurances, leading to a chronic state of dysphoria and adaptive failure punctuated by symptoms of unregulated emotions.

Intent to communicate may be thwarted by lack of control over the means of communication or the inability to formulate a communicable message. Harmony between nonverbal emotional expression, verbal message, and the emotional experience selected for revelation, depends on the integration and organization of several convergent factors. Differentiated emotions must be adequately regulated and cognitively rationalized before expression is undertaken. When emotional differentiation is inadequate and the regulatory mechanisms are fragile or incapable of withstanding the onslaught of intense emotions, affective dysharmony will result. Affective display is disproportionate to the gravity of provocative stimuli. Cognitive processes are disorganized, and the goal of the behavior and the intent of the message are unclear. When the social milieu mirrors this confusion and disorganization, the individual's function will further deteriorate, and the vicious cycle continues. In contrast, faced with a firmly supportive and unperturbed social environment, the psychological forces of restitution will seek to reestablish the previous state of equilibrium.

DISTURBED THINKING AND CONCEPTUALIZATION

Thinking is the goal-directed ordering of concepts which are formed by processing of sensory data, their integration with previous concepts and percepts, and their generalization and categorization. Thoughts may be simple or complex. They may remain private or be expressed verbally or behaviorally. Even when unexpressed, thoughts direct the ongoing interactions of the individual with his environment influencing his perception of himself and his surroundings. Disturbed thinking may result from deviant ordering of concepts or disorganization of the process of conceptualization and peculiarity of the concepts themselves. Logic is the most advanced form of order relating the concepts to each other. The individual's thinking may be assessed for its adherence to, or deviation from, the rules of logic. Regardless of whether or not the laws of logic reflect the innate neuronal substrate, the constant communication and discourse is an important factor in establishment of these laws as the common ground for ordering of concepts. When concepts are based upon the common, invariant properties of the environment, differences among individuals may be due to lack of sufficient experience, limited abstraction and generalization, errors in judgment, or disinterest in their elaboration and clarification. On the other hand, concepts derived from interpersonal relationships and subjective experiences are variable, relativistic, in a perpetual state of flux, and to a lesser or greater extent will remain individualistic. Every culture is the depository of the most common concepts of its members. These concepts are expressed through the words in its language, its mythology, its arts and philosophy, and the kind of relationships among individuals which are fostered or prohibited by it. Every infant is born into such a conceptual milieu and is exposed to its influence. However, in spite of the similarity of the background, the psychological makeup of each individual remains uniquely his own. This individuality results from the vast interactional potentials between two sets of factors: the dissimilarity of the life experiences and existence of each person, and the variability and plasticity of concepts relating to the interpersonal and subjective worlds. Because the sense organs are biologically responsive to a limited range and intensity of stimuli, the sensory stimuli received from the environment and the subsequent image of the perceptual, physical world remain constant over time and across individuals. In contrast, no such sense organ with its fixed boundary exists for the reception and incorporation of aspects of the interpersonal universe. Instead, the whole organism and his unique manner of interaction and adaptation act as the perceiver of social and cultural influences. Moreover, the common features of sociocultural surroundings are neither as permanent nor as precisely delimited as the invariant properties of the objective physical environment.

Although disordered logic and bizarre conception may be found in views held about both the motivational and physical worlds, the more prominent and common symptoms are those relating to the subjective and interpersonal domains. Even in those cultures where the inanimate world is viewed as possessing certain motivational properties, the interplay of such forces is regulated and ordered. Furthermore, although each individual may maintain a belief in the capricious nature of supernatural forces and entities, his ideas about his own relationships with his immediate social group are derived from the more concrete mutual interactions within this network. It is the disturbances of these relationships, and the disordered concepts associated with them, which create the deviant and deficient reality of the individual's subjective and social experiences.

To the extent that the subjective reality and its description can be accounted for by the individual's specific situation, deficient reasoning is not a reflection of disordered thinking. For example, the relative helplessness and dependence of children may give rise to their belief that a certain environment is hostile and rejective and their peers are their persecutors. This oversensitivity to unfriendliness can hardly be viewed as pathological or paranoic. Nor would we designate a child as grandiose when, with very little intellectual potential, he aspires to become a famous scientist. It is with the passing of time, accumulation of experiences, and abstraction from (and organization of) sensory data and their origins that the child begins to distinguish between dreams and reality, the inner imageries, and the outer images. The child's construct of the subjective reality may be inadequate for his age and the variety of interpersonal experiences provided in an average environment. Unless the environment is extremely limited and inordinately pathological, distortions and bizarre conceptions reflect organizational failures of the central processing of the cognitive-emotional mechanisms. Hence, disordered thoughts reveal the cumulative effects of past failings and misdirect the flow of future experiences. Furthermore, because the motives behind the actions initiated by the individual are inarticulate and poorly organized, the feedback from others also remains vague and ineffective, and the incomprehensible communication widens the gap between the two parties. The individual becomes insulated against the modifying influences of the communal standards, and his thinking and conception take on a more private character. At this point, the interactive process comes to a halt. The mutual alienation between the individual and his social milieu removes the individual as a continuous force for change and accommodation to the socially held viewpoints and puts an end to the persuasive power of the community. Ebbs and flows of undifferentiated and contradictory needs and emotions flood the consciousness, undermining efforts for goal-directed thinking and organization of sensory data. Environmental messages are ignored, subverted, or unintegrated with previous experiences.

Designation of disordered thinking encompasses the undifferentiated, uncontrolled emotions, incomprehensible communication, unfathomable motives, and fragmented subjective experiences. When language is fully mastered and cognitive processes developed, the individual can give an account of his motives and personal perceptions, and his logic can be challenged. With children, it is only by observation of the interactions and assessment of the adaptational efforts that inferences regarding the child's thinking and its logic can be made. Errors in perception, concrete conceptualization, and a self-centered view of the physical and social universe are characteristic of children's thinking. However, at every stage of development, behavioral organization and adaptational tendencies are unmistakably observable.

5

Normal Social Development

Every human infant is born in a social milieu and his survival, both biological and psychological, is dependent on such an environment. It may therefore be assumed that the capacity to respond to interpersonal cues and to develop social ties is among the important biological endowments of human beings. Although we do not have the necessary genetic information as yet to support such a hypothesis, we may observe seemingly innate tendencies on the part of the infant, which, if not directly causative, can be said to encourage and set the stage for socialization. We do not and cannot know how a human infant might have developed under a radically different set of circumstances, but we do know that even in vastly different forms of societies and with various philosophies of child rearing, the task of socialization of a child begins with the earliest interactions between him and his human environment. These interactions require social receptivity and reciprocity and are dependent on the presence of certain factors in the individual as well as in his surroundings.

STATE OF AROUSAL AND ALERTNESS

The first necessary condition for an infant to learn or to exercise a social response is to be alert, attentive, and in a state of arousal compatible with reception of a particular stimulus. It is further required that the state of arousal last long enough, and the stimulus be repeated often enough for a meaningful pattern to be extracted from the interaction. The social milieu of each infant is replete with stimuli, even though they are fragmented and discontinuous. A normal neonate fluctuates between states of high and low arousal and alert versus drowsy or sleepy states. However, it has been noted (Bennet, 1971) that when the environment provides age appropriate and meaningful stimuli, the neonate is more likely to maintain a state of alertness. The more alert the infant, the more likely that meaningful patterns can be extracted. Infants who are superaroused do not relate to their environment with ease. It is reasonable to assume that extreme hypersensitivity to sounds and/or light may, in ways still unknown, interfere with the smooth development of social connectedness. Although the drowsiness of the infant may act as an inhibiting factor in eliciting stimulation from the environment, alertness and attentiveness are important instruments in activating such stimuli. This state of affairs is observable in visual behavior and its consequence.

VISUAL BEHAVIOR

The infant's strategy in showing aversion or disinterest is not well developed and cannot be easily perceived in the first week of life. As early as the second week of life, however, the infant turns away or closes his eyes in order to avoid looking at someone or something. By around the second or third month, eye-to-eye gazing becomes a powerful technique in social contact and regulates the amount of social stimuli received from others (Stern, 1974). Around the same age, further facilitating effect is exerted by development of the social smile. Because the baby can evoke and respond to a smiling face, his caretakers are provided with cues to his preferences, his enjoyment of certain interactions, and his ability to reciprocate (Sander, 1962). This expressiveness is strengthened by other movements such as assumption of certain postures and motions of legs and arms. Cooing and babbling are heard from the infant in response to the sound of the human voice. What is perceived as the infant's desire to imitate behavior of the caretaker seems to have a powerful binding effect on the adults and to assure maintenance and repetition of the interaction.

SOCIAL AWARENESS AND SELF-AWARENESS

As developing eye–hand coordination allows the multisensorial exploration of inanimate objects, eye contact and reciprocal smiling provide beginning awareness of the fundamental difference between inanimate objects and people. Although objects can be pulled, held, pushed, and disposed of, they do not smile, imitate one's motion, or disappear in spite of infant's best effort and reappear on their own account. Within a very short period of time, the infant learns to differentiate among various people and to show his preference for certain individuals in the most nonambiguous manner. When it is clear that the infant's responses are discriminating, it can be inferred that differentiated representations of past events, perceptual configurations, and social cues have been consigned to memory and may be retrieved. What is abstracted, generalized, and stored from previous interactional opportunities becomes the cornerstone for the concept of a significant other or others. Between five to eight months of age, indication of the presence of a notion of significant others may be observed in those responses which have been variously referred to as stranger-fear or wariness. Such responsiveness to familiar figures and active avoidance of or passive nonparticipation in interaction with strangers are regular and predictable features of the infant's behavior, and enable us to logically infer the differential significance of certain others for the infant even though he cannot deny or confirm our inferences. By the end of the first year of life, the infant's behavior reveals that he has come to view objects and people as permanent features of the environment; he now searches for his toys, and watches for his mother's return. His memories of past experiences are projected into the future as expectations, and he has accumulated enough of these experiences to have developed a concept of himself. The integration of the desirable and undesirable experiences of interactional events provides the first unarticulated notion of self vis-à-vis the external world of objects and people. An indication that the child can recognize himself as a separate visual gestalt is noted between 15 and 18 months when children show awareness of their own image in the mirror. This self-recognition comes about at a point when visual perception has developed to the degree that various forms and configurations are differentiated and the notion of the self as a distinct object is attained. When, in the course of interaction with the environment, the child comes to discover his own ability to affect changes in others' behavior, or the shape and location of objects, he has laid the foundation for the core of the integrative and directive axis of himself as a separate individual. His knowledge of his own responsiveness to the world, as well as his ability as a causal agent, provides him with the early experiences of a conscious, self-reflective being. Self-control and self-direction become possible along with comparisons and identification with other follows.

EMOTIONAL DEVELOPMENT

Emotional development runs parallel to development of self-awareness and social interaction. The experience of emotions in children can be only inferred from their expressive activities and later on from their verbal reports. Observations of infants' responsiveness have revealed that various facial expressions can be differentiated in infants during the first few months after birth (Emde *et al.*, 1978; Lewis *et al.*, 1978). By around two-and-one-half months of age, a social smile can be elicited from infants in response to a human face, and signs of anger can be noted by around six months of age. The wariness or cautious withdrawal in the presence of unfamiliar individuals is detected before age one, and there are indications that sensitivity to disapproval by others and empathic distress appear by the age of two. Fear as a response to danger can be elicited when the infant's cognitive ability allows him to evaluate a situation as potentially harmful. For example, it is known that infants perceive depth much earlier than they begin walking. On the other hand, avoidance and fear of precipices appear after the child has started independent locomotion. Still later, the threat of danger or the nearness of it is a sufficient cause for avoidance behavior. Positive emotions can be observed when the infant is engaged in interaction with others or involved in exploration of his environment. Presentation of certain novel stimuli heightens the child's interest and attention, and surprise and joy can be easily noticed. During the second year of life, when the basis of self-evaluation and differentiation is more consolidated, such emotional reactions as guilt, empathy, and embarrassment are identifiable. Emotions are not only expressed but differentially experienced.

Development of emotions cannot be separated from the increasing differentiation of interpersonal relationships and the responsiveness to emotional cues of others. During the first 2 to 6 months of life, the caretaker's reaction to the infant's behavior is the determinant in eliciting or maintaining his emotional responsivity, though later on the infant initiates and sustains the social exchange by actively engaging his caretaker. By about one year of age, demands for social interactions or refusal to be engaged are more assertive in nature. Depending on the caretaker's affective state and spontaneity, and the pleasure which is derived from the interchange, the infant's skills in emotional expression and social interactions are facilitated or hampered. His experience of his emotions exerts a powerful influence on the organization and evolution of his behavior, just as emotional expressions regulate the responses elicited by the child and effect the type of social milieu which surrounds him. Such influences are at work when the infant's anger heightens his motivation to overcome an obstacle, or when his experience of shame or embarrassment acts as an incentive to develop self-control. Expressions of interest and excitement on an infant's face will hardly be ignored by his caretakers, and the duration of contact is increased or the interesting spectacle sustained to accommodate the infant's desire. The heightened awareness created by fear facilitates learning about danger, and the task of anticipation and recognition of dangerous situations broadens the child's cognition.

The relationship between cognition and emotions is a complex one. Emotions cannot be separated from the overall manner with which an individual reacts and interacts with his animate and inanimate environment. Emotional experiences may facilitate or hamper cognitive growth, or their intensity may block learning of new patterns. By the time that language is developed and emotional states are conceptualized as shared, the verbal report and the expression of emotions are, to a large extent, under the individual's conscious control and responses are more communal and stylized. Around four years of age, children are able to identify psychological states of others as well as report on their own, and they can bring their emotional expressions into harmonious relationship with their statements. As emotions become more differentiated and organized, they, in turn, facilitate the child's understanding of various aspects of the situations in which he finds himself and his ability to cope appropriately with them. When emotional experience is diffuse, it dominates the child's consciousness, and the likelihood of effective and skillful action is diminished.

Regulation of emotion may be achieved by expression, dissociation, or neutralization and all these strategies may be calibrated and adaptive, or disorganizing and maladaptive. When cognitive processes are capable of the evaluation and integration of emotional experience, the possibility for adaptive regulation is enhanced. When emotional experience is so intense that the evaluative function of cognition is impaired, the regulation may be achieved by defensive dissociation. Conversely, when evaluative processes are immature, the emotional state causes immediate emotional discharge which, when intense, may act as a disorganizing influence on behavior. Adaptive regulation of emotion is determined by the interaction between experiences and learning, and the cognitive ability of the individual. As such, this regulation can be expected to undergo an evolution from the more primitive to the more advanced stage throughout developmental period. Tolerance for negative emotions increases with age, and at the same time, various coping strategies are developed which will decrease the impact of the emotion-eliciting stimuli, downgrade its import, or extract a more balanced meaning from it.

COMMUNICATION

The notion of an inborn capacity for social relatedness implies the concomitant capability for communicative behavior. Though it can be argued that every piece of observable behavior may be viewed as containing a message, where the intent to communicate is obscure or cannot be verified, it is of little interpersonal value. Communicative skills are nurtured, modified, and corrected by constant interactions as the means of social cohesiveness and incorporation of individuals into a social network. Although nonverbal cues play a significant role in intimate communications among group members, language is the most important tool of wider communication. Before language is acquired, nonverbal cues are the only channel through which the infant's messages are broadcasted, and the caretaker's sensitivity to them is the only assurance for their correct interpretation. However, even after language acquisition, nonverbal cues are used to give verbal messages emotional coloring and to enhance or qualify their meanings. The quality and clarity of verbal products can be assessed by reference to communal standards, but the dimension added by nonverbal cues is not easily verifiable. For this reason, even verbal communication between two people has nonquantifiable and yet important elements. Nonverbal communication before speech development must be differentiated from the expression of an emotional state which signals the infant's needs in a nondiscriminating manner. These signals are of immense survival value, but do not carry information which would modify or regulate the infant's social world. In contrast, eye contact, the social smile, and the anticipating posture of infants have regulating effects on the quality and quantity of his social contact. The infant's sensitivity to communication can be inferred from his attentiveness to facial features, the interruption in his activities upon hearing human voice, and the relatively long time span during which this attentiveness lasts. Sound production, even cooing and babbling, is a valuable tool in eliciting change in interaction and sustaining social contact. With the first articulated speech sound, a new level of demands is placed on the caretakers. They become aware of the infant's first steps toward entrance into the communal communicative network and are expected in turn to try to understand the infant's verbal messages. Acquisition of speech is a social as well as maturational landmark. From the first appearance of one word messages to mature speech production, the social milieu is called upon to decipher the meaning, shape the nature of utterance, correct the form of statement, and help the child along by patient repetition of simplified vérbal messages addressed to the child. Although the child's nonverbal communication is not ignored or rejected, the emphasis and attention is slowly shifted toward verbalization. Gestures and mimicry, unaccompanied by speech, require the presence of both communicants within the visual range of each other. Such limitation decreases the opportunities for solitary exploration of the environment by the child, freedom of movement for caretakers, and/or the amount of communication between the child and his social surroundings. Verbal messages can be sent over a longer range, and the listener is not as restricted. Furthermore, the overwhelming reliance on verbal tags to convey information about internal states, conceptions, and impressions makes it virtually impossible for adults to understand the thinking processes of a nonverbal child—even if the child, in some ingenious way, has found a combination of nonverbal means to communicate with them. Thus the child's conceptualization is deprived of a crucial test of communal validation and the modifying effect of externalization.

Verbalization of impressions gathered from social interactions provides effective means for influencing and regulating the subsequent nature of interaction (messages intended to control and change another's behavior are the most frequent type of conversation between the child and parents). Declarations of love, hate, disappointment, or encouragement and praise are meant to change or reinforce the child's behavior, but assertion of love, hate, dislike, or disobedience are similar attempts on the part of the child to modify parental behavior.

CONCEPT FORMATION AND SYMBOLIZATION

The child's concepts are formed as the result of integration of sensory data received from his interactions with the physical and social world. For any concept to be formed, a certain amount of sensory information must be received, similarities in configurations must be discovered, and generalities must be abstracted. Furthermore, at each stage of development only certain aspects of the external world are apprehendable or of basic utility to the child. For example, before the notion of object permanency has taken hold, other characteristics of the objects are ignored and unattended to. Indications of concept formation appear long before language comprehension or production exists. However, once linguistic skills are developed, the thinking process is influenced by language, communicated via verbal means, and becomes intertwined in the matrix of sentences and their structures. Symbolization, as an inborn propensity of the central nervous system of the species, is the process by which a thing or a concept comes to invoke or assert the existence of another object or concept. As Lennenberg (1967) points out, a pattern or order of sounds or a temporal formation which underlies language comprehension or production, is best suited as symbols. Because not only symbolization but also other cognitive processes are common characteristics of the human species, communication becomes possible. The learning of common symbols and the extension of vocabulary and the syntactic order of sentences are indicative of this shared characteristic. The fundamental similarities of the environment, coupled with the universality of the basic endowment of members of the species, provide the regularity of course and pattern of cognitive development and concept formation. At an early stage of life, objects are perceived not only by their own properties but also as the result of the motor and affective activities of the child. Adults recognize inanimate objects by their geometrical, technical, and physical attributes. Concepts formed on these dissimilar foundations show certain divergencies, thus the image of the universe created by the child, and that discovered by adults, is not identical. However, the child's reality, though somewhat puzzling to the adult, is an organized and lawful reality. Its concepts are based on the diffuse and global qualities of objects. Because objects are comprehended only as what Werner calls "things-of-action," they do not preserve their essential characters in various temporal and spatial positions. This kind of subjectivity does not allow the child to construct a fixed view of reality. At the same time, this fluidity is a guarantee against premature and rigid closure of any conceptualization. Because so much of the child's motor and affective exploration and activity is directed toward people in his surroundings, his earliest notions of inanimate objects are akin to his concept of animate objects. Things are viewed as if they were people who could move, be responsive to one's desires, and punished for their frustrating actions. Furthermore, the only kind of causality conceivable for a young child is that of motivation, desires, wishes, and dislikes. Thus, the child's universe is populated by animate, motivated objects, and the order of things depends on motivational forces emanating from a prime mover or movers. The perceptual properties and configurations are determinants of the child's relationship with objects, and grouping of objects is done in the pragmatic manner through which the child relates to his environment. Concrete similarities and continuity of experience are used to classify, and when abstraction takes place it is on the basis of qualities which may undergo changes in different situations. Therefore, these abstractions are not stable and do not hold true under different circumstances. A corollary of this type of classification is the fact that objects giving approximately similar impressions are grouped together. Essential and nonessential aspects and characteristics are not differentiated. Therefore, categorization of objects into what, for adults, is contradictory or illogical units is acceptable. Because different aspects of objects achieve prominence in the child's mind according to what configuration or function is attended to, certain attributes which are viewed as opposite by adults do not appear so to a child. For example, a child may declare that a small boat can float because it is light, and a huge cargo ship remains on the surface of the water because it is heavy. Here the words "heavy" and "light" are not opposites, rather, by "heavy," the child means strong, and by "light," it is the weight to which he refers.

The child's language is a reflection of his thinking, and his thinking is the outcome of his experiences in the world. He experiences the world in a subjective and global manner. Affective evaluation and emotional needs are important factors in organizing the child's perception of the animate and inanimate world. Because needs and affective components are unstable, the child's concepts and percepts are also in continuous change. As the child grows older, from this global and diffuse conception of the world, more objective and stable concepts begin to emerge and separate. Children begin to differentiate between inanimate and animate objects, between their own desires and what moves other people. As relationships among concepts are discovered, the manner by which thinking processes operate becomes closer to adult logic. However, this is a slow process. Thinking may be directed and logical in one area and remain illogical in several other respects. Imageries based on sensorimotor and affective factors comprise the bulk of nonsocialized and undirected intelligence, while socialized thought is influenced by reality, adapted to it, and shaped by the need for communication and communal feedback. In socialized thinking, reason and logic are the modes of operation; private thought is not based on demands for proof, and personal analogies and idiosyncratic memories are the bases for beliefs and convictions.

To the degree that language itself is viewed as a part of external reality, the child's concept of verbal stimuli is similar to his concepts of other objects. Names are viewed as another attribute of things, and the arbitrary nature of them is not noted. Words are accepted at their most concrete level, and their shades of meaning are not easily discovered. Furthermore, they may be distorted according to the child's own interests and motives rather than the concern for their common meaning. The fact that the place of a word in a sentence may change the intended meaning is not understood, and the world reflected through language is as overwhelming as the one received via other modalities. It is when the nature of language and the relationships between words, things, and concepts are understood that information conveyed through language may become as significant as information discovered by experience. Such purely ideational information as moral prohibitions and imperatives can be comprehended by the child only after he has come to differentiate between the message and its medium.

Social development can be viewed as complete only after the child's experiential background and his intellectual abilities have prepared him to engage in socialized discourse and have brought his behavior under control of socially comprehensible motivations. The rate of movement and the ultimate level of social development show a range of differences among individuals; however, the direction of movement is from the global, undifferentiated, and dependent existence toward well-articulated and solid identity in interdependent relations with the social surroundings. The random experiences of the infant will eventually become integrated into giving him a sense of self. This self, from its inception, bears the mark of interaction with others and will in turn influence others through its own unique existence. The linguistic milieu which exists before the child's birth will shape his modes of discourse with others, but it will also provide him with a flexible tool to impress his own unique perception of the world on his environment.

6

Psycholinguistic Development: Functioning and Dysfunctioning

Language, viewed as it must be for the practical evaluation of problems in human communication, consists of holistic acts that involve complex, interconnected operations and determinants— physical, perceptual, cognitive, emotional and social, as well as linguistic. They are subjective acts to the extent that their meanings derive from the individual's interpretations of inner and outer experience and from their communal validity which is a matter of degree from person to person and situation to situation. They are objective acts in that they utilize a code with conventional referents and rules of grammar. Thus, in making judgments about aberrations of human communication, their primary and secondary components and systemic effects, one must consider *all* of their aspects interactively, from both the standpoint of the patient's phenomenological world and the standpoint of the congruence or incongruence of his acts with the shared rules and practice of communication in his particular community. When the patient is a child, one must consider one other, highly complicating factor—the patient is somewhere along the road of developing the mechanisms of communication and of learning its conventions from his immediate and extended community. Therefore, one's judgments also must be based upon comparative assessment of where his communicative behavior stands at this point in his growth, again in the total and each of its interconnected aspects, with regard both to what is to be expected according to general norms of development and what can reasonably be expected in the context in which he is growing.

It is with the general development of language that we are concerned in this chapter. Our approach is a broadly conceptual one, and we will not attempt to provide a normative chronology of specific developmental milestones. Such information is readily available in abundance in child development texts. Rather, we will describe the principles and operations of language as a holistic phenomenon, and very generally outline the order and variability in its development. Fortunately, we need not undertake the task of synthesizing the content of divergent disciplines and theoretical viewpoints in order to present a holistic picture. Recent trends in developmental psychology and psycholinguistics have been toward an organismic understanding of the complex, multifactor growth of symbolic thought and communication in the child. The approach is almost monumental in its complexity, and our necessarily cursory and selective discussion of it reduces matters to somewhat simplistic terms, doing little justice to the articulate bodies of thought upon which we have drawn. Thus, we refer the interested reader to the most recent originals, for starters, particularly the volumes by Bloom and Lahey (1978), Moerk (1977), and Morehead and Morehead (1976).

Before proceeding, a brief description of the evolution of recent thinking in the area is pertinent, since it highlights fundamental aspects of language and its development. The focus of developmental psychology is upon the application of psychological principles of growth and learning as they apply to the acquisition of language—that is, language as a developing psychological dynamic. Linguistics, on the other hand, takes as its domain of study the properties and structure of language itself, regardless of their psychological context. The wedding of the two disciplines, *psycholinguistics,* has been essentially an effort to dovetail what is known or postulated about human behavior with what is known or postulated about the composition and semantics of language. Developmental psycholinguistics attempts to carry this effort to the study of the successive, interrelated events of psychological growth as they affect linguistic development, and vice versa. Initially, such efforts resulted in head-on polemic conflict, which in turn led to progressive syntheses as each discipline had to relinquish or modify some of its cherished assumptions and hypotheses in order to accommodate insights from the other.

The fundamental conflict was waged over the age-old issue of nature versus nurture, now applied to language. Bates (1976) aptly summarized the matter as follows:

> For decades, British empiricists and American learning theorists claimed
> that language was entirely determined by the environment: the child

selects speech models from the environment, imitates them, and is reinforced for those imitations that most closely approximate the model. . . . In the late 1950's and early 1960's, linguists . . . and psychologists . . . moved away from the empiricist approach to a nativist model of language: the child is biologically equipped with certain clues about the nature of language and sets out actively searching his speech environment for structures that correspond to those clues . . . the effect of context is minimal. Although a rich or impoverished environment can affect the rate of development, the crucial structural aspects of language are not derived from the environment but are imposed upon it. (p. 412)

At the present time, the pendulum is swinging closer to the middle, with the recognition of innate biological capacities of the infant to develop linguistic forms, parallels between the structure of early sensorimotor learning and subsequently emerging linguistic structure, and a renewed emphasis on the critical importance of environmental contexts in the learning and use of language. Growth in language is considered explainable in terms of three interrelated aspects: (1) content—cognition, concepts, meaning; (2) form—words and syntax; (3) use—the pragmatics of linguistic communication, or the relationship between context and meaning and the practical uses to which language is put (Bloom and Lahey, 1978).

Considering these three aspects, one can arrive at a developmental definition of language that embodies the scope of observation called for in clinical practice. First, however, it is necessary to distinguish between the terms *language* and *communication*, since we are not using them interchangeably. In our discussion, both refer to information exchange between the individual and his environment, communication being the overall category and language being one mode of communication. In the developing exchange between the child and his environment, other modes are primary in the early stages: facial and bodily expression, gesture, and nonlinguistic vocalization. With the gradual acquisition of language, these early modes lose much of their importance, but remain as ancillary and reinforcing to verbal communication. However, in the realm of emotional expression, they remain the primary carriers of meaning throughout life. Furthermore, language is not only a tool of communication, but also a mode of cognition. In this role, it is preceded developmentally by visual-motor imagery, which Bruner (1975) described as enactive (representation based on action) and iconic (representation based on pictorial imagery). Here again, language eventually becomes the primary mode, although imagery remains as ancillary to much thought and as the dominant mode in fantasy.

Language, then, serves as the means by which concepts are

symbolized and a channel through which the structure and content of thought are developed, communicated, corrected, and expanded. In this way, the two general functions of language are intertwined and reciprocally related. Also, because most words are totally arbitrary symbols, bearing no necessary resemblance to the characteristics of their referents, they allow for the representation of phenomena that never have been directly experienced by the individual or are completely hypothetical and conceptual. They are not bound to concrete particulars and, thus, permit highly abstract and generalized thought and learning. By the same token, however, their meanings must be derived from conventional association and so must be learned from the community.

As symbols, words are meaningful only in that they are associated with concepts. In Bloom and Lahey's terms, "language represents ideas about the world." Implicit in this idea is the assumption that, developmentally, the concept precedes its linguistic representation. "It is logically necessary that concepts develop before words; otherwise the labels supplied by adults could not be attached to any content and would remain a meaningless sound soon to be forgotten" (Moerk, 1977). Words are learned first as labels for ideas of objects experienced by the child—their observed movements, their physical, spatial, and temporal attributes. Gradually he comes to acquire words and syntactical combinations of words to represent his notions of relationship—contingencies and causes and effects within the ken of his experience. His ideas grow in complexity and abstractness as does his language, the one affecting the other and being affected by it in turn. The referents of his expanding conceptual-linguistic system consist of phenomena in his inner world of physical and emotional states, desires, fantasies, etc., and the outer world of physical and social objects, attributes and events, and of relationships within and between both worlds. Eventually, through the instrumentality of linguistic symbolism, his thoughts can extend into the unknown and intangible, the theoretical and paradoxical, the metaphysical and spiritual, pushing the limits of understanding. Thus, language potentially is representative of the totality of human experience.

The form or construction of language can be defined in a number of ways: in terms of its underlying psychoneurological structures and processes, its physical properties and their anatomical counterparts, or its semantic-syntactical composition. With regard to the first, except for the very broad principles of psychoneurological growth (differentiation and plasticity), the highly complex realm of neurologic-linguistic processes is beyond the scope of our discussion. Although the psychological operations of language to which we will refer later (perception, association, memory, etc.) have their cerebral counterparts, it is not reasonable to assume that they are analogous to neurological structures or events. The state of affairs in the study of the psychoneurological aspects of language and its development was summarized by Lenneberg (1967):

> When the psychologist studies behavior he might propose certain theoretical categories which appear self-evident to him. . . . They might be considered phenomena that have psychological reality. . . . However, these categories do not have clear-cut neurological correlates. . . . On the other hand, many of the simple processes of the neurophysiologist have very poorly definable behavioral characteristics. (p. 63)

The development of the psychological operations necessary to language acquisition are dependent upon and timed to the maturation of certain structures in the brain, but the specific relationships and processes involved are still, at best, little understood.

By contrast, the physical properties of language and their corresponding anatomical mechanisms are quite clearly understood. Fundamentally, a language consists of a limited set of sounds (phonemes), which are differentiated from nonlinguistic sounds and from each other by their specific and measurable acoustic-phonetic characteristics. Phonemes, of themselves, have no meanings, but are combined to form morphemes, the smallest meaningful units of language. Morphemes, in turn, consist of base words and affixes (prefixes, suffixes and inflectional endings), which combine to make up all the words of the language. In addition to the phonetic combinations of sounds in speech, variations in acoustic stress or intonation convey differences in intent (e.g., to question or to declare), and emotional quality. The anatomical mechanisms that are required for the reception and production of all these physical features are innate in the human organism and observable from birth (Lieberman, 1967; Eisenberg, 1967; Eimas *et al.*, 1971). They develop via physical maturation and practice according to a fairly definable schedule. Of particular importance here are the perceptual-motor capacities that correspond to the temporal-sequential aspect of speech. The acquisition of effective linguistic communication is dependent upon the rapid and accurate auditory discrimination and motoric encoding of fine phonological differences in predetermined temporal order.

Whereas the conventions that dictate the combining of phonemes to form morphemes and words are arbitrary, the body of rules that governs the use and ordering of word forms in statements—the grammar of a language—is based to a significant extent upon conceptual logic. The syntactical arrangement of words in phrases and sentences reflects a common view of the arrangement of events and relationships in reality. Moerk states the case for this premise as follows:

> Since language is a code, it has to be about something whenever it is intended as referential communication. . . . Since language serves as a communication device for speakers, the transformations of and relationships to reality, their internal representations, and their expression in coded form have to be relatively homologous, consistent, and shared. This applies to all steps and variables that intervene between reality and verbal product. Otherwise, individuals could invent their own private language, which would be meaningless or at least misleading for the communication partner. (pp. 153–154)

Developmentally, it has been shown that the emerging use of words and syntactical structures is congruent with the child's sensorimotor experience. A number of recent writers, such as Brown (1973), Bloom (1973), Schlesinger (1974), Bowerman (1976), and Moerk (1977), have studied and described the close parallels between the generalized concepts apparent in the child's sequential behaviors and the early use of word forms and syntactical arrangements. Although a good deal of disagreement remains regarding how and to what extent the child's preexisting cognitive structures affect his learning of syntax and vice versa, it is evident that his grasp of object and event relationships provides the conceptual matrix within which he learns which word forms, in which combinations and sequential arrangements, are applicable to which occurrences.

The child comes to the task of language acquisition with a set of concepts about object and event relationships that are relatively few compared with the myriad of such instances that he witnesses daily. They form the fundamental rules of conceptual logic that regulate his interpretation of his sensorimotor world. They include ideas of object permanence, location in space and time, movement and action, causality, and possession. As he hears and begins to use varied word forms in combination, he already has some awareness of the conceptual relationships that underly the syntactical ones. Thus, not only can he comprehend and repeat specific word combinations heard in conjunction with observed events, but he has some meaningful basis for generalizing similar word combinations to different but related events. For instance, told that "The milk is all gone," as he holds up his empty cup, he learns not only to repeat "Milk gone," when the same situation occurs again, but eventually to apply the same semantic form on his own to different situations with different objects and words—"Water gone," "Teddy bear gone," "Daddy away," etc. He has gained the linguistic form to express his notion of object absence or disappearance. Similarly, over the course of many exposures to word arrangements that reflect his understanding of sequential occurrences, he acquires the means to represent agent–action(subject–verb), agent–action–recipient object (subject–verb–object), attribution (adjective–noun), and so on, until he eventually has mastered that limited number of the rules of grammar with which to generate infinite possible meaningful representations of his experience.

At some point in this process of syntactical learning (from the outset or later, depending upon which writer you read), the child's understanding of what happens in the world is affected by what is said to him. His concepts of causal relationships, for example, may be modified by the agent–action–object statements made to him. Thus, the structure of his thinking may be modified by the structure of the language to which he is exposed. As his linguistic proficiency increases, language becomes the most proficient means of thinking about and learning new ways of conceptualizing the relationships among things. Thus, language acquires pragmatic value for organizing, manipulating, and expanding cognitive structures.

In the realm of communication, it seems unnecessary to state that language is a useful instrument. However, the ways in which it is found to be useful by the child play an essential role in both motivating and directing its development. In very early development, the content of communication is simple and straightforward and carried by facial expression, movement and gesture, and gross vocalization (crying, cooing, etc.). As the child's physical, emotional, and social needs become more differentiated, abstract and complex, so the means of communicating them must become more articulate and abstract. Each communicative act must come to carry more complex units of meaning sequentially and simultaneously. The growth of language fills this developing need.

In the pragmatic sense, usefulness implies intent, which in turn implies an expectation of consequences. Though the crying of the hungry infant is useful in the sense that it communicates a state of need to the mother, it is initially a reflexive behavior, lacking in pragmatic value for the child. It does not become a communicative device of his until he gains some awareness that he is an agent causing things to occur. It is in this early, relatively amorphous, recognition of behavioral effect that the child first evidences a general intent to communicate. He comes to grasp very broadly that behaviors, which arise automatically from his inner states, have gratifying results, and he gives vent to them intentionally. *Expression* becomes the first definable pragmatic function of his communication. With the gradual differentiation of self from others, and the simultaneous differentiation of his needs and the means to satisfy them, he begins to use, with more specific purpose, differing behaviors to attain differing ends. He starts to guide the behavior of others according to his wants, and the second basic function of communication emerges—*direction*. Concomitantly, he develops a need to point out or identify for others those particular objects that he desires. Thus is born the third basic function—*reference*. Out of these three fundamental uses of communicative behavior eventually emerge the finer, multilevel, emotional, social, and cognitive functions of linguistic communication—requesting, informing, questioning, declaring, negating, and so on.

Defining language in terms of its communicative functions necessitates looking at it in relation to the contexts in which it is used. The external context, at least, affects and often dictates the purpose of the language act. When he means to communicate, the speaker has it in mind to influence the context in some way. His intent may be initiated by an inner state (need or desire), which is of itself unrelated to the immediate circumstances, or it may be itself the result of an effect produced by a contextual object, event, condition, or communication. For instance, when a child states, "My tummy hurts," the situation and whom he is addressing will, at least partially, determine whether he is seeking a remedy or sympathy, avoiding the lima beans on his plate, looking for a way out of an unpleasant task, or refusing a command to eat. Thus, it is in reference to the context that one defines the many subfunctions of language and of communication generally, which often occur in quite complex, simultaneous combinations.

The context also bears directly upon the content of the communicative act and the means by which it is carried out. On the basis of prior communication of one kind or another, or on the basis of features of the situation that are readily observable, the speaker presupposes what the listener is aware of and unaware of. Accordingly, he determines which thoughts must be explicitly included in the message and which may be left to implication. Further, the speaker's perception of the listener and the situation affects his use of verbal or nonverbal means to convey the full intent and meaning of his message. Moerk conceives of these factors in terms of a three-dimensional relationship, involving verbal acts, nonverbal acts, and those aspects of the context that are apparent to, or known by both communication partners. The more shared awareness that exists and is recognized by the speaker, the less information is actively encoded, either verbally or nonverbally. Much can be left unsaid and undemonstrated between close friends talking of common interests. The nonverbal means must carry the heaviest load of information when the verbal means are difficult or unavailable—for instance, among the deaf or between a parent and two-year-old child. The verbal means bear the greatest weight when the partners are separated and unacquainted (e.g., strangers on the telephone), or when the discourse is purely hypothetical or abstractly logical (e.g., two philosophers arguing a new point of metaphysics).

The grammatic form and tonal emphasis of what is said is affected by the context as well as the purpose of the communication. The speaker selects word forms and syntactical structures and lends them emphasis according to whether he intends to make a request, ask a question, declare a fact, negate a statement, etc. At the same time, however, his choice is influenced by his estimate of the circumstances. This estimate includes his presuppositions about the listener's awareness. For example, seeking candy from somebody who is already eating candy, a child might declare, "I want that." Whereas, with no candy in evidence, he would state, "I want candy." His choice also includes his consideration of the anticipated effect of his communication. Thus, the child might pose his request in the form of a polite question ("May I have candy?"), a forceful imperative ("Give me candy!"), or perhaps an exclamation ("Oh! Candy!") depending upon his perception of the social setting. At times, the selection from among various possible expressions of the same thought may be dictated predominantly by emotion, but it still depends upon an accurate perception of the context for its relevance and effectiveness.

In the framework of development, it is apparent that the uses which are served by the child's communicative behaviors are associated with a complexity of interrelated variables—perceptual-motor, cognitive, emotional, and social. Only to the degree that a child is able to perceive, comprehend, remember, encode, and execute word and sentence forms and coordinate them with nonverbal expression is it possible for him to state things flexibly in ways appropriate to his developing needs in a wide variety of contexts. Concomitantly, his expanding understanding of contexts and their implications, together with his emotional adaptation to them, is a decisive factor in the adequacy of his communication. By a process of differentiation and learning through observation, experimentation, and feedback in interaction with others, he develops the requisite social concepts and grows in his cognizance of the needs and reactions of others and of the implications of his own behaviors for others. Thus, the intricacy and effectiveness of his language uses increase, in reciprocal fashion, with his interpersonal relatedness.

GENERAL CHARACTERISTICS, PROCESSES, AND COURSE OF PSYCHOLINGUISTIC DEVELOPMENT

As we have stressed by defining language in terms of holistic, multifaceted acts of thought and communication, its development is characterized by *interactivity*. At all levels of development, from the very earliest observable acts of intentional nonverbal communication to mature acts of linguistic discourse, the growth of language entails an intricate interaction of capacities, skills and environmental influences, mediated by the child's evolving comprehension of himself and the world around him. Linguistic development is but one aspect of a systemic phenomenon of growth, each internal and external element of which affects and is affected by all the others in turn. It follows from this idea that, in seeking reasonable explanations for individual differences among children in the development of language, one must look at the totality of reciprocal factors at work in each child. Further, one must consider each child's growth in relation to his particular environment.

The process of human development, both biological and psychological, proceeds from the global to the complex. This process of *differentiation* is accompanied necessarily by the ongoing organization and reorganization of structures. In the realm of psycholinguistic development, these processes occur hand in hand with the increasing *symbolization* (abstraction) and *generalization* of concepts and conceptual hierarchies. The result is a continually expanding mesh of sensorimotor-cognitive linguistic structures that is, at best, difficult to adequately describe in its complex progression. Each of the developmental processes provides the necessary condition for the others to take place, and is simultaneously facilitated by each of the others. Thus, the whole is characterized by a *systemic continuity* of growth, in which the interactive steps shade off imperceptibly one into the next. Even though development is often conceived in terms of stages that occur in separate areas of functioning, the fact is that there are no distinct boundaries between functions, no sharply demarcated advances in their growth.

Beginning with the innate orienting reflex to visual and auditory stimuli, and facilitated by an early capacity for discrimination in all of the senses, there is an active exploration of the environment that leads the infant to respond differentially to different global classes of objects and events (e.g., inanimate versus animate, human voice versus other noises). On the basis of a repeated differential response to a particular type of event, one can infer that the child has formed a cognitive representation of a class, abstracted from the actual events according to the consistently recurring features that impress him. Such discriminatory behavior is apparent in the neonate, so it can be said that the child's world is broadly differentiated and given some degree of cognitive organization very early in life.

The child's initial explorations rely heavily upon the senses of touch, taste, and smell, but during the first year of life there is a shift in emphasis to the visual and auditory senses. With the movement away from direct-contact experience to experience through the distance receptors, the process of abstraction and symbolization is begun. The objects of the child's visual and auditory attention are experienced in far greater flux than those that he manipulated with his hands and placed in his mouth. They present themselves to him from varying distances and perspectives and in varying contexts. From these repeated, but inconstant, instances of the same or similar objects and events, a child must abstract constancies with which to construct mental representations. It is by these cognitive images that he recognizes such objects and events under varying conditions in the future. In this process, he differentiates categories of experience from each other and organizes his concepts accordingly. As new objects, events, and relationships come to his attention, and he discovers finer discriminations and similarities among them, he must use increasingly abstract mental images to represent the increasingly differentiated and generalized classes of experience that he is forming.

The process of symbolization necessarily involves generalization, and vice versa. A conceptual class is not limited to a stored representation of a single, concrete instance of its referent, nor does it consist of representations of all concrete instances of the referent that the child has encountered. Over time, and with repeated encounters, he formulates an abstracted idea of a dog, for example, which embodies what are the essential features of that object–class for him. Not only can he reassociate the concept with each dog, or toy dog, or pictured dog that he has already seen but, by means of the symbolized concept, he will be able to identify any new doglike phenomenon that he happens to meet. Generalization is present even in the early establishment of his sense of object constancy, when he comes to recognize an object for what it is, no matter the changing contexts and perceptual configurations. So, too, even an object class of one involves a degree of generalization. Mommy becomes identifiable as Mommy, in spite of changes in appearance, context, mood, etc.

As the child's complex of concepts widens and is arranged hierarchically in terms of more generalized categories, there is a growing need for more generalizable images or symbols to represent them. Enactive or iconic imagery can fulfill this function only up to a point, before it is taxed beyond its capacity to carry abstract meaning. Thus, imageries are not very effective means of representing either highly generalized categories or the increasingly subtle characteristics by which conceptual classes are distinguished from, and related to, one another. In terms of sheer quantity, the elements of the growing conceptual network would come to exceed the capacity of enactive and iconic imageries, because these images are reflective of, and thus to some extent, tied to concrete characteristics of the particular objects or events for which they stand. The nature of cognitive development itself, then, demands a more arbitrary, flexible, and simplifying system of representation. Ultimately, a code of pure symbols or words of one form or another, whether subjective or conventional, must be generated or acquired if the child's growing mass of experiential information is to be meaningfully organized and his cognition is to go beyond the logic of the immediately real, to the logic of the hypothetically possible.

As was noted earlier, the cognitive and communicative functions of language are reciprocally related. Thought provides the content of communication, and communication, in turn, provides the means whereby ideas and logic are learned from the external world. Because of this reciprocity in development, and because of the increasingly arbitrary nature of the symbolic code with which the child comes to think, communicate, and learn, the elements of that code must be *conventional* and *consistent* in their form, meaning, and usage. Words, from the standpoint of their use in conceptual organization, might be subjective *or* conventional and a private code could be partially effective in the process of concept formation. In fact, there is ample evidence of a high degree of subjectivity in the early verbal referencing of children, and many of their emerging "words" are quite unconventional in form and meaning. It is reasonable to assume that the child uses such subjective words in organizing his thoughts as well as in speaking.

The establishment of consistency or stability of form and meaning is obviously necessary to both the effective communicative and cognitive uses of words as arbitrary concept labels. However, whereas conventionality *and* consistency of symbolization are prerequisite to effective communication, consistency alone would be sufficient were words to function solely as cognitive symbols. Private "words" could quite adequately serve the purpose of concept designation provided they maintain their distinct forms and meanings over time. The point at which such a private code would become useless, and even a hindrance, to the development of thought is when verbal communication becomes important for the validation and learning of increasingly abstract conceptualizations. Normally, the development of consistency and conventionality go hand in hand and is dependent upon the child's growing competencies in auditory perception, memory, and vocal encoding. As his verbal productions become more stable, and he learns the rules and limits that govern the adult formation and use of words, the child's linguistic code becomes steadily more conventional and, thereby, shareable. Thus, more or less unshareable thoughts are opened to consensual validation or modification and expansion through communicative verbal learning.

Because a multitude of factors interact reciprocally in development, the course of language acquisition is irregular. The normal variations in physiological, psychological, and environmental conditions that occur during growth produce varying interrelated effects which in turn cause marked variations, not only from child to child, but also within each child, in the timing, content, and manner of language learning. However, there are broad regularities in the order of events and in the learning strategies of children and the teaching strategies of parents which allow one to outline the route of language acquisition that children generally take.

In much of the clinical writing on deviant language development, there is an emphasis on the first appearance of recognizable speech as the starting point of linguistic behavior. Implicit in this emphasis is the notion that the child quite precipitously begins to comprehend and use linguistic symbolism when he says his first comprehensible words. Also related to this idea is the common assumption that the child understands and intends the conventional meanings of the words that he regularly uses, from that point on.

Actually, the association of meanings with verbal sounds has earlier and more gradual beginnings, and the learning of conventional meanings is a more gradual process. During the first year, children begin to show meaningful discriminations among intonational patterns and some words in adult speech. At about the same time or slightly later, private "words" that have apparent associations for the child emerge from his babbling. The meanings attached to these early linguistic events are for the most part subjective, though parents may learn to comprehend their significance.

It is during the second year that the child begins to utter conventional words, but his semantic associations are by and large not in line with the adult's. Initially, the child tends to overextend his words so that "daddy," for instance, might refer to all adult males, or "kitty" to all four-legged animals. Further, when the child at this juncture learns a word in relation to an object or event, the association may be made with some peripheral or accidental aspect that impresses him rather than with the essential features of the referent. Thus, "kitty" might become the label for anything that feels furry when touched. It is only gradually that his words come to coincide with their exact conventional references.

The movement toward syntactical usage has its beginning prior to the time that the child initially combines two words grammatically. First, individual words are used to express relational meanings that, later in development, are made explicit in sentences. These utterances are called *holophrases* or single-word sentences, and denote a variety of intents (i.e., to point out, request, direct, or declare). A child's use of "bottie" (sic: bottle), for instance, might be translated: "The bottle is there"; "My bottle"; "I want the bottle"; or "The bottle is empty; fill it," according to the situation and the child's behavior. Subsequently, he starts to use words in succession that are semantically related but not yet syntactically connected. He might state, "Bottle milk," and, thereby, more explicitly convey a request in words. From this point, there is but a short step to syntactical word combinations. Gradually, the length and complexity of the syntactical utterances increases, and the child acquires the forms to express more intricate intentions and meanings, and learns the use of alternate forms to say the same thing with differing connotations.

In learning a vocabulary and a generative syntactical framework, the child is not simply a passive imitator of adult speech, but an active student and experimenter in language. There is little doubt (except among strict nativists) that imitation plays a role in linguistic learning, but it is not just that of echoing adult models or rehearsing new words and expressions by rote. Both immediate and delayed imitation may be observed in the child's acquiring of linguistic skills and, in conjunction with the instructional and corrective activities of adults. Early on, children echo and repeat themselves in acquiring the phonetic structures of words. By means of jargon, they rehearse the intonations and flow of adult conversation. However, such rote activities are soon superseded by more active learning strategies. For example, some children have been observed to imitate selectively, seemingly in order to establish the meanings and uses of words and syntactical structures. Their echoing is neither of words nor phrases that are already used consistently in their spontaneous speech, nor of those that are totally new to them. Rather, they imitate those words or phrases that they are just beginning to use spontaneously and cease imitating them once they have been mastered (Bloom *et al.*, 1974).

There is suggestive evidence that such imitative behaviors help the young speaker to abstract new basic forms or rules of grammar from what is said to them (Whitehurst, 1973). It has been observed, also, that the meanings of words and expressions are not acquired simply and directly by learning associations with the objects and events that they signify. Object–concept–word relationships are gradually constructed and differentiated through games, in which the child experiments with words and their referents and tests his expanding vocabulary in a variety of contexts (Brown, 1956; Wittgenstein, 1958). Through simultaneous verbal and motor play, the properties of word referents are conceptualized, and word associations are refined. Further, by matching words already associated with particular objects with different, but somehow similar, objects, the child experimentally generalizes and delimits his semantic categories. Likewise, by trying out the expressions, learned in particular behavioral situations, in other contexts, the child learns their appropriate applications. Thus, the child gradually brings his language into line with convention and elaborates his conceptual grasp of the world at the same time.

In these activities, adults and older children are the child's models and foils, providing the examples and corrections by which he shapes his linguistic usage. The mother, especially, is an active language instructor for the child and employs various teaching techniques in this role. During infancy, she responds differentially to, and so encourages, the child's differential vocalizations. She imitates early vocalizations and, with much gesturing and exaggerated expression, comments, points out, exhorts, soothes, scolds, and even engages in question and answer soliloquies for his benefit. As he advances, she models and often actively elicits verbal behavior. It is a regular occurrence to hear a mother urge her toddler to wave and "say bye-bye" as someone is leaving, or to hold up an object and repetitively state: "This is a spoon; say spoon." In the discourses between the mother and the child who is beginning to acquire syntax, the conventions of conversational information exchange are developed—taking turns in speaking, using references that are related to the other speaker's statement or question, adding information, and seeking clarification. Concomitantly, words and grammar are being exemplified, expanded upon, and corrected.

The role of parents, adults in general, and even older children as language teachers is taken on almost as if by instinct. In questioning, directing, expanding, and responding to the child's utterances, they automatically adapt the form and content of their own address, so as to take into account the child's level of conceptualization and syntax. They simplify, use clarifying redundancies, overemphasize, change the normal pitch of their speech, and exaggerate meaningful patterns of intonation. This process is accompanied most often by more than the usual nonverbal expression—gesturing, pointing out, dramatizing, etc. Most importantly from the child's point of view, adults tend to limit their references to things in the immediate environment to which they can call the child's attention, or to which he is already attending. Thus, they instruct him directly and concretely in the relationships between words and syntactical structures and their referents and uses. Once again, linguistic and conceptual learning concur.

THE FUNCTIONING AND DYSFUNCTIONING OF PSYCHOLINGUISTIC OPERATIONS

Functioning

Up to now, we have been using the term *function* with reference to the uses or purposes of language and language acts. Here we use *functioning* to denote the workings of those psychological operations necessary to the normal reception, comprehension, and production of linguistic forms at any point in development. These constructs are implicit in, and requisite to, the manifest behaviors that make up language acts, but are not directly observable in themselves. However, something of their functioning or dysfunctioning in a given linguistic event may be deduced from the nature of the input, accompanying behaviors, and response produced.

A linguistic act of a child, say, responding to a verbal request to name an object, cannot be analyzed without recourse to concepts of auditory perception, auditory association, memory, and motoric encoding, among other things. Having attended to and adequately heard the request, the child must discriminate its phonemic and morphemic components and register them in accurate temporal sequence. He then has to maintain them in memory while the intonational and syntactical patterns are decoded and analyzed in relation to contextual cues and past experience in order to determine their meaning and the intent of the speaker. Assuming that he is familiar with the object and already has stored its name in his memory in association with its conceptual class, he must now retrieve or remake the associations between the visually perceived object and its abstract class and label. Finally, assuming further that he is motivated to respond, he must encode the name motorically and execute it vocally, again with accurate temporal ordering of the phonemic components. Of course, the cognitive and expressive operations would become much more complicated if the situation were to involve more than simply identifying and naming. If he wanted to explain something, not only would there be more complicated operations of association and recall, but also additional operations in the selection and encoding of sequential grammatical structures appropriate to his intended meanings and his estimate of the informational needs of the listener.

The above-mentioned processes are the basic psychological operations involved in the reception, cognitive processing, and expression of vocal language. There are a variety of theoretical models in the literature which delineate subfunctions in each of these three major categories and plot their relationships to each other and to the visual-motor modality. Here, we will limit our discussion to the auditory-vocal components that are implicated, in one way or another, in dysphasic anomalies. Overall, it is apparent that the order of events in a full linguistic act proceeds from the receptive, through the cognitive, to the expressive. Therefore, defect at any one point will affect in some manner those processes that follow it. However, this is not the total picture. A defect in a later operation also has consequences for those that precede it.

The perception of auditory signals occurs after the sounds have been transmitted to the brain via the mechanical and neural apparatuses of hearing. However, attention is vital to the perception, registration, and comprehension of any sounds. Wood (1975) stated the importance of this factor as follows:

> The most critical component of auditory processing is attending behavior. If an individual is unable to or elects not to attend to the source of the stimulus or the stimulus itself, any auditory processing which involves sorting, coding, storage, and retrieval is of no consequence. If the attending process is interrupted or lacks establishment, the processing which follows will result in distorted evaluation of the signal or the message. Only those signals which are considered by the receiver as interesting enough to demand attending behavior for a sufficient period of time to permit message analysis can be considered codable, sortable, storable, and retrievable. (p. 115)

Even though attending behavior is requisite to auditory perception and, consequently, comprehension, it is evident that a reciprocal dependency exists also. In the neonatal period, the infant already displays a differential interest in the pattern of sounds made by the human voice (Eisenberg, 1967), and as soon as two weeks after birth, the human voice is singularly effective in arresting the baby's crying (Wolff, 1966). Within two months, the mother's voice is differentiated from the voices of strangers, and there is indication of some discrimination among intonational patterns (Boyd, 1975; Culp and Boyd, 1975). As the child grows during the first six or seven months, it becomes increasingly apparent that differences in the mother's tone of voice (soothing, scolding, questioning, etc.) affect him differentially. Thus, though the orienting reflex to speech may be basically innate, there is soon evidence to suggest that the infant's attention and discriminatory reactions to voice qualities are, at least partially, attributable to the associations they acquire through the ministrations and reactions of the caregiver. Voice qualities become of interest to him, and so are attended to and discriminated. Whereas, without the initial reflexive attention to the human voice there would be no discrimination, it is also obvious that there would be no attention to specific vocal characteristics were there no discrimination and no meaning to sustain such interest. Finally, for there to be differential meaning, there must be capacities for differentiated association, memory storage, and recall.

Thus, meaning becomes a factor in auditory attention and discrimination as well as the distinctive acoustic features (volume, pitch, etc.) of vocal sounds. The reciprocity of attending behavior, perception, and cognitive processing continues as the child advances toward an understanding of language proper. We have discussed the temporal-sequential aspect of phonemic discrimination in Chapter 3, and it will suffice here to add that the establishment of meaningful linguistic behavior by the child depends upon the development of increasingly fine and consistently ordered discriminations of incoming speech. Without such perceptual refinement, spoken language would remain a more or less amorphous phenomenon, capable of transmitting only very gross emotional messages, and about as effective in sustaining interest as prolonged but inconsequential noise.

With the perceptual discrimination and registration of a language event (a spoken word, phrase, or sentence), the processing of language shades into its cognitive operations. The message must be analyzed for meaning, but for this analysis to take place the utterance must be maintained in its sequentially differentiated form. The maintenance mechanism involved is referred to as *short-term auditory memory*, and its capacity is measured by both the number of linguistic elements (syllables or words) and the complexity of the syntactical sequences that it can handle at one time. However, recent research has shown syntactical complexity to be the more salient factor in the growth of short-term memory span. It is not so much the number of words that determines the extent to which a child can accurately recall a sentence, but the presence or absence of complicating forms. For example, the sentence: "Paul is a boy scout, and Paul knows how to tie knots"; is more readily and accurately imitated than the shorter, but more complex form: "Paul, a boy scout, knows how to tie knots" (Meynuk and Looney, 1976). As the child develops in other aspects of language processing, so he advances in the capacity to retain and repeat forms of increasing length and complexity and to grasp their syntactical relationships and associated meanings. Here, too, the principle of reciprocity between operations applies. It is a time-worn fact in cognitive psychology that meaningful (i.e., familiar) verbal material is better recalled than meaningless material. It is easier to maintain familiar words and syntactical forms in short-term memory than unfamiliar ones. Hence, to the extent that a child analyzes and gleans meaning from the sentence, he retains more of it, more accurately. The growth of immediate auditory recall span, then, must be conceived of as a gradual, step-by-step affair, involving syntactical analysis and comprehension in addition to the simple retention of perceived sequences of sounds. Conversely, if auditory retention were hampered in some way, so would be comprehension.

The comprehension of speech entails operations of syntactical and conceptual association, memory, and recall. When a child processes a single word for meaning, he need only recall the connection between the word and the concept it signifies. When he processes a sentence for meaning, he must recall three types of relationships— between the individual words and their stored conceptual counterparts, between the order of the words and their abstracted counterparts (categories of syntactical form), and between the syntactical form and its conceptual meaning. When all works well, this intricate associative-recall operation is accomplished in microseconds.

To some extent, linguistic comprehension might be regarded as a matching operation. However, it is not simply one-to-one matching, but a matching of the particular with the general, in order to recognize the meaning of the particular. Essentially, this matching process is what is meant by the somewhat elusive term *transformation* in the psycholinguistic literature. Immediate sensory patterns (spoken words and sentences) are transformed into generalized categories of abstract structures, each related to a category of meaning and capable of being transformed back into a meaningful sensory pattern. Most lexical and syntactical comprehension, then, involves the generalization and categorization of concepts and relationships among concepts, with few possible exceptions. There are, for instance, those words and phrases that are used as routine social conventions—hello, goodbye, excuse me, thank you, etc. Yet, even these are associated with classes of social situations and concepts of friendliness and politeness that lend them meaning. Then there are automatic emotional expressions, including cursing, but these also are related to generalized concepts of frustration, anger, fear, and so on, which make them understandable even when they are used out of context and without accompanying physical expressions of emotion. A proper name, too, though applicable to a singular object, is associated with a conceptual category of one that carries with it the person's features, qualities, and relationship to the listener. Thus, while the degree of generalization varies, the associative recall of conceptual categories is involved in one way or another in the comprehension of all linguistic acts.

The part played by memory in the process of comprehension is readily apparent in what we have said so far. It is to be added that associative recall is not an evenly facile operation, but its operation fluctuates according to the listener's familiarity with the words and forms he hears. The semantic-conceptual and syntactical elements of language that are learned and reestablished continually through hearing and use become more or less permanently and readily available memories. In fact, familiarity with basic syntactical relationships becomes such that the listener is usually in the position of probabilistically anticipating the complete form, and often content, of the speaker's utterance before he has said it all. Words and forms that are heard and used less frequently are less available and more difficult to recall in connection with their conceptual meanings. Thus, one may recognize the phonemic configuration of a word and experience a vague sense of knowing the meaning, but be unable to grasp it. Of course, the listener is not always dependent upon sheer, unaided recall in making the link between spoken forms and their conceptual meanings. There are often ancillary cues in the context of what is being said, in the accompanying gestures or demeanor of the speaker, or in the immediate environment, which help in the establishment of meaningful connections.

On the production or output side of psycholinguistic processing, associative-recall operations are utilized once again, but in the opposite direction from those used in comprehension. This reversal of direction generally makes a significant difference in the ease with which the operations are accomplished. Unless the speaker is simply repeating what he has just heard in the same form in which it was said, he is faced with additional steps of associative recall and selection of words and syntax. To the degree that what he wants to express is abstract or unrelated to the immediate context, he has the task of transforming generalized and sometimes vague ideas into specific and comprehensible form. Added to this problem is the cognitive work entailed in estimating the informational requirements of the listener and of choosing, from among a wide assortment of lexical and syntactical possibilities, the words and combinations which best suit the effect the speaker intends to create. The difficulties which may be encountered in these complicated operations are attested to by the groping statements, repetitions, and awkward phrasing that one hears in spontaneous monologues of even accomplished adult speakers.

Much has been said in the psycholinguistic literature of the gap between linguistic comprehension and expression in children. The notion that comprehension precedes expression developmentally is founded on the readily observable fact that the child responds behaviorally to words and sentences before they appear in his expression. However, there is an opposing argument based upon the equally observable fact that the vast bulk of what is said to the young child is anchored in the here-and-now, and related to concrete objects and visible occurrences. Therefore, the child comprehends at least as much, if not more, on the basis of what he is aware of nonverbally than what his linguistic grasp of the utterances made to him may be. Thus, the gap between purely linguistic comprehension and expression may be more apparent than real (Bloom and Lahey, 1978).

As the child grows and becomes less context-bound, and relies more upon language alone for understanding and transmitting communications, both comprehension and expression become more complicated. This is particularly so in situations where there are few or no referent objects or events present to indicate or reinforce meaning. However, the complexity of the added operations required for expression still make for a real gap in efficiency between comprehension and expression. Upon hearing a word, the child need only recall its conceptual referent. To use it, when it has not just been spoken by another, he must retrieve it on his own from among other conceptually related or phonetically similar terms that he knows, and apply it to the situation. So, in becoming an independent experimenter and user of words, the child takes on more arduous operations than are involved in being simply a receptive pupil. The added difficulty of expressive word retrieval and association is evidenced by the commonly observed broader range of receptive versus expressive vocabularies. In the matter of syntactical comprehension and expression, the same disparity prevails. It is easier to perceive and understand a sentence than it is to gather all of the parts together and combine them appropriately oneself. Moreover, as we noted above, this difficulty pertains to the unaided speech of adults as well as to the developing speech of children.

The final psychological operation of linguistic expression, motoric encoding, parallels auditory perception in that it requires the temporal-sequential ordering of phonemes, morphemes, words, and phrases. Now, though, they are represented to the efferent pathways that control the musculature involved in the production of speech sounds. In this operation, structure must be imparted and maintained according to the delimited characteristics of words, phrases, and sentences as well as their phonemic and syntactical arrangements. To this process is added the encoding of intonation patterns and word stress. The successful accomplishment of this task necessitates both effectuating and inhibiting operations, coordinated to produce the full meaning and effect of the utterance. Coordination is also entailed in bringing together both the verbal and nonverbal channels of expression, so that words, gestures, facial and bodily movements are synchronized in a total communicative act.

Dysfunctioning

Since language is a holistic phenomenon and its development is marked by systemic continuity, a significant block or defect in any one of its multiple, interactive aspects will have some form of consequence, often reciprocal, for the manner in which the child performs and develops in other aspects and in totality. An aberration in concept formation, social perception, emotional adaptation, or linguistic operation will affect the style and/or adequacy of thought, relatedness, communication, and learning. Here, our discussion is limited to primary defects in the development of linguistic form. Further, it is limited to those anomalies, defined as *dysphasic*, which derive from faulty operations in the perceptual, cognitive, or expressive processing of vocal language.

Beginning with the receptive side, we note the temporal-sequential imperception found in many dysphasic children, and the interactive failure in attending behavior that it incurs. The effect of such imperception upon the learning of words and their conceptual associations would depend not only upon how grossly the incoming words are distorted, but also upon the consistency or inconsistency with which they are experienced. If the same mistakes in perception were made consistently, the child would develop a distorted, but privately meaningful, vocabulary, on the order of idioglossia. However, since the rate and clarity of speech production normally varies considerably, and since attention and discrimination in auditory imperception are also usually variable, there is little chance of a consistent idioglossia developing on an auditory basis alone. In most cases, it is apparent that spontaneous or trained lipreading is involved in the establishment of idioglossic speech. Given auditory imperception, without lipreading, there will be difficulties with attention to speech sounds with comprehension and syntactical construction. To the extent that the child lacks consistent words to relate meaningfully one to another, his language will lack grammatical structure.

It is obvious that in a child who perceptually distorts speech sounds, immediate auditory recall will be phonemically inaccurate. The child can retain and repeat words only as accurately as he experiences them. Yet, since such imperception affects attending behavior and comprehension, both of which influence immediate retention, the span of short-term auditory memory will tend to be limited as well. On the basis of clinical observation, it can be said that the degree of limitation is quite variable from situation to situation and child to child. Some severely imperceptive children, though producing gibberish when brought to attend to a sentence-repetition task, can reproduce approximately the same number of syllables as in the sentence. However, Meynuk and Looney's (1976) study yielded evidence to suggest that at least some language-disabled children are limited sufficiently in immediate auditory retention so as to hinder the acquisition of all but the simplest syntactical rules and their associations. The same authors note that children normally reduce the utterances they imitate to the level of syntactical structure that they have mastered. Considering this point, and the interactive implications of comprehension and attention, it is very difficult to determine if a child understands less because he immediately retains less, or retains less because he understands less. In looking over both the research and clinical literature, it is evident that, whichever operation is more at fault in any single case, impaired immediate recall and impaired comprehension generally go hand in hand. This is true whether or not there is any apparent defect in auditory discrimination. Further, dysphasic children who show auditory-comprehension defects tend to be restricted in *both* the syntactical accuracy and length of the utterances they can retain at any one time.

When a dysphasic child can imitate accurately single words, and, possibly, to some extent sentences, defective phonemic perception is automatically ruled out even though comprehension is impaired. It was on this basis that Worster-Drought and Allen (1930) and later, others, drew the distinction between "word-sound-deafness" and "word-meaning-deafness." In the latter case, the problem necessarily involves a deficiency in the process of word–concept association, since immediate retention is not so limited that the child cannot repeat at least individual words. In such an event, however, one must question whether the deficiency in association is because the child cannot make connections between perceived words and the concepts he has already learned nonverbally, or whether he does not have the concepts to begin with. If the concepts are not there, all learning, verbal and nonverbal, is somehow awry, and one must consider retarded or disordered thinking as the basis for the lack of understanding.

When a child demonstrates by his appropriately discriminatory and meaningful nonverbal behaviors, that he has an adequate level of conceptualization for the acquisition of words and can echo but does not understand or learn them, there are two possible explanations. First, the child is unable to recognize the familiar phonemic configurations of words, no matter how often he has correctly perceived or immediately imitated them. Either he is unable to store memory representations of the words, or he cannot recall and match them with their immediately perceived forms. Second, though the words themselves, when heard are recalled and recognized, he cannot make connections between them and their associated concepts. In this instance, the difficulty could be either in a momentary inability to complete the linkage between word and concept or in a failure to establish word–concept connection in memory in the first place. At first glance, it would seem that the inability to make immediate word–concept associations would preclude having learned them, and that the distinction is thus superfluous. However, in all but the most severe cases, children with such problems do develop some language and can show apparent difficulties with associative recall and word recognition, most often with a characteristic variability. Failures in association or associative recall can pertain not only for words, but also for the increasingly complex conceptual relationships entailed in the development of syntax. Therefore, a child may fail to abstract or store adequately the general rules of language, and thus be lacking in the receptive analysis of sentences, although recognition and comprehension of single words is relatively intact.

In any instance of receptive dysfunctioning in dysphasic children, expression will also be defective, at least to the degree that one or all of the receptive operations are impaired. As a child is unable to perceive, recognize, or understand linguistic forms consistently, so he will be deficient in their use. On this point there is no disagreement in the literature. However, by taking the position that all developmental dysphasia is receptively based, some writers implicitly deny the possibility that a child can be solely, or predominantly, expressively dysphasic. When expressive problems alone are apparent, they are relegated to the realm of anarthria (Eisenson, 1972; Lenneberg, 1962). The premise for the assumption that all dysphasia is receptive in origin stems from the principle that the development of comprehension precedes that of expression. De Hirsch (1975) made this point explicit in declaring: "Input always precedes output, and the deficits on the input side cause the problems." However, it must be remembered that intact expressive processing does not inevitably follow upon intact reception.

Word-loss or anomia in dysphasic children is a case in point. In this phenomenon, the child cannot find the right word to name an object, or is at a loss for a specific word to express his meaning in spontaneous speech. In many such instances, the child shows immediate recognition of lost words when he is given verbal multiple choices, indicating that there is nothing markedly wrong with his perception, conceptual association, or storage of the words. Furthermore, that he then can complete his statement quite adequately with the word he has recognized, suggests that his initial groping was for the word itself and for a syntactical structure. Here, receptive defects cannot be invoked to explain the problem. It is quite clearly one of expressive retrieval.

In a similar vein, some dysphasic children exhibit extraordinary difficulty in putting together syntactical structures, though they show little apparent deficit in understanding what is said to them, even in the absence of gesturing and overt contextual cues. However, receptive shortcomings in the learning of syntactical rules cannot as easily be eliminated here, as is learning in word retrieval problems. Whereas the awkwardness may be the result of particular trouble in assembling and encoding sentences, there is no practical way to discern whether or not this is the sole reason for the poor construction. When it is quite variable, it is likely that expressive operations are implicated. When there is consistent misuse of grammatical form—such as inflections, verb tenses, plurality, etc.— it would seem most likely to reflect ill-learned grammar. On the other hand, spontaneous expressive missequencing, of the sort that resembles adult literal or verbal paraphasia, apparently occurs in the encoding operation and is usually highly variable and not connected with the misperception of language just spoken by another.

In practice, the matter of identifying specific dysfunctional operations is fraught with uncertainties. In some instances, by controlling nonverbal factors and eliminating what operations are apparently intact, one can come to a reasonable estimate of how a particular child's language is impaired. Using such functional analysis, one can observe marked differences between expressive and receptive functioning on the whole. Also, at times the distinction between word–sound and word–meaning "deafness," or defective word storage and word-loss or anomia, is readily observable. Even finer distinction may be made relatively apparent through extensive cross-modal analysis. For the most part though clearcut classifications of operational defect are generally more elusive than they are immediately apparent, and the clinician must have a tolerance for perplexing ambiguities. In addition to the complicating matter of reciprocal effects among operations, one often faces issues of motivation and resistance beyond one's effective control.

Dysphasic Development

A child's dysphasia does not exempt him from the general principles and processes of development, but it does have implications for the fashion in which he responds to the needs that his own growth imposes on him, and to the needs, expectations, and reactions of those around him. He is still a holistically functioning and gradually differentiating organism, subject to the complexly interrelated forces that press upon and shape development. The dysphasic child requires some means of accounting for, organizing, and communicating his experiences, and thus of compensating for his linguistic deficiencies and the inner and outer problems they pose. The individual mechanisms and overall style with which he accomplishes this task will depend upon the latitude and severity of his dysfunctioning, and the innate and learned traits and capabilities that develop in interaction with his particular set of circumstances. From a clinical standpoint, his moves may be adaptive or maladaptive or both, solving issues or creating more problems for both himself and those involved with him. Finally, in his state of holistic and interrelated change, the child's linguistic anomalies, and compensations themselves, change as he grows.

Because of the systemic nature of psycholinguistic development, the dysphasic child's problems in acquiring the conventional forms of language necessarily effect their pragmatic and contextual aspects and content. The nature and degree of the child's dysfunctioning will influence not only how he learns to communicate, but also the content and extent of his communication. The trouble a dysphasic child has in deriving meaning from, or transmitting meaning through, speech tends to reduce its value to him as an instrument of communication. He is prone, most naturally, to look to other modes of communication in the give and take with his environment. Given relatively intact visual-motor functions, he will incline toward their greater use in comprehending the communication of others or making his own intentions known. Thus, this manner of compensating will work to magnify and prolong his reliance upon nonverbal channels and upon referents and cues in the immediate surroundings. In turn, this dependence tends to restrict the range of what he can communicate about. To the extent that he is bound to devices which cannot effectively carry information about the absent and the unobservable, the past and the future, he will be more or less confined to understanding and expressing messages about the concrete here-and-now.

Since all but the most severely impaired receptive dysphasics do learn to grasp and use some language, they are not completely context-bound. Nevertheless, their interest in and, hence, attention to and use of language is most often lower than normal. The loss of the initial orienting reflex of speech and the similar loss of the early words of some dysphasic children, dramatically attest to this. Even those dysphasic children who produce a great deal of speech, with varying degrees of incoherence, show a lack of attention to the informational value of vocal language *per se*. Because of such attentional deficit, many dysphasics become actually linguistic underachievers relative to the language they might otherwise acquire in spite of their defects. In this regard, as in all others, a receptively impaired child is at the greatest disadvantage. He is functionally, and usually motivationally, handicapped in what he might learn as a passive observer and an active experimenter in linguistic communication. A child whose problem is predominantly expressive, may learn receptively to a greater degree, but will be lacking in the inherent interest and motivation to undertake the more arduous role of experimenter. Moreover, such attentional deficits are prone to become habitual and aggravate a dysphasic problem as the child moves out into the world and into school.

On the other side of the language acquisition process, the child's natural teachers frequently react to his anomalous behaviors in ways that reinforce or exacerbate his difficulties in linguistic learning. The orientations and behaviors that parents and siblings develop toward dysphasic children are as divergent as their personalities and circumstances. Yet, in the role of language instructor, they display remarkable commonality in their proclivity for adapting to the young child's level of functioning. It is this same adaptability, together with a lack of results from their efforts, that can work to maintain the dysphasic's deficiency in motivation to engage in remedial learning. Since the child responds better to nonverbal communication, they tend to emphasize this channel and reduce their verbal communications to him. Further, in many instances, they become so accustomed to his anomalous usage as to understand him quite well and thereby further solidify his deficient communicative behavior. Thus, the dysphasic may train his trainers to hamper what progress he is capable of. Although this is a fairly common event, the interpersonal dynamics of dysphasic children are much too diverse to draw meaningful generalities other than to note that they are particularly susceptible to mistaken feedback about why they have trouble. This false information occurs all down the line, from parents to professionals.

The cognitive development of dysphasics is also highly diverse and related to all of the reciprocal factors that affect the cognitive development of other children—intellectual, emotional, and environmental. However, the interrelated nature of cognitive growth and language acquisition implies that impaired learning of the abstract symbolism afforded by words will affect the child's concept formation and thinking. Recalling the postulations of Inhelder (1976) and de Ajuriaguerra *et al.* (1976), it would seem that when the child reaches the point of needing arbitrary mental representations in the abstract development of his thought, he will be hindered to the degree that consistent words and syntax are unavailable to him. However, the matter is not at all that straightforward. First, that level of abstraction involved in the purely formal operations of thought is not reached during childhood, but begins developing in adolescence and extends into adulthood. Then, even in highly intelligent adults, the formal operations are not uniformly dependent upon pure symbolism. They entail gradations of abstractness–concreteness and combined image–word processes, according to the topic and the sort of logical thinking in which one engages. Further, not all imagery is uniformly concrete and incapable of carrying symbolic generalization, and even nearly total ineptitude in language does not necessarily impede abstract thinking across the board witness the cases of so-called idiot savants. So, one cannot prognosticate with any assuredness about concrete-mindedness on the basis of developmental dysphasia alone. It is because the process of symbolization and symbolic association itself is impaired that growth in abstract thinking is hampered. In the manner of Myklebust's (1952) notion of "central aphasia" in childhood, all symbolic activity would have to be affected, and here the distinction between linguistic dysfunctioning and general mental retardation is blurred. A child thus affected is lacking in all means of categorizing and organizing ideas and, therefore, of interpreting all experience—verbal and nonverbal.

The linguistic behavior that any dysphasic child does acquire is a product essentially of what is intact in his language processing and of his compensation for what is not. The compensation that takes place is of two sorts—organic compensation, which results in the direct amelioration of the operational defects themselves, and the compensatory psychological mechanisms that the child employs in an effort to overcome or get around what is lacking to him in communication. Organic compensation occurs as a result of the plasticity of the developing cerebral cortex. Briefly, this entails the propensity of the brain to shift functions from defective to intact and, more or less, uncommitted areas. In Penfield's (1965) view, the cerebral functions relating to perception and language are established through a process of facilitation: "As the child begins to perceive and to speak, electrical currents must be passing in corresponding patterns through the cortex and underlying brain. After each time of passage it is easier for the passage of later currents along the same trail." This facilitation results in the "trail" or structure becoming more or less fixed in its commitment to the function involved. With the development of language, wider and more complex structures are fixed, and the uncommitted cerebral portions diminish.

When facilitation in one cerebral location is impaired, the current seeks to gain an alternate route, so to speak. To the extent that other routes are not already committed or likewise impaired, the function can be established. Thus, in acquired childhood aphasia, the younger the child and the more restricted or focal the damage, the more rapid and complete is the recovery of linguistic functioning and development. In developmental dysphasia, the same process applies, but on the whole it is apparently less easily or more slowly accomplished. A number of explanations have been put forth for this difference, including the possibility that the cerebral defects are necessarily bilateral and diffuse, or that congenital defects interfere with fundamental learning processes in such a way as to impede the evolution of more complex learning processes. Whatever the case, it is the rule that the defective conditions do ameliorate gradually with age, so that even those severe, receptively impaired cases that Gordon (1966) termed "centrally deaf" often improve to the extent that the original diagnosis may be questioned later on.

The compensatory mechanisms that the child develops to circumvent his deficiencies in communication can be placed in two general categories—those that occur in the service of defensively avoiding communicative difficulties, and those that occur in the effort to understand or speak despite the difficulties. The former are the behavioral stratagems and emotional defenses that arise primarily out of the child's experiences of frustration, anxiety, and ineffectuality with linguistic interchange. They may vary from situation to situation or become more or less permanent traits that characterize his overall interpersonal adjustment. Commonly, they include withdrawal, oppositionalism, evasion, purposeful distraction, silliness, and so on. The mechanisms used to overcome difficulties are dictated by and, in one way or another, reveal the nature of the linguistic anomalies underlying them. Some are primarily ancillary

and nonverbal, such as the reliance upon situational cues in comprehension, and gesturing to make up for gaps or distortions in
expression. Others are directly verbal. For example, on the receptive
side, the child may use what bits and pieces he grasps of a speech
act to guess at the speaker's intent, sometimes responding accurately and sometimes incongruously. In expression, he may circumlocute, or engage in a process of assonant associating in his attempts
to retrieve words, or use semantically approximate terms to fill gaps.
Such compensatory moves are also quite variable—laborious and
mixed with paraphasia and agrammia in some instances, or embedded in adequate discourse in others.

Both organic and adaptive linguistic compensation are interrelated with intelligence and learning, as well as with the breadth and
severity of dysfunctioning. On the whole, as dysphasics develop,
their dysfunctional operations, naturally, tend toward increasing
efficiency, whereas the children simultaneously become more and
more proficient at circumventing recurrent anomalies. It is apparent,
too, that emotional adjustment facilitates learning, and hence
amelioration and compensation, whereas maladjustment generally
impedes it. Another factor in linguistic progress was observed by de
Ajuriaguerra and his colleagues (1976), in their two- to three-year
study of dysphasic development. The greater utilitarian value of
some areas of linguistic functioning over others in ordinary discourse is a more potent force in remediation than intensive training.
The areas in which verbal and nonverbal contextual cues and holistic
structural patterns are major factors in conveying meaning (comprehension, narration and syntax), progress more rapidly than those
involving more specific skills (auditory perception and motoric encoding). Thus, a process of pragmatic selection occurs in compensation. In our own experience, many intelligent dysphasics, who are
not significantly dyslexic as well, come to use reading as a compensatory tool in learning linguistic structure and meaning, in some
instances actually visualizing the printed forms of words and sentences as an aid in organizing verbal expression. It has also been
apparent at times that dysphasics, with particularly keen ability in
analytic thought, apply this ability to language as they grow older,
and so actively establish syntactical relationships that are normally
learned automatically.

Coupled with the amelioration of and compensation for dysfunctional language operations, is the normal process of developmental differentiation. Although faulty, dysphasic children's linguistic systems grow more differentiated and complex as they learn.

At the same time, the expressive anomalies they display tend to become more defined and specific as they diminish. The appearance of symptomatology on the whole in four- and five-year-olds is more amorphous than in schoolage patients. The impression is that the younger children most frequently are either hypoproductive or produce a good deal of gibberish, whereas older children are prone to show specific problems with word retrieval, paraphasia, and awkward grammar.

Overall, the forces for psycholinguistic development are strong, and the prognosis for dysphasics generally is in the positive direction. Yet, there are numerous, complexly interrelated givens in this. We have mentioned repeatedly the latitude and severity of dysfunctioning, not only in the auditory-vocal but also in the visual-motor sphere. This dysfunctioning must be considered in conjunction with cognitive capability, attentional behavior, and motivation. On the negative side of the picture, there is the particular disadvantage facing dysphasics of meeting the communicative expectations and demands of others. Although most of these children have the inherent capacity to respond with appropriate ideas and behavior, they are hampered in knowing what is wanted, or in expressing it, or both. Some are more successful than others in getting around communicative obstacles, but all are subject to a sense of difficulty and incompetence in this, most central aspect of psychological growth. Moreover, they usually have little way of knowing, directly, why they meet such difficulty, and are hindered in expressing the problems and conflicts they experience. Thus, they tend to define themselves predominantly as they appear in the eyes of others— stupid, stubborn, bad, or even bizarre. From this standpoint, first and foremost of the corrective factors in the treatment of any dysphasic child is an accurate understanding of the fundamentally linguistic origin of his problems, on the part of all who deal with him and eventually on the part of the child himself.

7

Disordered Thinking

In his monograph on group of schizophrenias, Bleuler (1911/1950) stated that the abnormality in the verbal behavior of schizophrenic patients "does not lie in the language itself, but rather in its content." Nevertheless, he described disturbances of communication ranging from irrelevancy to inattentiveness to the interlocutor and even refusal to speak. Because disorders of thinking processes are usually inferred from anomalies in the content of written and spoken language, Bleuler considered the methodology seriously defective, but did not offer any alternative methods.

Influenced by the then current associationist school of psychology, Bleuler defined disorders of thought as disturbances of association, and viewed two such anomalies as characteristic of schizophrenia: an unusual increase in the flow of associations (thought pressure), and pathological diminution or absence of ideas (blocking). Moreover, the nature of associative linkage was said to be unpredictable and incomprehensible because ideas have "no recognizable connection with the preceding ones." Concepts are fortuitously related, idiosyncratically formed, and without communally accepted focus. Conversely, an idea may be of such private overriding value that it intrudes into the patient's conceptualization and singularly determines the nature and direction of his thinking. As the result of such rigidity of focus and domination of one concept or constellation of concepts, the patient's thinking becomes impervious to external stimuli and is unmodifiable by experiences and consequently nonadaptive.

Since Bleuler's time, other observers have reported on other peculiarities of adult schizophrenic thinking (Brown, 1973; Maher, 1972; Rochester, 1977). Because patients are unable to organize their percepts and concepts around a fixed axis, categorization or classification is based on the generalization of everchanging attributes. Concepts are fluid because the haphazard inclusion of nonessential, and even incongruous elements does not allow permanent demarcations to be drawn, delineating concepts or relationships among them. This peculiarity is revealed in the patient's assignment of undue significance and meaning to innocuous environmental stimuli and in his perception of variability in such commonly accepted invariants as time, space and other fundamental aspects of the objective world.

The anomalous logic and bizarre conception may be pervasive or encapsulated. At times, concepts relating to the inanimate world are not faulty, but the patient is unable to apply similar logic to his notions about the interpersonal or intrapsychic domain. For example, although the patient may implicitly accept and acknowledge that the transmission of sound waves is hampered by barriers in space, this acceptance does not stop him from asserting that he hears the voices of faraway people talking to him. Attempts to explain this incongruity and to harmonize the cognitive dissonance results in further confusion and more bizarre conceptualization. A challenge for justification may be raised by others, or be felt by the patient himself, when he becomes aware of the discrepancies in his own logic as applied to different conceptual domains (Rapoport, 1951). When the patient is able to isolate a part of his experience and related concepts into a self-contained and self-sustaining system, the distorting influence of the system on the general thinking processes is limited. On the other hand, when a more severe form of disorganization prevails in the conceptual world, the patient disregards the immutable physical laws and interprets his physical surroundings in a distorted fashion similar to his social environment.

Attempts to define disordered thinking of adults in terms of principles applicable to all patients, or to describe a pathogonomonic pattern of distortion in conceptualization have not been very successful. Tests of concept formation have revealed that some patients have difficulty generalizing from the particular, and others are overinclusive and engage in excessive generalization (Kasanin, 1940; Fromkin, 1975). Conceptual categorization might be made on the basis of dissimilarities rather than common attributes, and organization of concepts into hierarchical abstract structures may represent inordinate difficulty for the patients. Some patients are unable to differentiate between the figurative and literal meanings of proverbs. Others speak in metaphors of their own invention. Detached and objective conception may be impossible because the patient is in a state of emotional turmoil and sees the world around him as mirroring his own subjective states, or he may feel cut off, alienated from his surroundings, and incapable of drawing any conclusion or forming any principles from his visions.

When the formal characteristics of adult schizophrenic thinking are assessed in terms of lack of abstraction, and concrete, perception-bound generalization, anthropomorphization, and the like, the resemblance to the normal child's thinking is striking. However, the schizophrenic patient is not viewed, even by the laymen, as childish or ignorant, rather he is placed in a distinctive deviant group because of how he thinks. It is the patient's notions about people and their motives, his opinions about how he is influenced or can influence the social and natural phenomena which are clearly bizarre. For instance, the patient may assert that he has been singled out for a special mission or an unusual punishment, or that others can read his thoughts and manipulate or withdraw them. He may express an unshakable conviction that he can correctly identify motives of other people and marshal the most insignificant gestures or chance statements as evidence for his contention.

Disturbances of association in adult schizophrenia are inferred by Bleuler from the observation that patients' thoughts "no longer follow the old preferred ways, that is, the logical pathways indicated by past experiences." This position is further amplified by Heinz Werner (1965):

> Schizophrenic thought lacks a unity occasioned by central objective ideas. Each individual partial content represents an unlimited plethora of subjective experience and there is absent the organization by means of which the experience of an objectively functioning mind is centralized and brought under rigid control.

In early papers on schizophrenia in childhood, the diagnostic criteria, including thinking disorders, were transposed from the adult variety to what was viewed as a downward extension of the disease entity to childhood. Potter (1933) spoke about incoherence and diminution of speech and blocking, condensation and perseveration of thoughts and concepts. However, at least in the case of blocking or thought withdrawal, Bleuler had cautioned "children, imbeciles, hysterics, each for a different reason are very easily dominated by their affects and are prone to blocking." Other undisputed signs of disturbed thinking in adults such as thought insertion or thought broadcast may be reported by normal young children because of their inability to differentiate between reality and fantasy and their naive assumption that their intent cannot be detected from their behavior, leaving their minds open for others' inspection.

Identification of an individual's thinking processes as deviant rests upon the premise that in spite of differences in experiential background, the cognitive processes of all individuals are fundamentally similar and that each individual strives to report and express these underlying processes in a socially comprehensible manner. However, both the unfolding of cognitive processes and the communal manner of reporting them are developmentally directed and controlled. Continuous social interaction is required to shape and modify the thinking processes, and an awareness of the dependence of communicability upon the shared order and system of verbal presentation must develop before comprehensible discourse can be achieved. Because rigid application of the standards developed for identifying adults' disordered thinking is likely to produce many false positives in children, this major diagnostic criteria of psychosis has received diminishing attention in child psychiatry. However, because the criterion has not been openly discarded, it has continued to play a major part in the diagnosis of childhood psychosis, particularly by the beginners who have learned the central importance of the symptom in their work with adults. The situation is further beclouded by the fact that although the presence of the symptom is viewed as a significant point in favor of the diagnosis of psychosis in childhood, its absence is not used to exclude the condition.

Organization of concepts and their use in problem solving are of such central importance in the general adaptation of the organism that no assessment of overall functioning can be complete without evaluation of thinking processes. However, it must also be remembered that the child's notion of reality and his mode of conceptualization are different from what accumulated experiences and maturation create in an adult. For example, a four-year-old child asserts that a chair "looks mean" because he considers the physical universe as both animate and expressive, but for an adult, intents and emotions are characteristics of living beings. A schoolboy whose concept of death is not of finality and nothingness says he wishes to die so that he can go to school in heaven and have God help him with his homework.

A valid assessment of conceptualization and its dysfunction in childhood must be based on those aspects of the child's behavior which express his thinking in every stage of his development. The child's verbal communication is only one of several factors which need to be evaluated. In the following discussion, we have tried to point out the conceptual underpinning of children's behavior and inferences which can be made by observation as well as verbalization about the normalcy or pathology of thinking processes.

DEVELOPMENT OF THINKING

The act of thinking begins with symbolic transformation of the sensory data. These data include the stimuli received from the sensory channels as well as the sensations and the qualitative information which do not have distinct sense organs for their reception, such as states of arousal and experiences of emotions and reflective consciousness. Because sensory data are experienced as forms and patterns rather than as the flux of light waves or sound waves, an organizational tendency within the central nervous system may be hypothesized. This organized processing of information operates on all data received by the central nervous system and allows for the grouping of the recurrent forms and patterns into significant categories. This is the first step in the formation of conceptual symbols. As this process of transformation becomes automatic, the symbols come to synthesize, modify, and direct our reactions toward future experiences. This act of symbolization, which is essential to thinking, is at first in representational form, although later, it takes on a verbal cast. With acquisition of language, words become tags for conception, and their temporal sequence in a sentence is used to reveal the state of affairs as experienced by the speaker.

Shortly after birth, the infant's behaviors indicate that certain segments of the objective world have acquired significance for him and the stimuli arising from them are the raw material from which early concepts will be formed. Signs of attentiveness to the perceptual configuration of the human face and voice appearing within the first few weeks of life show that the most fundamental elements for survival—both physical and psychological—are those selected for early consideration. Division of the objective world into people and nonpeople precedes the discrimination between the familiar caretakers and strangers. Later on, indications of conceptual elaboration of these elementary notions are manifested through the differentiated responsiveness of the toddler toward specific adults and the constellation of behavioral patterns reflecting the formation of emotional bonds and attachments.

Inanimate objects invite the child's attention by their perceptual and, somewhat later, functional qualities. They fall into groups because they are movable or immobile, make noises or are silent, are squeezable or hard, and edible or nonedible. As the child grows older, his opportunities for manipulation of objects and exploration of their functions increase, and such dimensions as shape, color, size, volume and meaning of sounds, and myriads of other attributes are experienced. Although sensory data form the basis of the child's conception, concepts then become the mold by which slices of sensation are interpreted and shaped.

Early indications of distinction between self and others appear by about three months of age (Lewis and Brooks, 1978). Shortly thereafter, the continuity of self and permanence of others is apprehended. Distinctive affective reactions are observed during the second half of the first year of life. A variety of sources, including memories of past events and their imaginative reconstruction elicit short-lived affective states which color the child's perception and conception, and direct his subsequent interaction with his environment.

The basis for concept formation is generalization from repeated experiences of similar nature. When it is the perceptual quality of objects which determines their grouping, the resultant concepts are concrete and limited in scope and applicability. On the other hand, conceptual groupings are of a higher order of abstraction and more universal. Concepts extracted from similarities—even the nonessential ones—are more stable than those formed on the basis of differences because objects may be different from each other in a variety of ways whereas their similarities are more limited and therefore more manageable. A further characteristic of generalization based on similarities is that they can be modified and corrected when the perceived similarities are proved to be nonessential or impermanent. For example, a preschooler may classify his battery-operated toy train with things which are alive because it moves. However, once he realized that without the battery it cannot move, he will exclude the toy train from the category, and thus his concept is modified. Apprehension of gross dissimilarities is the first step in classification and generalization. When young children are asked to identify similar aspects of two objects (for example, an orange and an apple), they insist on reporting their differences and may either declare that they are totally unlike each other or report such things as, "They both have seeds," or even point out their functional similarities: "You can eat them both." Some objects or events are grouped together by virtue of the fact that they have a similar emotional impact on the child. For example, a child who has experienced fear in relation to a particular object shows the same phobic reaction in encountering other objects which only vaguely resemble the first one. The extent of conceptual organization and synthesis which is generated by affective dimensions remains uncharted. In normal children, examples of emotionally based conceptualization may be seen in dynamization of inanimate objects, the attribution of intentions to all phenomena, and the egocentrism of perspectives. However, such disharmony and dissimilarity of views between the child and adults do not constitute an unsurmountable obstacle for communication and interaction. The continuous processes of accommodation and assimilation of environmental events and stimuli will eventually lead to an awareness of the consensually validated concepts, ensuring a functional level of adaptation in every stage of cognitive and emotional development.

The task of developing a sense of reality is carried out by the normal child on several interdependent and interpenetrating planes. Experiences of the first year of life result in the discovery that inanimate objects are permanent fixtures of the environment, and self and others are distinctly separate entities. Equipped with these three fundamental notions, the infant sets out to build three conceptual domains consisting of physical, psychological, and social reality. Within the span of another year, he manages to consolidate a sense of himself—his gender, his status as a child, his preference for and affiliation with a family group, and his effectiveness and competence in negotiating his way around his small universe. He learns to communicate with others and comprehend their messages; he can feel their joy or pain, and he is sensitive to their disapproval and disapproves of himself in turn for infractions of their rules. He gains enough knowledge about the physical world to orient himself in space, have an awareness of time, and discover the functional utilities of various objects.

From this point onward, the main thrust of a child's attention is turned to discovering the relationships between things and concepts, and the motivating forces directing the occurrence of events and appearance of phenomena. At first he is aware only of the part played by himself. He attends to or ignores, reaches out or withdraws from objects and events, and his desires and needs are the only crucial forces. As he discovers the separateness of others, he comes to take note of the role that their needs and desires play in making things happen. It is the extension and generalization of this understanding which imparts to the inanimate world a psychological and motivational dimension. The uncertainties about these other forces, the clashes of wills attributed to others—both animate and inanimate—are reflected in the child's verbal statements. The tentativeness of his conclusions and thoughts is expressed by such words as "perhaps" and "maybe" which appear in the child's vocabulary during the third year of life. By using modifiers like "I think" or "I believe," the child indicates an awareness that his views may not be shared by others. This awareness also allows him to be consciously misleading.

The child's unstated hypothesis during this period is that movement indicates life, and living creatures are endowed with will and purpose. The moon, overhead, is walking along with the child, and the sun tires and takes a rest at night. Because he realizes that his wishes are not the prime mover of events, he comes to believe that the collective desires of people, or the mysterious creator of the universe, rule all events and phenomena. The trees bear fruit so people can eat, the stars appear in the sky so people can realize that they ought to go to sleep. God makes the oceans so people can have water. This stress on human motivation and purpose as the explanatory causes of all happenings prepares the way for construction of a more sophisticated social reality with legal, moral, and ethical rules and values. This grasp of the importance of social reality is the basic foundation of the child's psychological and social survival and growth.

Laws of physical causality and objective attributes are abstracted from repeated experiences with them, and observations of their relationships with each other, as well as from the communal understanding and explanation regarding their nature and function. In an advanced technological society, the child may be told about the force of gravity and its manifestation. However, even in a primitive community, repeated experience will convince the child that things thrown will eventually be attracted to the ground.

Construction of the multiple dimensions of reality requires the ability to group one's impressions in such a way that an articulate concept can be abstracted from them, and then to organize these concepts so that a communicable statement can be made about them. Even though all concepts and impressions are not shared with others, the advent of language wraps a verbal envelope around all concepts. The communication of concepts exposes them to the critical light of the cognitive evaluation of others and, thus, ensures their comprehensibility and validity. The necessity for the communicability of thought makes it imperative for the child to organize and order his concepts in a discursive manner. This requires a gradual shift from global impressionistic convictions to the rules of evidence and a hierarchical scale of values and significance. Instead of leaping from premises to conclusions, which is characteristic of the child's intuitive thinking, there is a demand for step-by-step progression from causes to effects and from premises to conclusions. Personal analogies and representational symbols must give way to verbal symbols and logical relationships. Although this mature form of reasoning is achieved only gradually, and is only partially applied to the social and interpersonal spheres, it does provide a system for the analysis of communal reality as well as an instrument for the critical evaluation of one's own personal views and ideas. As long as the child's thinking remains what Piaget (1926) calls "ego centric," the lack of such a self-evaluative system results in self-contradiction and distortion. It is commonly observed that children invent explanations and continue in their distorted views in spite of being exposed to the factual information. This is the consequence of the limitation placed on their logic by their specific form of conceptualization.

DISTURBANCES OF THINKING IN CHILDHOOD

Disordered thinking in childhood cannot be identified by a lack of correspondence with mature adult logic nor by the concrete forms of concepts and their interrelationships. As it was noted earlier, perceptual bound conceptualization and functional grouping are the normal strategies of the child's thinking, and his reasoning is influenced by his egocentrism and his inability to evaluate evidence objectively. Normative scales may identify lags and gaps in individual development, but they do not reflect disorganizations and deviations in concept formation. Conceptual deviation in childhood is characterized by the absence of constant and predictable organizing principles, problematic communication, failed assimilation, ineffectual accommodative strategies, and, thus, overall maladaptation. Indications of disorder and disorganization of thought in children are manifested in three aspects of their behavior discussed below.

Physical Activities

Even before cognitive processes are verbalized, the child's self-initiated activities and interactions with the environment reveal a certain level of systematized understanding and conceptualization of the nature of the social, psychological, and physical universes. Repeated encounters and interactions with the dependable structural and functional properties of the environment, and interpretation and synthesis of such experiences are the basis of this generalized comprehension. Although the quantity of encounters necessary for formation of particular notions is not known, it is reasonable to assume that, within the context of the average life situation, sufficient degrees of experience are accumulated within certain time spans. For example, it is noted that by the time a child begins independent locomotion, he has already developed the notion that the presence of a palpable platform under his feet is necessary for walking. This appreciation is revealed by the observation that children at this stage normally avoid walking off edges into empty space (Campos *et al.*, 1978). Even when a verbal child states that he is a superman and can fly, the desire to put this conviction into practice is checked by the common sense of the body. The absence of the sensible utilization of bodily experiences with the environment is indicative of failure to organize and integrate sensations with their antecedent events and consequences. Avoidance of pain is another natural reaction of the body. Severe forms of self-injurious behavior are another example of the lack of body intelligence which is observed among very young psychotics. However, it must be noted that self-stimulation and evocation of certain sensations may be seen in association with sensory deficits or in an impoverished interpersonal context. Blind infants may press on their own eyeballs and neglected infants may bang their own heads. In both of these instances, the activity serves a specific purpose, and other stimuli and sensations can attract the child's attention and terminate the undesirable behavior. In contrast, self-injurious behavior of psychotic children is exceptionally resistant to treatment and modification. At times, it appears to be the child's preferred activity.

Certain stereotypic motions or mannerisms of various parts of the body, such as arm-flapping, may be a reflection of the child's inability to integrate a set of sensations into the rest of his behavioral repertoire. Even interminable repetition fails to satiate the child's desire for the same sensations, and no variation is sought in an effort to experiment with and explore other possibilities. This paucity of exploratory tendencies is observed in other areas of the child's behavior and interactions with the animate and inanimate objects, and it contributes to the impoverishment of the child's adaptational potential.

As the child grows older, the nucleus of concepts resulting from sensations and activities of the body is supplemented by an elaborate array of emotional reactions, interpersonal relationships and communications, and learning. This complex edifice is referred to as self- or body-image. When the sum total of sensations and physical experiences does not form a cohesive and stable biological matrix for later psychological and social concepts, the concept of self is easily disorganized. A child incorporates the concrete meaning of an adult's statement and declares himself the dwelling place for the devil. Another child is not above imitating animals' cries or manners. A six-year-old girl becomes frightened because she believes that since she is called "sweet," she is an ice cream and will be devoured. For certain children, certain portions of bodily experiences remain unintegrated and are felt as alien. A seven-year-old boy describes a creature who lives inside his chest and expands to monstrous proportion or is contracted to the size of a peanut without any warning. Another child draws a machine that is imbedded in his right arm and operates his right fist.

Manipulation of Objects and Representation of Reality

The infant's interest in the exploration of objects is aided by the rapidly developing functional utilization of the grasping reflex. Before the child is able to inquire about the nature and purpose of various artifacts around him, observation and exploration begin. Intersensory integration of visual, tactile, auditory, and kinesthetic stimuli allow the child to seek the source of sound, to reach for what he sees, and to submit what he grasps to visual scrutiny. A further attempt at exploration is the infant's active experiment to discover objects that are edible. Some materials are rejected because of their taste, others due to their smell, their consistency, or their temperature. However, for the most part, the reactions of the caretakers help the child define the classes of edible and nonedible objects. Therefore, an additional dimension of social information will need to be incorporated into the sensations acquired by direct manipulation.

The normal child begins by assuming that all surrounding artifacts are approachable and can be manipulated at will. Learning from the processes of exploration and the outcome of his experimentation will limit his options and reduce his expectations, but, at the same time, his tentative hypothesis about the nature of the universe acquires solidity and certainty. This orderly process of classification and concept formation is reflected in the predictability of the child's behavior in most familiar situations. A toddler is cautious when in the presence of a mysterious looking machine but confidently reaches for objects that he knows. As the child becomes more certain of his own knowledge, he playfully assigns arbitrary functions or identities to objects, or roles to persons, in order to reproduce a reality inspired event or to imitate aspects of human interactions. His use of toys or other objects and his role-playing reflect his preconceived plan as it unfolds. Although for the duration of the play the actual identity and attributes of people and objects are ignored, the child remains aware of the pretense involved in the game; he may suspend his fantasy play and reassign roles, and all the while he is in control of his own reactions and movements.

Disordered concept formation and disorganized thinking may be detected in a child's inability to make systematic exploration, gain functional knowledge of objects, form a game plan, or maintain an awareness of the pretense in his play activities, thereby revealing his lack of mastery over his own reactions. Some children become frightened of a role that they themselves have assigned to an otherwise innocent object. Others are unable to relinquish the arbitrary function that they have assigned to an object and resist its use in any other form. The disregard for functional or perceptual attributes of objects bars the formation of an appropriate concept and the classification of elements of the physical surroundings, and, at times, repetitive and stereotyped use of a few objects occupies the patient to the extent that the larger environment goes unnoticed. The psychotic child's play activities are a series of uncoordinated and random events. Neither functional, esthetic, nor conceptual harmony and purpose can be detected in his selection of toys, nor can it be said that a common theme or thread runs through the succession of events represented in the play activity. At times, after the child has selected his toys for the purpose of play, incongruous emotions or preoccupations take over, and toys and their arrangements assume a subsidiary and irrelevant part in the ensuing activities. For example, a child may use any toy as an instrument of aggression against himself, his playmates, or the imaginary figures in the game, and any arrangement of toys as a backdrop for violent interactions and threats. The child's imaginative play rarely depicts a coherent version of reality. The same fragments of situations appear over and over again without the slightest variations. When the child finally moves on to a new pattern of activities, the fragments of the previous patterns reappear without any effort at reorganization or incorporation to the new level of conceptualization. Even though the child's resistance to any change and intrusion gives the impression that he has an unchangeable vision of the overall picture in mind, the unfolding of his activities and the haphazard inclusion and exclusion of objects and imaginary events do not reflect a coherent succession of events nor a purposeful selection of materials.

Graphic representation reveals the disordered conceptualization, particularly when the subject is the drawing of the human body. At times, essential or nonessential details of the face and body are drawn on the paper in random fashion with or without lines representing the contour of the body or delineating the space which contains these elements. Segments are drawn without any hint as to their connection with each other, and their spatial relationships are distorted or totally disregarded. Bizarre ideations concerning what is contained in the body may be openly displayed or covered under excessive and inappropriate shading of the area, to be revealed only under questioning.

Reproduction of geometrical figures such as the Bender Gestalt Test may show total lack of organization to the extent that images are superimposed upon each other, or the pull for embellishment and elaboration may be irresistible to the child, resulting in figures which are no longer identifiable.

Of course, deviant conceptualization and the consequent disordered and bizarre graphic representation can be ascertained only when the child comprehends the nature of the demanded task and is motivated to comply. Moreover, it is with the help of the child's verbal explanation that some ideational peculiarities can be reliably judged.

Verbal Communication

In children, verbalization begins as the utterance of a single word, a phrase, a sentence, and finally a succession of disconnected statements expressing the child's fleeting emotions, desires, knowledge, or subjective experiences. The majority of the spontaneous utterances of a toddler are not addressed to any particular individual even though they appear in social contexts. As socialization proceeds, goal-directed communication becomes more necessary, and an increasingly larger portion of verbal output is formulated according to the rules of social discourse. However, verbal accounts of preschoolers remain low in communicative value because the child's span of attention is short, his ability to clarify his concepts is inadequate for the task, and his awareness of the listener's needs is underdeveloped. Moreover, intense emotions, both positive and negative, physiologic states (such as hunger, fatigue, full bladder, or pain), and even fortuitous events, tend to interrupt the child's train of thought, and the thread of conversation is easily broken. Even under patient questioning the normal child may be unable to explain how he has leaped from one statement to the next, and his inventive answers usually becloud the issue rather than clarify it. Assessment of the communicative intent and the flow of associations of young children requires more ingenuity and active participation from the listener than is the case with adults. Of course, the difficulty is magnified manifold when the child's communicative skills are impaired.

In psychotic states, when a total inability to organize percepts is present during the preverbal stage, language does not develop at all because even the early utterances of infants are dependent upon some degree of integration and discrimination of stimuli and generalization and abstraction based on experienced events (Menyuk, 1975). Some children learn to say a few words without showing a grasp of their functional significance and utility so that the limited vocabulary is uttered in a haphazard manner and never used for the purpose of communication. Concomitantly, the verbalization of others is totally disregarded or its purpose and significance is not comprehended by the child. Even when the psychotic child appears to listen to what is said to him, he lacks the internal conceptual model or template by which verbal messages are deciphered and understood, or gaps are discovered and filled. At times, only the fact that the child repeats the last segment of the speaker's message indicates that he has heard what has been said to him. This echoing, whether immediate or delayed, is used by normal children in the early stages of their language acquisition. However, the overall communicative strategy of normal and psychotic children reveals fundamental differences in this aspect of verbal behavior (Shapiro, 1976). The psychotic child repeats the fragment of communication without any effort toward incorporation of the fragment or creative changes in it. Moreover, in cases of delayed echolalia, the child utters the successive sound patterns whenever a particular configuration of events or percepts present themselves with no realization that his listeners do not share his perceptions. The metaphorical use of speech reveals that such a child does not understand the limits and contours of concepts identified and symbolized by each word or the temporal order of words, and he fails to discriminate between the essential and incidental attributes of the context within which a certain word is utilized. Disorganization of the cognitive processes hampers the development of symbolization and comprehension of the syntactic and semantic aspects of language and their relationships to the experiences of the individual. Furthermore, because the communicative function of speech and the communality of our language form is not recognized, the child fails to profit from the modification and correction afforded by the social feedback.

Some psychotic children learn to recite songs and commercials or read complex words, but the words thus learned are not attached to their proper referents, and they are exhibited in inappropriate context or uttered as a defensive technique in order to ward off social intrusion and terminate interactions. At times, verbalization is stopped when the child realizes that his listener is intent on maintaining the interaction. The quality of voice and facial and bodily gesture remain nonexpressive because the subtle differentiations and specializations associated with expressive functions do not develop. The monotony of the voice is punctuated only by angry, high-pitched screams or unhappy whimperings. Gestures may be limited to leading adults in the general direction of desired objects or indicating the child's refusal to engage in interactions. Discovering the child's intention is a guessing game for the uninitiated and is learned only through trials and errors over long years by the family. The child's handicap in interpersonal relationships is thus shared by the social milieu, and estrangement and alienation is mutual and self-perpetuating. Socialization is severely hampered, and the burden of accommodation and adjustment is disproportionately carried by the social environment.

For those children in whom disorganization arises after language has developed or for those in whom it has not been severe enough to interfere with language acquisition, the disordered thinking is reflected in the peculiarities of higher-level concepts and the content of verbal messages. The conceptual deviancy is most readily detectable in the child's report of his own subjective experiences, his understanding of social reality, and the dynamics of the interpersonal relationships. Both concepts of self as an object to others (social self) and as a subject (psychological self) are unstable and without a clear boundary. Interpersonal relationships are bewildering and, for the most part, avoided; therefore, no clear and consistent picture of self or others can be abstracted from them. Because the subjective basis of concept formation, namely, the individual's emotional states, is undifferentiated and unregulated, the generalizations based on experiences do not provide a cohesive and stable picture of reality. A nonsignificant part of an object, situation, or fortuitous event acquires vital importance because it has been observed simultaneously with the experience of an emotional state. A set of inferential categories of relationships is formed between these aspects of the environment and the subjective experience. Because the emotional experience is global and lacks gradation and qualitative differentiation, and because the fundamental attributes of events, objects, or situations have gone unheeded, the inferences made are subject to constant changes. Unlimited numbers of pairings of objects and events are made and unmade; concepts overlap and intermingle, and the child's subsequent behavior toward the environment is unpredictable. A child refuses to remain in the examining room because the design on the curtains has yellow spots "like a tiger," and then he cringes and turns away when a tissue paper is offered to wipe his nose because "it is white like the curtains." The child's anxiety has dictated both conceptual categories; in one the yellow spots have determined the identity of the curtain or its fear-inducing quality; in another, the white background is viewed as fundamental.

Because conceptualization is directed by affectivity, barely distinguishable similarities and vague resemblances of stimuli are used for classification, and temporal simultaneity and spatial contiguity are viewed as proof of causal relationships. At times, the resemblance is only in the similarity of the emotional impact created by dissimilar events on the child, and a change in affective state will destroy the category. This fleeting and unsubstantial image of reality is of no help to the child in building a solid self-concept, and the absence of an integrative core hinders further organization of affects, percepts, and concepts. Conventional concepts co-exist with bizarre and anomalous notions without exercizing any corrective or modifying influence on them.

The child's disability extends to the interpretation of behavior and the decoding of the communicative messages of others. A single aspect of anothers' behavior—at times the more peripheral or insignificant part—absorbs the child's attention and elicits such strong reaction that the flow of interaction ceases or is deflected from its intended course. For example, a child is made apprehensive by the tone of voice of the speaker and is unable to attend to the verbal message. Another child is angered by the fact that he has not been addressed by his nickname, and his subsequent interactions—both verbal and nonverbal—are dictated by this initial reaction. Personal interaction with a psychotic child creates much bewilderment and confusion because the nonpsychotic member of the interacting pair can predict or direct neither the course nor the outcome of the encounter. Because the child misreads the intention and misinterprets messages directed toward him, the interaction results in frustration for both parties. The child's tendency to withdraw is reinforced by the hesitation of others to engage in interaction with him. Interactional deprivation further hampers the construction of a sense of social reality and allows the distorted concepts to go unchallenged.

The psychotic child's communication mirrors the confusion that he experiences regarding various dimensions and images of reality. The experienced self or "me" cannot lay claim to a solid depository of knowledge, abilities, feelings, and attitudes, and the shared premises which allow for social discourse are lacking. Concepts are elusive and unstable because of their purely subjective origin and are idiosyncratic and bizarre because they are directed by the ever-changing and overwhelming global emotions. Lack of appropriate ideational substrates to anchor the felt emotions results in superficiality of affective responses and their unheralded appearance and sudden dissipation. Certain themes break through the child's verbalization, and unrelated material intermingles with the goal-directed social discourse. A fleeting percept, a memory trace, or a statement or gesture by the listener interrupts the child's verbal account, and the unrelated topic intrudes into it. Requests for justification or rationalization of the verbal comments go unanswered or simply invoke expression of confusion and reveal the bizarreness of the child's thought processes. The psychotic child's subjective interpretations or his conceptual reality exert such overwhelming influence over his perception that the readily apparent contradictions and incongruities are ignored; unmodulated impulses are expressed without heed to the essential attributes and requirements of reality. The boundaries between the subjective reality of fears, desires, and personalized elaboration and the shared social and physical realities are not firmly drawn, or the distinction is repeatedly lost. The young patient goes to an uncommon length trying to defend himself from or ward off his imaginary world, and he remains frightened by his nightmares long after they have happened.

As long as the psychotic child is unaware of the peculiarities of his views, he attempts to communicate them to others and thus expose them to the modifying influences of the social exchange and interaction. However, when such articulation is beyond the child's ability, or the social reactions which he receives discourage further exposition, or the stress remains unrelieved, the child will withdraw from social interactions. Since the construction of a coherent cognitive scheme for organization and evaluation of reality is necessary for adaptation, the child attempts to construct such a system in isolation. Excessive daydreaming by these children is the manifestation of such a lonely struggle toward the creation of a coherent conceptual system. Unfortunately, the child's brooding and his prolonged fantasizing do not lead to the discovery of problem-solving strategies. A limited number of ideas and the associated chronic unpleasant emotional states absorb the totality of the child's attention, and a sense of entrapment by these concepts and affects increases the child's anguish. Because both the external and subjective realities are unpleasant, threatening and intermingled, fights and flights are equally futile and depressing. Whereas for normal children, daydreaming provides an adaptive mechanism for dissipating the overflow of strong emotions, in psychotic children undesirable emotional states are strengthened by the solitary brooding, resulting in periodic unprovoked outbursts.

Even when certain aspects of reality remain unaffected by the distorting glasses through which the environment is viewed, the child's preoccupation with the general ambiguity of his inner states will diminish his interest (and ability) in exploration and learning. This results in gaps in general information and delays the formation of complex concepts, causing the overall underdevelopment of the cognitive processes. The presence of incongruous elements of primitive logic alongside more age-appropriate ideations makes the task of conceptual organization more difficult. Affectively generated and motivationally organized thoughts are bizarre and confused; ideas based on social interactions and communications are underdeveloped or distorted, and learning is hindered by deficiencies in interest, concentration, and objective evaluation.

The psychotic child may be reluctant to talk as a part of his general tendency to withdraw from all interpersonal activities. His speech may remain low in communicative value because of his disregard for the needs of his listener or his unawareness of the separation of himself and others which leads to the assumption that his intents and meanings are known to others as they are known to him. His communicative skills may be underdeveloped in that he does not comprehend that words must have shared meanings in order to be understood, and their temporal orders must reflect the relational order between things and events. He may use pronouns without having provided the reference in prior verbal or immediate physical context, inconsistent and vague references, or he may even condense several words together to make a neologism. His wandering attention may interrupt the flow of his speech or introduce unrelated elements to his socially directed verbalization. The content of the child's communication may reveal his anomalous picture of reality and the chaotic nature of his experiences. The topic of his spontaneous conversation is usually determined by his threatening vision of forces beyond his control and his inability to liberate himself from his imaginary enemies. Even when the child speaks as if he is the director and modifier of his immediate universe, his strategies are limited to destruction and intimidation of those whom he views as threatening. The child's responses to questions may vary from logical, age-appropriate answers to some, to confused, evasive declarations to others of equal simplicity or complexity. The accounts of his dreams and daydreams may evoke fear and anxiety in him as if they are being presently experienced. The child's behavior in these circumstances shows that the distinction between the conceptual reality and the actual state of affairs is repeatedly lost. The patient's descriptions of his moods, desires, ambitions, or social affiliations indicate his inability to see himself in various roles, to report on his own inner states in the past or present, to detach himself sufficiently to be able to project himself into the future, or to stand apart from others long enough to form an opinion about his relationships with them.

Based on such ambiguous, unstable, and deficient conceptual organization, all aspects of the child's behavior fall short of their adaptational goal. Furthermore, social responses to the deviant conceptualization and maladaptive behavior are dictated by each individual's own perceptions and conclusions rather than communally accepted standards. The interactive result of such bafflement and confusion is the state diagnosed as *psychosis* by the professionals and suffered by the child, his immediate family, and the community at large.

8

Diagnosis and Evaluation of Disordered Thought and Language

By definition, dysphasic behavior originates in the processing of the formal components of language—in a child's perception, decoding, comprehension, storage, retrieval, or encoding of words and syntactical arrangements of words that he hears in his environment. Defects in any one or more of these operations result in abnormalities of communication, either in what the child does and does not do in response to the communication of others, or in expressing himself, or in both. Although dysphasic defects secondarily bring about or contribute to difficulties in the way the child conceives of and reacts emotionally to himself and the world about him, they are not caused by such difficulties. Psychotic behavior also is comprised of aberrations in the child's communicative functioning, both receptive and expressive, and may affect the formal components of his developing language as well. However, psychotic disability originates in the child's conceptualization of and emotional reactivity to self and environment. In short, both dysphasic and psychotic functioning have systemically interactive consequences for the development of communication and for the child's psychological and social adaptation and survival, but for fundamentally different reasons. Although at times the behavioral manifestations of each are quite similar, and mixed cases are not unheard of, the distinction in primary dysfunctioning bears directly upon one's approach to planning and treatment and is vitally significant to those who must understand daily the child's actions and look to his needs.

The first step in the clinical assessment of the child's communication is the determination of the developmental normalcy or deviation of his behavior. Then the differentiation must be made between simply lagging, or retarded, functions and those anomalies that represent distortions in the linguistic means of communication, its conceptual content, its motivation, and its use. At this point, one must address questions of functionally why and how the child's communicative behavior is aberrant, sorting out the relationships among the form of his behavior, its content, and its pragmatic or interpersonal aspects, and coming to some cause-and-effect judgments. Finally, the severity and pervasiveness of pathology, related limitations on behavioral flexibility and adaptiveness, and implications for future development must be evaluated. Because of the variable, complex, and reciprocally interrelated nature of the various facets of communicative functioning and development, one always must be ready to doubt immediate diagnostic impressions and assiduously avoid conclusions based on theoretical concepts, and undertake examination with an active awareness of the following issues:

1. The fluctuations and extreme limits of developmentally normative behaviors.
2. The multiple determination of behavioral patterns and the wide range of factors and levels of organization contributing to them.
3. The diversity of pathways which may lead to any one given pattern of behavior, and the often subtle interplay between internal and external influences that shape and sustain the pattern.
4. The capacity of the developing organism to devise detours when the main path of development is blocked by specific defects.

Normative evaluation must be undertaken in terms of broadly applicable and individually tailored criteria. The child's behavior is judged according to the ranges and limits of general developmental expectancies—criteria derived from the study of maturing functions and behaviors acquired over the general course of childhood. This analysis can tell us roughly what the child is doing or not doing in relation to established schedules for major developmental milestones, or to what degree he deviates at a given moment from the average performances of his statistically normal age group on tests of developing functions. The clinical value of such information is, however, quite limited. Marked deviations from developmental norms and age-related test standards are signals that something is amiss, but by themselves they afford no insight into what that something is. According to such criteria, retardation or loss of function may be grossly identified, but specific pathological processes and organizational factors are not apparent on this basis alone. Moreover, the fact that a child does not fall significantly below such broadly quantitative norms does not rule out the possibility that his communicative behavior is defective in relation to his own general intellectual endowment and the milieu in which he is being raised.

Dysphasic or psychotic impairment can occur in any child, regardless of intellectual capacity and regardless of the intellectual richness or poverty, values and beliefs of the milieu. To be judged defective specifically in its form, content, or use, communicative behavior must deviate from what can be expected reasonably in terms of the child's own overall capacity and environmental input. A distinction is to be made, for instance, between a retarded ten-year-old who behaves like a six-year-old across the board, and a retarded ten-year-old of similar endowment who speaks like a three-year-old or shows the objectivity and reality orientation of a toddler. Likewise, one must question the communication of a gifted six-year-old of highly educated and articulate parents whose language contains gaps and errors of syntax that would be overlooked in the expression of an average six-year-old from a less stimulating environment, or one who grossly fails to appreciate the informational needs of others when he expresses his thoughts. In assessing the soundness of a child's conceptualization of reality, one must account also for the conceptual realities of his community. The child of a family imbued with the beliefs of a spiritist sect, who states that his mood is determined by good and evil spirits, is in an entirely different position than the child of a rationalist environment who is convinced of the same thing. Likewise, a child in the care of a psychotic parent may convey the parent's conceptual distortions and not be basically psychotic in his own right.

Once one has established that a child's communicative behavior is not in line with his intellectual and environmental givens, there still remains the issue of what is predominantly wrong. All too frequently, it is not what appears to be wrong at first glance. For example, marked incongruities in a child's response to verbal overtures may be determined primarily by an inability to process accurately and learn the conventions of verbal interchange. Secondarily, his communicative failures and the feedback they generate give rise to a highly threatening view of social situations and a tendency toward disorganizing rage or anxiety reactions. The latter, being the most visible and alarming behaviors, triggers the psychiatric referral and dominates the parents' complaints and the child's response to the demands of clinical examination. An identical pattern of behavior could be produced by fundamentally disordered interpretations of reality, and secondarily distort the organization of the child's verbal communication. Often, too, the compensatory mechanisms adopted by dysphasic children in the service of avoiding or circumventing their defects, resemble the anomalous behaviors of psychotic children. A dysphasic child's attempts to approximate or find substitutes for missing words can be difficult to distinguish from a psychotic child's use of neologisms or incongruous statements. Nonresponse or inaccurate response to miscomprehended directions can be taken for a lack of orientation to the immediate situation. Efforts to express an idea by talking around it, or by stringing together related ideas when the precise terms are unavailable, may appear as evidence of poorly controlled or tangential thinking. The possibilities for diagnostically confusing pictures are many, and one must tolerate the immediate ambiguity in the process of evaluating the interrelated functional bases for the aberrant behavior.

The ambiguities to be met in the diagnosis of communicative impairments are related partly to the breadth and severity of the deviant behavior. Psychosis, by its definition, is a relatively severe phenomenon, but the impairment involved does vary in terms of the continuousness and pervasiveness of the thinking disorder, and the degree of communicative and linguistic behavior that the child maintains. Some may suffer obvious breaks only under emotionally exacerbating or unstructured conditions, while others are more or less continuously out of touch. The disorder may be blatantly apparent in all areas of cognitive functioning, or relatively limited to interpersonal concepts and judgments. The child may be completely unresponsive to communication or respond with varying degrees of incongruity, and linguistic behavior may range from muteness to garrulity. The deficiencies of dysphasic children can be so broad as to include all aspects of communication, verbal and nonverbal, or limited to particular processes such as word retrieval. Severity ranges from total or nearly total inability to comprehend and respond to the communication of others, to mild anomalies that shade into the normal vicissitudes of development.

At the level of broad and severe impairment of communication where there is no appreciable responsive or expressive behavior, it is virtually impossible to state with any surety whether the functional basis for the problem is primarily one of dysphasic defect or psychosis. The child offers too little behavior for differential analysis. In the absence of deafness and severe motoric impairment, the lack of communication and language is actually an enigma, no matter what name one gives to it. While something may be detected of the level and appropriateness of the child's conceptual structures from the manner in which he deals with objects, one can say nothing definitive of his *capacity* for perceiving, comprehending, or expressing language. In the case of a loss of communicative behavior where there is evidence of premorbid development and the circumstances of the loss are clear, generally a substantial suspicion can be formed of what has gone wrong (e.g., in the case of an acquired aphasia). Even here, however, the specific nature of the linguistic, cognitive, or emotional disabilities involved become apparent only to the extent that the child offers some behavior for evaluation. In the case of congenital noncommunication, there usually are no clearcut pathogenetic events, and nonexistent behavior, *per se,* is not self-explanatory. One must rely upon what a child does in order to ascertain why and how he is prevented from doing what is expected of him developmentally.

At the mild level, the recognition of dysphasic problems as contributing or causative factors in psychological maladaptation is also an obscure and confusing proposition. In a number of instances of older children, adolescents, and even a few adults whom we have seen, defects in linguistic processing had played a major role in the formation of debilitating emotional and behavioral patterns. There were residual traces of dysphasic anomalies, but they now posed little or no direct obstacles to communication or learning, and their significance became evident only in retrospect. In earlier life, the patients' difficulties in understanding others or in making themselves understood linguistically had gone unrecognized for what they were. Now they had been largely compensated for and were barely noticeable in clinical examination, but their accumulated emotional sequellae were obvious. Moreover, the recognition of what had been wrong earlier went a long way toward helping some of these individuals undo distortions of self-view that stood in the way of their relating effectively with others.

It is in the middle range of severity that anomalies of language processing are most readily evident for what they are, and more easily distinguishable from those of disordered thinking. The child has enough language to display the end products of faulty processing and efforts to compensate, and to afford direct evidence of his thoughts. Nevertheless, even here the distinction between discrepant language and thought is apt to be obscured in the midst of the motivational and interpersonal problems that accrue from dysphasic impairment. More often than not, the presenting problems of dysphasic children are the secondary accompaniments of the linguistic deficiency. Such children tend to be noticed initially because they are withdrawn, explosive, overanxious, depressed, etc., rather than specifically because there is something wrong with their understanding or expression. It can easily happen that the linguistic failures are seen as effects rather than causes of the maladaptive behavior, and confused with disordered thinking. There is the matter, too, of mixed conditions. One can meet dysphasia together with any variety of emotional disorder, and when the disorder is of psychotic proportions, the issues of diagnostic assessment are particularly thorny.

In the following section we will present, in generalized terms, our experience with behaviors that derive from dysphasic and psychotic malfunctioning. The cases from which these generalities have been drawn represent a wide spectrum of backgrounds and environments, intelligence and education. The observed commonalities were embedded within differing individual contexts and styles, and ran the gamut in terms of the pervasiveness and severity of pathology and of adaptivity. Whereas basic functional defects and deficiencies are consistent, their behavioral manifestations and secondary concomitants vary according to age and the interrelated factors and forces that lend each case its individual characteristics. Because of the rapid rate of development in language and communicative skills during the first five years of life, it is clinically practical to divide the diagnostic issues into those pertaining to early childhood and those of the middle and later years, even though no sharp chronological demarcation exists in practice.

COMMON BEHAVIORAL CHARACTERISTICS

Dysphasia in the Early Years

Linguistic functioning has its beginnings in the innate perceptual capacities that are evident in very early differential responses to auditory stimuli. Thus, a lack of such response would constitute the first manifestation of dysphasic impairment. However, for it to be noticeable under ordinary circumstances, the child would have to lack discriminatory power to the extent that there would be an obvious obliteration of attending behavior. This is essentially what happens in the sometimes observed loss of the orienting reflex to the human voice, but even this phenomenon is usually noted retrospectively in the light of later and more commanding failures and difficulties. Generally in prespeech-age children, unless the problem is so severe as to grossly affect the child's interaction with the environment, it is likely to go unnoticed. Therefore, those cases that may be brought to professional attention during the stages before children are expected to engage in some form of meaningful verbal behavior are usually so grossly impaired and unresponsive that they afford little basis for differential diagnosis.

The issue of delay in the appearance of expected linguistic milestones is somewhat ambiguous. Because of the normal variations in the timing of developmental events among children, and the variable lags and spurts in each child, it is often difficult to define what constitutes a real delay except in the most marked cases. Considering the complex interrelated nature of the determinants of developmental time tables, what could be seen as "within normal limits" for one child might constitute a real linguistic delay in another whose particular potentials and environment would portend a faster rate of development. The trouble is that it is next to impossible to account for all of the reciprocal factors in any one case and so to predict the normal variants of timing that should apply. Of course, the greater the deviation from established developmental expectancies, the more one can feel assured that linguistic behavior is abnormally lagging. Many children who are diagnosed as dysphasic in later years do show substantial linguistic delays in retrospect. Yet, at times, so do children who have no current lags or anomalies of language. Further, even definitely retarded language development is not exclusively a signal of dysphasic impairment. For these reasons, lateness or seeming lateness in achieving linguistic milestones cannot be considered, *per se*, a sufficient condition for diagnosis, nor should one rule out the possibility of dysphasia simply because there do not seem to have been any marked linguistic delays in a child's history.

Once dysphasic children attain some degree of linguistic behavior, the faults in their processing and learning become more discernible and characteristic, and one can begin to differentiate specific functional defects. In the receptive sphere, there may be an

inordinate paucity of response to verbal communication, or a prone-
ness to seemingly random or incongruous responding. Parents are
sometimes heard to complain that the child does not listen to what
he is told—"Just does what he feels like no matter what we say."
Though such behavior is not necessarily indicative of dysphasia, it
warrants investigation of the possibility of impaired auditory perception and comprehension. Most often, one sees a confusion or inconsistency of reactions to simple verbal statements that has persisted
well beyond the point when the child would be reasonably expected
to understand them. A key point in the evaluation of all such faulty
responsive behavior is the child's motivation to comply with what is
addressed to him. When the child is making an obvious effort to
decipher what is wanted, the task of evaluation is, of course,
simplified. However, frequently young dysphasics will tune out
situations in which they are confused, or grow seemingly negativistic, oppositional, whining, or even exhibit tantrumlike behavior.
When such behavior occurs in evaluation, a good deal of patience
and painstaking variations of verbal and nonverbal cueing in informal interactions are usually the only way to tease out the nature of
the problem.

Since linguistic comprehension generally is very heavily dependent upon contextual cues in the early years, and especially so
among dysphasics, one must be acutely aware of the relationships of
accurate and inaccurate responding to those peripheral indicators of
meaning that are present in the situation. These indicators include
not only referent objects, but also the examiner's gestures, body and
eye movements, facial expressions, vocal intonation and emphasis.
A slight, unconscious nod of the head or glance in the direction of a
named object may give the child enough of a hint at what is
intended for him to react accurately to a direction. Whereas, without
such visual reference, he appears at a loss. At times, inconsistency
of response can be seen to have its origin in the variable use of
extralinguistic cues by the speaker, or presence and absence of
concrete referents. Many children, too, pick up one or two words in
a direction and guess at the intent on the basis of directions or object
uses that have been observed by them, habitually, in the past. For
instance, an examiner, being careful to afford no gestural cues, tells
an imperceptive four-year-old to "sit in the chair," or "close the
door." Because the patient responds correctly to these and similar
directions, it is concluded falsely that there is no apparent receptive
difficulty. However, what the child has done is to pick up the key
words "chair" and "door" and then responded with what he has

learned is done usually with chairs and doors. By varying directions from the usual, one can often see this mechanism in action (e.g., the child sits on the chair no matter whether he's being told to touch it, stand on it, push it, etc). Similarly, some young dysphasics will simply point to objects named in directions rather than carry them out, or show their confusion directly by trying a number of activities in the hope that one will hit the mark. Also, the variable accuracy of response often is due to highly fluctuating attention and to the variability of defective auditory perception itself. Add to this the tendency of speakers to slow down and enunciate in an exaggerated manner when they are not immediately understood by a child, and it is apparent that there are numerous possible combinations of reasons for the children to show their receptive anomaly at times, and at others to respond quite accurately. Furthermore, by intentionally manipulating the situation, the examiner can often clarify issues of linguistic versus conceptual miscomprehension.

The expressive behaviors of young dysphasics is frequently limited, though some may be downright garrulous, even if they are difficult or impossible to understand. When they do speak, imperceptive children display the inconsistencies in auditory discrimination and sequencing that they experience in the words that they utter. For many, single word sentences and naming behavior make up the great bulk of verbal activity for an inordinate length of time, and this activity may be markedly restricted in quantity as well as distorted in form. Others undertake relatively long, jargonlike utterances with some recognizable words scattered here and there, and may become quite frustrated by the listener's puzzlement. On the other hand, when the child's defective linguistic comprehension is not due predominantly to auditory imperception, the distortions of word form will be minimal. He may clearly echo words or even phrases or short sentences, but with little understanding. In fact, not infrequently, such children resort to echoing parts of directions in evaluation sessions when they cannot grasp the meaning.

The effects of the limitations of a dysphasic's immediate auditory recall are most apparent when the child is asked to repeat sentences and phrases. Of course, before the child can echo word combinations, such a defect can not be elicited through imitation, but when immediate retention span widens, one can note the restrictions in the accurate retention of simple phrases. In the absence of or in addition to noticeable imperception, the quantity of words repeated at any one time may be markedly below expectation, and as the child develops there usually will be limitations in the complexity of word combinations he can echo. There will be gaps and errors of word sequencing or inaccurate word substitutions. Often number repetition is effected, although this seems a less frequent occurrence than difficulty with the imitation of syntactical combinations.

Problems with long-term memory storage and/or recall are often the most obvious, even during the early stages of language growth. Some young dysphasics, though not all, show an inability to learn words in association with their referents. With such children, one can teach the name of something until the child has apparently established a semantic connection and can respond repetitively to the question: "What is this?" Yet, just moments later, after one has turned to teaching another word or even an intervening nonverbal activity, the apparently learned name has been totally lost. The child can no longer respond to a request to identify the object, and may or may not show apparent recognition of the word when it is spoken. Depending upon the severity of the problem, the child does eventually learn some words and perhaps even stock phrases, particularly those that are most useful to him or have strong emotional valence, but the range of his receptive and expressive vocabularies is curtailed.

Much more common, in our experience, is the behavior associated with anomia or word loss. Here the child's problem is predominantly composed of failure to retrieve previously learned word forms when he needs them to express a concept, rather than failure to establish words and semantic connections in his memory in the beginning. Thus, he will characteristically act as though he knows the term to name something or express a thought but is blocking it out somehow. If the word is supplied by the listener, he will immediately recognize it and use it appropriately. Usually the problem is quite variable, and a word that is missing at one point may be used with no difficulty at another. The mechanisms that young children are prone to use to compensate for this most often entail avoidance of some sort—shifting attention to something else, silliness, outright refusal, etc. However, given the intelligence and learning, they may display some of the compensating efforts of older children, such as talking around the term, using generically related, but inaccurate, substitutes or sound-alike words. At times, one hears seeming neologisms as the child reaches for a known word or simply invents a term on the spot to fill the gap. Also, offering nonsense replies to questions is a fairly common tactic that often leads to the impression of incongruous thinking. Gesturing and referring to contextual cues to help get their meaning across is used by some children but not by others.

Another related phenomenon of faulty linguistic memory that we have seen occasionally is the loss of verbal directions that the child has understood when they were spoken. Thus, he will respond to directions to perform a task correctly right after they are spoken, and precipitously become confused in the midst of carrying out the task. It is as though he has totally lost his grasp of the verbal formula underlying the activity as he is performing it, and he will begin to behave randomly or even nonsensically after definitely establishing that he knew quite well what to do. In a similar vein, some dysphasics appear to lose the intent of a question in the midst of answering it. They may ask for a reiteration of the original question, appear suddenly nonplused after a quite coherent beginning, or resort to attempts to regain directions that are peripheral or unrelated to what was initially asked. This occurrence is to be seen as the child develops the ability to respond at length to questions, and is therefore more likely in older dysphasics.

Difficulties with syntactical construction may begin to appear when the child starts using words in combination, but in the early stages they are hard to distinguish from the omissions and errors that occur in the normal acquisition of grammar. The young child's language, then, may seem simply retarded in this regard. The tendency is toward prolonged use of one-word sentences or the elision of verbs, prepositions, etc. However, except in relatively severe cases, syntactical usage grows in complexity and the mistakes gradually take on a quality that is different from that of normal linguistic development. The child may have problems putting words and phrases in their right places, and gross missequences litter his speech when he attempts utterances of any length. Elisions and inflectional errors are still common, but they appear in the contrasting context of more complicated constructions than would be expected of a simply retarded child. Furthermore, in most, there is a characteristic inconsistency in this, with usage relatively intact in one sentence and garbled in the next. Of course, the abnormality of the child's grammar must be judged both in terms of his intelligence and the forms of speaking that he hears in his environment.

Aberrations of speech articulation, beyond those of the distortions found in the imperceptive child (e.g., anarthria, stuttering, lisp) may or may not be present. Generally, these distortions, too, are difficult to distinguish during the early years and grow more obvious as the child's speech becomes more differentiated. Also, defects in the visual-motor sphere may accompany the auditory-vocal anomalies. They seem to appear in a great majority of instances, but there are far too many exceptions to make it a general rule. Often fine motor coordination is affected and the child's drawing may be unusually awkward for his age. Spacial perception may be faulty, though this phenomenon is not an invariable concomitant of either dysphasia or dysgraphia. Actually, any of the behavioral or neurological indications of organicity may or may not be noted.

As a result of their communicative mishaps and failures, young dysphasics gradually come to realize that they are somehow handicapped in their interactions with adults and older children. With this awareness, they come to react with either overcautiousness and social withdrawal or develop certain behavioral maneuvers that minimize their linguistic disability and its consequences. Although one must take care in discussing pure types, these two general forms of social behavior arise consistently enough to warrant description separately.

Overcautiousness and Withdrawal. These reactions do not become apparent in many young dysphasic children until their first encounters with demands outside of the home—that is, in nursery school or kindergarten. They may be manifested by a refusal to remain in the situation without their parents. Subsequently, some develop anxiety symptoms typical of older school phobias, whereas others may markedly limit their interactions with teachers. Frequently, a child may appear content in his participation in group activities, pay rapt attention to demonstrations, and laugh and play with the other children. Yet he becomes tense when approached by a teacher, looks frightened when spoken to, does not answer questions, and may burst into tears or a temper tantrum, or run away and hide when pressed for responses. Similar behavior is usually noted in the psychiatric interview. The child may be resistant to entering the room without his mother. Once inside, he may choose to play but avoid engaging in question and answer interactions. When he speaks, the mother may fall into the role of interpreter possibly revealing an idioglossic consistency to his distorted language. Attempts to put the child at ease may result in increased withdrawal, unless the examiner has some intuition of the child's basic difficulty and finds an approach and mode of communication that relieves the pressure the child is experiencing. Even so, some dysphasics persist in activities which seem calculated, or at least result in putting off adults and frustrating any effort at initiating social interactions.

Social relationships with younger children and selected members of the peer group tend to be more satisfactory than those with adults or older children. The child may find his needs for interpersonal activity gratified in the largely nonverbal companionship of such friends, since even the most verbal preschoolers do not expect that all of their queries will be answered or all their statements acknowledged. Verbal commentaries at this stage are prone to be self-directed, and many questions are rhetorical. Moreover, even children with high linguistic achievement are rarely critical of the problematic speech of their peers. In fact, some such children extend a protective attitude toward the dysphasic child and manage to guess or decipher the intent of his verbal messages, taking the role of intermediary between the dysphasic and others.

There are many variations on the theme of overcautiousness and withdrawal shown by some dysphasic children. Most often, the child's communication is understood to a high degree within his family, although one parent or sibling may show more aptitude for comprehending the child's messages than others. Generally, under circumstances with familiar people, the child is quite willing to participate in nonverbal activities and enjoys physical contact and play. However, there are some who show marked reticence even within the family and in nonverbal or peer situations. Further, the difficulties with language are not accepted benignly in all families, and the child's mechanisms are laid to a variety of malevolent or emotionally distorted attributes. Pressures, tensions, circular struggles, rejections, etc., are evident and the child's communicative problem becomes compounded early on by extraordinary fears of relatedness and a sense of ineptitude. One young child, seen intensively over a period of time during in-patient observation, had actually developed a language phobia within his family in reaction to somewhat hysterical, angry demands for him to express himself clearly. Given an unpressured, understanding approach on the part of a worker, he began to speak quite freely on the ward, revealing the anomalous nature of his language. Yet, whenever his mother visited, he once again withdrew and became minimally communicative.

Socially Outgoing Dysphasics. These preschoolers show a strong preference for social interaction and will tend to seek it out rather than remain alone. They are prone to imitate and maintain contacts with adults, and exhibit cute, funny, or even adultlike winsome ways that most adults find charming. In spite of their disabling communicative defects, they often chatter incessantly. It is only when an examiner controls the direction of the verbal interaction and demands specifically focused verbal responses by asking questions that hesitation appears. Often, though, the child will come up with a response that is linguistically comprehensible but irrelevant to the question. He appears to be attempting, sometimes rather cleverly, to lead the interlocutor away from the question and regain control over the direction of his own verbalizations. Frequently, the maneuver fails to cover up the basic reason for its use. Even if the questioner accepts the child's lead and shifts his questions according to the child's changes of topic, the responses may become more puzzling, either because the child continues to shift inappropriately or because his expression becomes increasingly distorted by jargon-like utterances, elisions, and missequences. When the questioner persists in following a particular line of inquiry, the child may grow increasingly restless and distracted, break off contact, engage in solitary activities, grow silly, or turn to another person in the room. Some children manage to reverse roles by questioning the questioner, others dance, sing, smile, show off, and cuddle up, or the like, and some directly express their desire for the questioning to cease. With older children, young outgoing dysphasics sometimes adopt babyish behaviors, hoping to evoke more protective and indulgent reactions in them. With peers and younger children, they are generally at ease, unless they are in the position of competing for adult attention and approbation where their disability places them at a disadvantage.

The voluminous amount of verbalization produced by these children, at times, brings their linguistic anomalies to the attention of adults sooner than might be the case with less talkative and withdrawn children. Yet, whether or not they are then brought to professional attention is a matter of how much their difficulty alarms the adults. Often such children find adults inclined to cooperate with them in circumventing the defects by repeating themselves, rephrasing and simplifying verbal messages, and compensating for the gaps and errors in the child's utterances. When the child's speech is so sparse that little opportunity for lengthy verbal interchange exists, the child must depend upon other means of engaging the adult's active interest in maintaining social contact. Some dysphasics of preschool age are able to make articulate use of gestures and mimicry in the service of their communicative goals, whereas others do not. The precise and effective use of nonverbal means of communication requires much observation and learning. It does not come effortlessly to the child. Early attempts and failures to gain understanding through nonverbal modes may discourage the child from further experimentation or a concomitant apraxia may prevent him from using meaningful gesture other than pointing to objects.

Young dysphasics' manipulation of toys and objects is usually appropriate to their age and intelligence. They investigate and examine unfamiliar objects and use play materials constructively or for acting out fantasy. Such stereotype activities as finger sucking or rocking may appear when the child experiences pressure to communicate verbally and is unsuccessful in diverting the examiner. Echoing is fairly common, but it is usually not the only form of verbal production the child engages in. It may appear only when the child does not comprehend a direction or question, or it may involve elements of mastery. The child may repeat words and phrases over and over in an effort to overcome his problem with comprehension or with being unable to retrieve them when they are needed. When appropriate rapport is established, even children with severe imperception and verbal learning problems will engage in efforts to clarify and commit words to memory by repetition.

Dysphasia in the School Years

The problematic behavior which occasions older children's referral for evaluation is nearly always academic backwardness and/or social and interpersonal impairment. Behavioral problems run the gamut of poor social skills, excessive confrontation with or withdrawal from peers, rebelliousness, inattention or disruptiveness in the classroom, dejected mood, low self-confidence, underachievement, and the like. Very rarely is there a question of linguistic dysfunctioning, though "possible learning disability" is a frequent notation on referrals from schools.

When one considers language as holistic phenomenon, it is not surprising that the visual-motor modality may be implicated as well as the auditory-vocal. Thus, upon examination, a great many of these children referred with specific deficits in reading and writing are found to have auditory-vocal anomalies as well. The latter usually range from the relatively mild to defects severe enough to cause the child significant problems in the classroom, resulting in debilitating anxiety, frustration, depression, anger, etc. They have gone unrecognized and their emotional concomitants are attributed to psychological problems and family dynamics of one sort or another. The defects in the visual-manual mode, though, are readily picked up in school, reading and writing being the primary focus in the early stages of formal education. Seemingly, "learning disability" is predominantly identified with dyslexia and dyspraxia, and the educational apparatus is more keenly attuned to these handicaps than to the frequently more disabling defects of auditory-vocal language.

Not all schoolage dysphasics, however, display reading or writing deficits. Some read and write up to grade level, though they often could be expected to do better on the basis of their above-normal intellectual capacities. Still others excel at reading and come to use it as a tool of compensation for the learning difficulties posed by their auditory-vocal anomalies. One bright eight-year-old girl displayed a puzzling variability in responding to questions posed during formal psychological evaluation. At moments, her responses to relatively simple questions were unexplainably vague or peripheral guesses, whereas at others, she was direct and right on target. Quite accidentally the examiner noticed that the quality of her answers was related to his sitting position. When he leaned forward and obscured the test manual in which the questions were printed, she had trouble responding. When he leaned back and she could read the questions (upside down), she became quite accurate. Such students may read vociferously and depend upon the blackboard and other written classroom materials to make up for their impaired auditory perception and/or comprehension. When these means are not available, they are in trouble and sometimes resort to evasive tactics or fall into disruptive behaviors.

There are many variations of relationship and discontinuity between aberrations of auditory-vocal and visual-motor language in school children. For instance, some dysphasics with particular difficulties in verbal encoding and expression make much better account of themselves when they write out their thoughts and, thus, are lacking in vocal participation in the classroom, but do better at the blackboard or in written examination. Some, who are adequate or even excellent silent readers, falter significantly when asked to read aloud. Many, while able to read well enough, have great difficulty with spelling or with formulating grammatical constructions vocally and in writing. In our experiences, though cross-modal linguistic deficits are very common among schoolage dysphasics, they are not inevitable. Moreover, there seem to be no invariable patterns of cross-modal weaknesses or strengths, though on the whole, problems with listening and speaking, and reading and writing are frequent concomitants.

The dysphasic anomalies shown by older children are generally more differentiated and specific than those of early childhood, and the compensatory mechanisms are usually more subtle and complicated. The receptive defects that are seen are, of course, customarily milder, or better compensated and seemingly less frequent, than those that are picked up in the earlier years. Yet, one may be surprised occasionally by a child who still shows a marked receptive problem that has gone undetected even through the early grades of school. Most commonly, such children have been seen clinically already and were misdiagnosed, their recurring difficulty showing little improvement in spite of elaborate psychodynamic workups and careful planning and treatment. It is in the expressive realm that the most marked and frequent obstacles are observed. Word loss and anomia appear to head the list, and limitations of immediate auditory recall, agrammaria, and paraphasialike missequencing and elisions are not far behind. Further, since the child's language has grown both in quantity and quality, he had wider means at hand for circumventing trouble linguistically than is the case among younger children.

For the most part, it is in spontaneous discourse that the child has the greatest opportunity for compensation and shows the least difficulty. Here, like the younger child, he can shift or talk around topics when he finds himself at a loss for words, but with his wider range of learning and experience his maneuvers are usually not as gross and are more apt to be accepted by adults. Also, older children are often quite adept at eliciting the unknowing assistance of listeners. This is particularly true of intelligent dysphasics with relatively large vocabularies. Their understanding of the topic is quite obvious, and listeners are often oblivious to or only vaguely aware of the awkwardness, inaccuracies, and gaps in wording and syntax, and are prone to make up for the deficiencies by filling in the gaps or supplying more articulate phrasing themselves. At times, a child is proficient in the use of very sophisticated terms and so is able to camouflage his variable loss of everyday words and phrases with high-blown verbiage. An obviously intelligent, underachieving nine-year-old defined a bicycle as "a vehicle driven by leg power, a means of transportation for one person." However, when pressed for further description, he went on: "It has—a—you know (demonstrating pedaling) to push with your feet, and—er—to—the thing to turn (again demonstrating)—the hand whatchcallit." In informal conversation, also, the child may restrict the length and syntactical complexity of his utterances, communicating passably, if tersely.

The classification of dysphasics as withdrawn or socially outgoing is still valid in the later years, but it seems that one does not see such clearcut extremes of incommunicative behavior or volubleness as in the younger children. Also, the distinction between interactivity with adults and peers is no longer widely applicable. During interview, the child is often quite reticent at first, but although anxious, establishes and maintains contact with the examiner. Although his initial responses may be monosyllabic or restricted to short phrases and proportionately unrevealing, when he opens up and starts to recount things at greater length, his difficulties with words and syntax begin to surface. Yet, even at this point, the defects of the more intelligent and better compensated children may be barely noticeable. It is in direct questioning, and particularly formal testing, that the impairments ordinarily become most apparent. Questions and requests for explanation may create such a degree of anxiety in some children that seemingly precipitous confusion sets in, or the child incongruously states that he does not know or does not remember things that should be at his fingertips. The anxiety itself works to undermine the child's compensatory efforts and the functional defects worsen. When a significant receptive impairment is involved, some answers may be clearly unrelated to the questions. In their efforts to understand, imperceptive or uncomprehending children frequently rely on opening words or key words from which to predict or guess at the speaker's intent. Depending upon the amount of information they are able to garner from what has been said, as well as from contextual cues, their successes and failures vary. Thus, they may appear variably tangential in their communication.

Problems with word retrieval produce a number of observable phenomena, some of which can be readily taken as disordered or even bizarre conceptualization. However, that the difficulty is essentially not with concept formation but with labeling and expressing ideas is apparent in both the gist of verbalization and in the organization of nonverbal activities. In the verbal sphere, since the inability to recall words fluctuates from moment to moment and occasion to occasion, terms that the child uses commonly may be only momentarily missing, or he may block on naming a concept as simple as "food" and readily express one as sophisticated as "nutrition." In his search for the correct terminology, the child often reveals a grasp of the concept although he can not directly label it. A ten-year-old girl, asked how a pound and a yard are similar, responded: "One's long and a pound's heavy—both—er—tell you—both rulers—like rule things—tell how long and how heavy." Then she showed immediate recognition of the word "measure" when the examiner mentioned it moments later. Sometimes a child will attempt to identify a missing conceptual category by enumerating objects that belong in it. One boy, trying to relate that he had visited the zoo, noted that he had been to the "lions, elephants, bears, monkeys." A seven-year-old, trying to state the similarity between a cat and a mouse, simply said, "dog, horse, lion, cow, pig, rabbit."

Efforts to supply missing words by using sound-alikes, generic substitutes, or words with peripherally associated meanings, often give the impression of illogic or bizarreness. However, inquiry will reveal that the word is distorted whereas the intended concept is accurate. Identifying a bird in an inkblot, an eight-year-old noted: "It's a bird because it has flags." When the "flags" were questioned, he responded: "I mean flaps—er—flappers." A verbal multiple choice showed that he was trying to suggest "wings." Odd phrases and inaccurate substitutions for words are used as temporary means of formulating ideas about situations and are not necessarily repeated when the same idea is described in a different context or even moments later in the same context. Game-playing and the manipulation of toys usually show that the child is quite able to organize his percepts in articulate, meaningful patterns, to integrate objects into preconceived designs, and to be detached enough from objects to rearrange them. Drawings, though they may give indication of perceptual-motor distortion, also reveal the general intactness of conceptualization. One must be wary, though, of falling into the diagnostic presumption that if a child does display disordered concepts or bizarre ideation, he is thereby excluded from the general category of dysphasia. Some dysphasic children may display degrees of seeming or real disorganization under stress, and some may be actually psychotic in addition to dysphasic.

Because language and auditory-vocal communication are integral in a child's adaptation to his environment, the linguistic impairments of dysphasia are central in the child's formulation of a sense of who he is—his qualities and his capacity to deal with social interchange and cope with the demands, expectations, and needs of others. As a very general rule, to the degree that a dysphasic is aware and understands the basis for his communicational shortcoming, and this awareness and understanding is shared by his caretakers and taken into account in dealing with him, his compensatory strategems will tend to be adaptive. Without the benefit of accurate professional judgment, the vast majority of dysphasics and their families and teachers lack such insight. Even those children who are socially outgoing and effective in gaining positive feedback from others are prone to vague uneasiness and doubts about their ability to cope, which are reflected in contrastingly maladaptive behaviors. The immediate causes of these behaviors remain hidden from the children and from the people around them, and they often are unable to give reasons for their behavior. Generally, the reactions of dysphasics to interpersonal situations are characterized at least partially by a perpetual need to avoid or reduce the potential stress of verbal interchange. Some, therefore, find it easier to associate with younger children or inarticulate adults, and most develop the defensive maneuvers that afford them the most control over interactions or allow them to evade particular demands for verbal performance. For example, a ten-year-old hid under his desk whenever it looked as though his teacher might turn to him with a question.

At times one meets an older dysphasic child who has a fairly clear idea of the functional nature of his disability. His verbal tactics and coping mechanisms are customarily quite advanced and elaborate, although they may not be totally adaptive. One boy of ten years, who was frequently at a loss for key words in explaining or describing things, displayed a proclivity for overdramatizing his handicap and his frustration. He did so to the point of purposefully bungling responses or histrionically protesting their inadequacy even when his efforts were quite passable. When his bluff was finally called, he noted in a straightforward manner: "I got trouble remembering words. . . . Nobody believes me. . . . I know what to say but I always forget words." Later, he also explained his apparent momentary absences in the middle of interchanges: "I remember a word and close my eyes and say the word over and over in my head." Although some youngsters can describe and complain about their inabilities accurately and directly, it does not seem to lessen their dismay or self-defeating moves in school when they fail in efforts to make themselves understood. Truancy, stubborn withdrawal, oppositionalism, and other avoidance tactics appear and become chronic, even though the consequences of these may be no easier to bear than the frustration experienced over their verbal inabilities.

Since the older dysphasic child's deficiencies have been present since childhood, he does not experience abrupt change or discontinuity in his abilities, nor, usually, do his parents or teachers. However, when the demands of new learning and performance in school complicate his compensations and exacerbate his sense of ineffectuality, or when the impotency and frustration of knowing what is wanted and yet being unable to supply it reaches a certain point, a break in adaptive efforts occurs. Few parents will describe their dysphasic child as a good student before an onset of truancy, or as a great conversationalist before he grew inexplicably reticent and noncommunicative. Most will seek and come up with other explanations for his behavior or remain simply perplexed. Of course, dysphasic children are at least as susceptible as other children to emotional difficulties arising out of all sorts of debilitating situations—parental divorce, death, abuse, and the like. If anything, they may be more vulnerable. Thus, many appear in the clinical examining room for a good many reasons other than those directly triggered by the linguistic impairment.

Psychotic Behavior

Even when a psychotic child is referred as a previously normal person whose behavior has become suddenly perplexing, one can obtain a history of chronic suboptimal functioning and maladaptive behavior in many areas. Most parents have already attempted various stretgies for correcting the child's shortcomings and have developed personal hypotheses regarding the causes of his behavior. At times their opinions have colored and influenced the facts presented as symptoms. The label selected for the child's problematic behavior, mentioned or not, determines the nature and the sequence of events reported in spontaneous description of the abnormal behavior. This all too human tendency on the part of the parents makes an unhurried and attentive observation of the child's behavior the most important element of the diagnostic workup.

Psychotic Preschoolers. Regardless of the type or etiology of psychosis, these children show reluctance, indifference, or total rejection of interpersonal activities which is most obvious in their relationship with their peers. They may remain totally aloof, allow themselves to be passively led, or shy away from interactions initiated by others. They may act indifferently toward their parents and siblings and enter the room with strangers without any indication that they are aware of the novelty of the situation. They may allow the examiner to lead them to a seat, take their coats off or pile various toys in front of them. Conversely, they may remain by the mother's side and even refuse to come into the playroom with her. Although some may make fleeting eye contact or keep their gazes averted, others look at the examiner steadily without showing any signs of social contact. They may be self-absorbed and oblivious to the encouragements of adults or may show unpredictable approach and unexplainable withdrawal. Though they may gravitate toward a particular child, adult, or sibling, they seem content to remain in close proximity to the person without any attempt at initiating or, at times, even responding to social advances.

Their speech may range from total mutism to immediate and delayed echolalia, and at times well-formed sentences. However, the speech is not goal directed and is a subjectively initiated and subjectively appreciated activity. The child's attention to his interlocutor does not last more than a few seconds, and it is not possible to know whether the child has comprehended the meaning of what has been told to him. When the child's language is well developed, the content of speech may be irrelevant, inappropriate, or without any communicative goal. He speaks for himself and follows his own interest without any allowance for questions to interrupt him and without knowing when he has satisfied the aim of his questioner.

Stereotyped activities may be self-injurious or simply a shield against intrusion by others. In either case, the child is reluctant to be distracted and may refuse vehemently to be stopped.

Play materials are ignored except for the object(s) which have special importance for the child. When encouraged to use the material, the child may make a half-hearted attempt to touch objects, but he will discard them immediately or throw them away without exploration and examination. At times a child may pick an object to carry around, to put into his mouth, or to smell, but refuses to play with it. On the other hand, he may engage in endless, repetitive, and disorganized shaking, moving, or banging of other objects, turning the lights or the faucets off and on. Some children may show a more elaborate and stereotyped pattern of play with a particular toy or set of toys. This pattern is rigid and the child resists any change in the ritualistic game by others, nor will he change the sequence or the nature of the game by himself. Temper outbursts, crying, screaming, or smiling and giggling may be noted without any provocation and may continue in spite of soothing words, embraces, or requests for explanation.

Psychotic Children in Mid- and Later Childhood Years. The presenting behavioral problem in these children may be a continuation of preexisting difficulties, an aggravation of earlier symptoms, or a dramatic change in the child's behavior. Social impairment is specially marked in the area of peer relationship. The child is isolated and withdrawn from the beginning or withdraws at the onset of psychotic disorganization. The peer group is viewed by the patient as threatening or rejecting and the usual altercations and confrontations among children are noted and catalogued with alarm. Even in an adult supervised setting, the child's interactions with other children lacks spontaneity and direction and remains fragile and transient. At times a psychotic child "adopts" another child as a friend in his fantasies and daydreams without any external signs of approach in the presence of the other child. Or he may expect his chosen playmate to acquiesce passively to his demands for interactions, and he becomes extremely angry and disappointed when he is rebuffed. Children who withdraw after a period of normal peer relationships begin to interpret their friends' activities as insulting, noncaring, or hostile and rejecting and justify their own withdrawal as reaction to these newly discovered insights. Whereas the child who has always been socially impaired indicates a desire for friendship and complains of loneliness, the newly withdrawn child claims to be content with his isolation and relieved from the headaches and anxiety engendered by others.

Some psychotic children are more at ease in the company of adults. Some prefer familiar figures, others show an equal and indiscriminate trust in all. Some learn and use appropriate formulas for greetings, remember special occasions such as birthdays and holidays, and initiate conversation. They also show extreme sensitivity to indications of adults' displeasure even though this displeasure may not be directed at them. Because of the strong expectation for unconditional acceptance, some children become disoriented and disorganized when they are pushed aside or rejected. For others, the mere presence of an adult is enough inducement for a one-sided, uninterrupted barrage of verbal output.

Children whose psychosis follows a period of normal socialization may exhibit distrust and cautious reticence vis-à-vis most adults, at times, even those whom they have known for some time. In these children's minds, adults are endowed with the ability to see through them to read their thoughts and to discover their secrets. This fear is reinforced when adults seek to alleviate their observable anxiety or comment about their expressed anger. Some children become belligerent in contrast to their earlier timidity. Others change from assertive and outgoing youngsters to placid and frightened individuals. However, even children who become belligerent do not maintain their aggressive stance for long, and it is common to see a child who bursts into tears, clings, or withdraws fearfully following a violent confrontation or temper outburst.

The relationships within the family may be a duplicate of social relations with others. Chronically psychotic children remain extremely dependent on their parents though siblings, close to the child's age, are ignored or approached without any regard for their wishes. Disorganization of later origin changes the pattern of family relationships in that the child may ignore his previously favorite sibling, cling to another one, and vacillate between demanding attention, seeking security, or angry rejection and confrontation with each parent.

Patterns of interest and activities may remain limited and rigid in a chronically psychotic child or diminish and contract in a later developing psychosis. Some chronically psychotic children give up one ritual in favor of another equally inflexible and stylized pattern; others remain attached to the same objects and the same level of fantasy play for years. Whereas the child may be encouraged to experiment with a new toy for a few minutes, he rejects further exploration and shows very little curiosity regarding new toys or games. Older children may give up their previous favorite hobbies and activities with the excuse that the activities were "childish" or boring, but they do not develop new interests, nor do they derive pleasure from their elaborate attention to the sequence of certain routines which they begin to follow. The child selects the color of his shirt or shoes, not because it is aesthetically pleasing or fashionable, but because it is the combination which guarantees good luck or wards off certain calamity. He walks to school along a certain route, not because he is interested in window shopping or viewing the scenery, but because his schoolmates do not frequent that street.

Observation of the child's behavior and evaluation of his thoughts and his adaptive skills reveals the primitive and inadequate nature of some and the disorganized and deviant quality of other aspects.

In children who have acquired language, the psychotic speech is syntactically and grammatically correct, though semantically perplexing. At times, the child plays with words as if there is no fixed meaning attached to the particular sound patterns. He combines portions of two words to make up a new one and uses the new combination in an arbitrary and even inconsistent fashion. For example, a ten-year-old boy refers to his music class as "learsing" because he is learning to sing there. A few moments later he uses the same word in response to a question about his father's occupation. Another child is instructed by his mother to say "please" when making a request. He then proceeds to open every drawer in the desk saying: "I am looking for a please." He says: "Please is something to eat or wear in your hair." Talking about a Tarzan movie, a nine-year-old girl stops in the middle of a word: "There is more Tar, I want to bring Tar in the room. I want to bring Tar in the bedroom." She denies that Tar is the same as Tarzan, but does not say what it is. Words are used as toys. They may be assembled or disassembled like objects, put next to each other, or taken apart.

Lack of interest in the rules of communication is apparent when a child who can use various forms of sentences correctly, expresses a declarative statement in the form of a question, ignores the answers, or does not wait for his communicative partner to finish a statement. "Is this chair broken? Is it really broken?" All the while the patient is scanning the room and making similar statements. "Is this a crayon? Is this a stove?" The inner self-directive speech is uttered loudly at times after the action is completed. "You mustn't kick! The teacher, he has to watch me like a hawk. Don't let people cough! She should get talkified, she kicks."

The conceptualization of events and their relationships are unconventional and incomprehensible. A ten-year-old boy is planning his future actions. He will have a child by his housekeeper when he is 20 years old so that when he decides to marry another woman at the age of 35 he won't feel lonely. His child will keep him company. A seven-year-old girl is perplexed about why you can't make children in a factory. Her aunt makes wigs in a workshop. "You could get pieces of arms and legs from the operating room and make new people with them."

In manipulation of toys, the realistic evaluation of their functional and mechanical nature is subordinated to their usefulness as a vehicle for expression of inner anxieties and private ideations. Some children find it impossible to detach their attention from certain aspects of their environment. Others exhibit a total indifference toward it. A psychotic child may gravitate toward a particular toy, or an object which has come to be symbolically significant, or he may assemble a variety of toys around him without any discernible goal or any further plan for playing with them. His graphic representation of geometrical or social figures may reveal his inability to visualize a plan of action, to give a realistic evaluation of objects and people, or to represent his disorganized perception of the world. When he is capable of self-observation and can give an account of his experienced emotions, intense fears, unbearable anger, or an emptiness bordering on lack of substantive feeling of self emerges. The patient's report of interactions and strategies for dealing with environmental contingencies reveals that the child's behavior is predominantly defensive and maladaptive. Because the patient's deficits are global, attempts at isolating the deficiencies, or establishing coping patterns in spite of them, do not succeed or are not entertained. Consequently, the child is left with limited options and his defensive behavior narrows his field of interaction still further. His fantasies increase, rather than diminish, his intense negative feelings; his brooding complicates, rather than clarifies, his thoughts. The maladaptive nature of behavior is attested to by the fact that defensive behavior does not facilitate or enhance psychosocial functioning and survival. They diminish or waste the patient's abilities, do not compensate for his deficits, and do not provide alternative pathways for his adjustment.

9

The Psychological Testing of Dysphasic and Psychotic Children

The distinctions and similarities between dysphasic and psychotic behavior that we have discussed thus far extend to the children's reactions and responses to psychological testing. The use of standard tests in making differential judgments about these children is, however, fraught with misconception and open to serious misinterpretation when test results and responses are accepted at face value and when preconceived categorical notions of test interpretation are applied.

Regarding the customarily employed standardized measures of intelligence which sample a variety of abilities across areas of cognitive and perceptual-motor functioning, there is a widespread tendency, in research and clinical circles alike, to consider first and foremost the numerical scores that are produced. Particular score patterns or discrepancies are frequently taken as diagnostic indicators of linguistic or psychotic dysfunctioning, and their absence is seen to militate against diagnosis of one or the other. In practice, one finds that dysphasic children may or may not produce significant gaps between verbal and visual-motor performances and that psychotic children may or may not display marked levels of subtest scatter.

Although some dysphasics do show the expected verbal-nonverbal discrepancy, a great many produce equally deficient scores in both areas, and some even show lower nonverbal than verbal. This is not surprising when one considers the fact that the difficulties with auditory-vocal language are sometimes accompanied by visual-motor impairments of various sorts, and sometimes not. One child may be hampered across the board, whereas another is unevenly defective, or intact, depending upon the type of visual-motor function involved in the test (e.g., drawing, spatial organization, sequencing, memory, visual-tracking, etc.). In some instances, dysphasics actually produce higher verbal than nonverbal scores, according to the relative severity of the deficits they suffer or their ability and motivation to get the message across well enough by talking around things and gesturing to meet scoring criteria in spite of glaring anomalies of grammar, sequencing, and even word-finding.

Psychotic children sometimes do function in such an in-and-out way as to produce a wide scattering of high and low scores on their test profiles and/or unevenly accurate and erroneous responses within subtests. However, many can respond well enough to the clearcut structure of such testing that their quantitative results are quite even. Though the distortions in their thinking may be apparent at times in their behavior during testing and in other ways, they offer enough to meet test criteria fairly consistently. Also, there are those psychotic children whose responses are so consistently distorted as to produce an even depression of test scores all along the line.

It is in the responses themselves rather than numerical notations of their accuracy and inaccuracy that one finds evidence of the underlying dysfunctional processes. However, in and of themselves, a child's answers to questions are usually not enough to reveal whether distortions are due to conceptual or linguistic disability. A child who, for instance, calls an obvious dog a "donkey" or a "god," may be exhibiting the end product of either a conceptual or a linguistic incongruity. In order to clarify the issue, the examiner must inquire into the intent of the response then and there. One cannot be certain whether in the child's thinking, an arbitrary and incongruous conceptual association has taken place, or whether the distortion represents an inaccurate linguistic effort.

The form of enquiry that is effective will vary from child to child and context to context. We have found that verbal multiple choices are often helpful, but just as often direct questioning or asking the child to demonstrate what he means will elicit the evidence needed to make valid distinctions. Slowing down and exaggerating enunciation, altering and simplifying the syntactical forms and words of questions, offering demonstrations and examples of what one means, and giving increasingly directive cues as one enquires, are all ways of attempting to elicit evidence of the linguistic or conceptual origins of deviant responses. The proclivity is for the psychotic child to continue in his deviant thinking with little significant effort toward bringing his response into line with what is expected. Dysphasics, on the other hand, usually either show recognition of the correct response or make attempts to express it more accurately. Often, in their circumspect efforts, one can deduce the logic of what they are driving at.

In examining the structure of the child's conceptual processes, and their congruence with objective possibility, by means of projective techniques, one must be equally cautious and inquire fully into the child's intent. With the most commonly used technique, the Rorschach (1921), psychotic children's conceptual illogic and lack of inherent cognitive organization are usually most apparent, even when there is little or no indication of it on structured cognitive tests. Yet, the naming and descriptive expression required in response to the inkblots also tend to bring to the fore the defects and compensatory linguistic behaviors of many dysphasics. The similarities between misnamed or ill-described percepts and reasoning, and disordered percepts and reasoning, or between the evasive or circumspect mechanism of dysphasics, and the ill-focused and countercommunicative activities of psychotics can lead to perplexity and often, arbitrary conclusions based on too little evidence.

In the following case material, we will present some details of psychological test response and inquiry, as well as general behavior and discourse, in order to illustrate the diagnostic ambiguities and distinctions that we have discussed.

CASE MATERIAL

JOEY (AGE 3 YEARS, 10 MONTHS)

Joey, the oldest of three children in a middle-class family, was brought to psychiatric attention by his mother about six months after he had undergone surgery for a hernia. His behavior, which prior to the operation had been troublesome, was now unmanageable for her. Without much apparent reason, he would break into tantrums, aimlessly screaming and lashing out at her or his siblings and throwing things around the room. As suddenly and spontaneously as they had begun, these episodes would cease, and he would behave so calmly as to give the impression that he was unaware of what had occurred. He was also prone to more intentionally destructive behaviors, such as poking holes in screens or raiding the refrigerator in the dead of night and smearing food around the house, and he had an upsetting fondness for knives, which he would brandish about whenever he found one within reach. About three days prior to admission as a day patient on a psychiatric unit, he had stopped sleeping at night and would not eat.

Joey had a clear history of seizure disorder, dating from age two months. His convulsive episodes were daily and treated with phenobarbital. At age one, however, they were still in evidence. Then Benadryl was used with apparent success for about five months before the mother reduced and finally discontinued medication without medical advice. His development had been unremarkable in all areas but one. He was said to be "slow" in language. The mother noted that recognizable "words" had first appeared at about 2½ years, but that he did not relate these utterances to any objects. In psychiatric examination, he was described as having limited comprehension of what was said, and as using mainly jargon with some identifiable word combinations here and there. His speech was thus largely unintelligible, but he behaved as though he had the intention to communicate. The mother also offered that he was "obsessed" with things, but the obsessions turned out to be related to his linguistic development rather than stereotyped or perseverative behavior. As an example of an obsession, she related that he had learned the word "telephone" and went around using it to label just about everything he saw.

Joey was seen for psychological evaluation about a month after he had begun attending the psychiatric nursery daily. There, he had stood out in contrast to his withdrawn and noncommunicative nurserymates, most of whom were diagnosed autistics. Although he could be quite negativistic, his full-fledged tantrum episodes were no longer in evidence, and his overall relatedness could not be described as that of a psychotic child. He engaged regularly in cooperative games with his teachers, called attention to what he was doing, and spontaneously sought to enlist others in his own activities, including at one point a sociable child who was visiting the unit. He was at least at age level in self-help behaviors and took common directions well. However, when requests or commands were put to him on a purely verbal plane or were unrelated to the immediate context, his compliance was highly variable. For instance, asked to "sit down," "throw the ball," or "look out the window," he responded accurately and without hesitation. Yet when questions such as "What do you do when you are hungry?" were posed, or when varying prepositional directions (i.e., involving "in," "on," "under," "over," etc.) were given without gesture, he gazed blankly at the examiner as though awaiting further cues. Given enough gesturing, he usually responded correctly. He spoke almost exclusively in one-word sentences, and sometimes engaged incessantly in naming things. Occasionally on the ward, he would surprise everyone with an articulate two-word combination or even a three-word phrase. He had one clear syntactical construction, though, that at times he used with consistency—"I can't do that."

In the evaluation sessions, Joey's naming activities revealed a fair vocabulary of common nouns which he applied with relative accuracy as long as he selected the objects to be named. Thus, paging through a picturebook, he spontaneously identified "apple," "coffee," "cake," "arf arf doggie," and "baby." Contrastingly, when the examiner pointed to each in a series of test pictures for him to name, he became noticeably reticent, labeled a couple, perseverated "cat" for a number of distinctly different animals, and finally grew stubbornly silent. As soon as another activity was introduced, he would verbalize quite freely, but whenever the examiner began directing his naming, the reticence and nonresponsiveness would return. Throughout the sessions, his utterances were only variably comprehensible. However, when listened to closely, his jargonlike talk turned out to be structured, multiform, and complex in its phonemic configurations. It was unlike the more amorphous and repetitive jargon one hears from a younger child. It was littered with idiosyncratic "words," such as "beseck," "bragane," or "isha," and a couple of idioglossic words with consistent referents (such as "temo" for "bird") were apparent. Although these bore no resemblance to conventional words, other terms in his jargon did. Interpreted in the context of the immediate situation, "fleet" or "fleese" became approximations of "please;" "soss" obviously meant "socks;" and "ive foon" indicated a knife and a spoon. In such instances, one could detect phonemic elisions, substitutions, and, occasionally, missequencing in his attempts at words that made perfect semantic sense in context. Sometimes, too, recognizable words were semantically overgeneralized, not an uncommon phenomenon in a young child, but in this case somewhat overdone. He had only a few descriptive words which he used to denote a wide variety of loosely related conditions. "Broken," for instance, meant not only a damaged object, but extended to anything that was disconnected, incomplete, gone, or even unopened.

Although Joey sporadically was heard to echo up to three-word phrases, he was unable to do so with any consistency upon demand. "See the dog" was repeated accurately, but "I have a ball" came out "I mo ball," and longer constructions were met with the same silence that arose during directed naming. Digit recall was accurate only when "1 -2- 3" was given in that order, which he also could recite spontaneously. To all random three-digit series, he responded by perseverating "three-thirteen," a response of unknown origin that he often used when acting as if he were counting objects. His gross motor coordination was normal, but he exhibited some lag in graphomotor coordination. He could roughly approximate a circular motion with an awkwardly held pencil, but attempts at straight lines wound up either as quick swipes at the paper or angular scribbles. Anything more complex seemed to be beyond him. Other nonverbal tasks involving shapes and spatial perception were performed well for his age.

The points at which Joey's behaviors in evaluation might have been taken as cognitively or socially disordered were few, and such an interpretation was contradicted when one placed them in the context of his overall functioning. They occurred almost exclusively around demands to communicate or perform linguistically and, in most instances, clearly represented attempts to overcome, circumvent, or evade the difficulties he showed with understanding the spoken word or making himself understood. Most cogently, there was a consistent intent to be in communication, obvious in his demeanor, gestures, and physical responses, and his seemingly nonsensical language often approximated words appropriate to the situation. Then, his nonverbal behavior was as ordered and appropriately directed as one could expect of a not-quite-four-year-old child. When, for example, blocks were introduced, he built with them, or when the examiner drew a partially complete person, he attempted to add parts logically—nose, eye, leg, shoes, etc. Finally, his history of unrelated tantrumlike behavior could be associated readily with the early evidence of seizure disorder, and such a diagnostic judgment was reinforced by his response to medication. The other problematic behaviors that he had shown at home could not be deemed simply evidence of a fundamentally psychotic orientation, given his chaotic familial circumstances and his disability in linguistic communication. Further, their rapid disappearance in a therapeutic environment supported the conclusion that they were reactive in nature.

MICHELE (AGE 3 YEARS-8 MONTHS TO 9 YEARS-3 MONTHS)

Michele was a boy, given a girl's name arbitrarily by his mother, dressed in girlish clothing, and raised symbiotically in a fatherless home with a chronically schizophrenic older sister. He first came to attention through his sister's psychiatric contacts since he apparently posed no extreme behavioral problems to the mother. When seen at a little over 3½ years, he was a quiet, highly passive, but not totally unresponsive child, whose predominant mode of relating to adults was in seeking to be cuddled. Aside from that, he initiated no interaction. In evaluation, he smiled occasionally when approached, but remained largely impassive or appeared frightened by some objects in the room. Although he displayed no markedly bizarre activities, he was strangely prone to compulsive-like routines, such as meticulously lining up the parts of puzzles or blocks and regularly not eating M&M's until he turned each piece so that the initials faced toward him. When the examiner tried to intervene in these behaviors, Michele would physically resist or withdraw. He was silent during evaluation but was reported by staff to have about a ten-word vocabulary that he used very sporadically to make needs and wants known. Usually, though, he just pulled or pointed to express himself. At times he responded to simple commands, but at other times, he seemed not to understand them even when they were accompanied by profuse gesturing and demonstration, and frequently had to be led physically by the examiner to perform imitative acts. Asked to put blocks in a deep box, he made an initial move but withdrew from the box with a look of fright. The fear did not dissipate until he was shown repeatedly where the blocks had gone, and even then he would insert them only partially and immediately pull them out. He would draw a fair circle, but when asked to imitate one drawn by the examiner, he drew the parts of a face in it.

Mike, as he came to be called more appropriately by the ward staff, fed himself independently, if messily, but had to be dressed totally and showed no toilet control other than taking his pants down before defecating on the floor. He was heard to echo the last words of some statements with some misarticulation, but only occasionally. His play, though not grossly inappropriate, was quiet, languid, and mainly solitary, though at moments he did parallel the activities of his peers. Gross and fine motor coordination were normal for his age, and there were no remarkable neurological findings. One could not reasonably rule out dysphasic incapacity, though there was suggestion in the incongruity of some behaviors that his lack of communication was not explainable solely on a linguistic basis. He offered too little by which to judge.

After a year of care and training, Mike was noticeably more responsive, but still relatively impassive, and showed little proclivity for starting an interaction or for questioning anything. Seemingly the only spontaneous behavior was to demonstrate that he knew something, although the circumstances at the moment had no relation to his demonstrations. For instance, he somewhat perseveritively broke into recitals of the alphabet in correct sequence, or quite precipitously counted or named objects in the room. He followed simple directions well, whether they were given with or without gestures, but invariably failed to complete more complex commands. Told to put a pencil on a table, then open a box and go to the window, he would begin accurately with the first part, make a move toward the second, and become quickly sidetracked into an unrelated activity. He made no attempts to call the examiner's attention to what had diverted him. On the whole, he appeared alert but showed a tendency to withdraw inwardly for brief periods.

Mike's use of language had advanced notably since his initial evaluation. He spoke in some phrases of two to four or five words, but for the most part restricted himself to naming things and was still relatively limited in the overall quantity of speech produced. Semantically and syntactically he was fairly accurate for his age, and though his speech was comprehensible, there was a tendency toward babyish articulation. He still echoed, seemingly more often than a year earlier, and usually to purely verbal questions. On a test (Terman and Merrill, 1960), he could not, or would not, respond to incomplete analogies (e.g., "Daddy is a man; Mommy is a ————"), or to questions that did not relate to something in the immediate situation (e.g., "What do you do when you are hungry?"), either accurately repeating much of the question or remaining silent. Yet, he was able to name pictures at a level commensurate with his age. When asked to describe what was happening in pictures depicting relatively complex activities, he was at his most voluble. Shown a picture of a grandmotherly woman in a rocking chair talking to children, with a pot boiling over on a stove in the background, he noted, "That's a picture for Mommy—oh—oh, Mommy, you spilled that, you spilled that!" His visual-motor functioning was near age level, and he displayed no marked defects in copying designs or recognizing and naming geometric shapes. It was becoming increasingly evident, in the complexity of the speech he did use and in the absence of specific linguistic anomalies, that the deficiencies in Mike's communicative behavior were not due to faulty language processing.

At age five years eight months, Mike was even more voluble and was now saying things with some spontaneity, though still with traces of babyish articulation. Two- and three-word phrases were the mainstay of his communication, and he uttered up to full five- to eight-word sentences at times. His syntax was at times a bit awkward, but there was no notable missequencing, and words were well constructed and accurately used, with the exception of an occasional idiosyncratic term that had no recognizable association to the context. The content of his speech was, however, another matter. He remained the most terse and least revealing in interview, but in response to test questions, he showed that he was only variably oriented to the topics at hand. When the questions were of the sort that would elicit factual information, he was at his best, but still fluctuated in relevance. The question, "From what animal do we get milk?" was answered: "Cow milk." "What shines in the sky at night?" elicited "Yeah, sure, it's dark out here,

M&M's." When the questions were concerned with practical logic, he was consistent in being irrelevant or peripheral at best, as follows:

Q. Why shouldn't we play with matches?
A. Yeah-why! I'm Mike.
Q. Why do you have to wash your face and hands?
A. Or head? Wash your head.
Q. What should you do when you cut your finger?
A. He cut your tied.

Finally, rehospitalized a number of years after treatment had ceased, Mike had progressed to a linguistically articulate nine-year-old, capable of performing in the genius range on some highly analytical nonverbal tests. His communication, however, now quite spontaneous and formally accurate, showed little regard for the informational needs of the listener. Further, his stance with the examiner was distant and imperious. His disordered logic, conceptualization, and judgment are exemplified in the following exchanges:

Q. Why are you here?
A. Because a social worker took me here with the police. She tricked me and my mother.
Q. How?
A. There's a girl in my building. She's seven. She does sex with boys, makes them get naked in bed and fucks and sucks them off. She did it with me and another boy, Howard. He's a black dude. We had lunch at the Hotel Grande.
Q. How did the social worker trick you?
A. Room number 612. Howard's *not* my father.
Q. How many days are there in the week?
A. Monday.
Q. How many days in one week?
A. 5, 3, 1.
Q. In which direction does the sun set?
A. Makes you hot and sweaty.
Q. Where does the sun go down? (Gesturing). The sun comes up every morning in the same direction and goes down every night in the same direction. Where does it go down?
A. Degrees.
Q. What is the thing to do if you lose a ball that belongs to one of your friends?
A. Then you can't find it.
Q. What should you do about it?
A. Then you can't play baseball.
Q. It was your friend's ball and you lost it. What should you do for him?
A. Then you *have* to play ball.

There was an overall trend in Mike's responses toward greater order, logic, and efficiency of thought as the questions and concepts with which he had to deal became more abstract and removed from the level of everyday experiences. Thus, questions which dealt purely with conceptual classification received focused answers, whereas those of more immediate practical or social quality elicited peripheral and subjective, self-related associations. This reaction was apparent, too, on nonverbal tasks, but in these areas, on the whole, he functioned with glaringly greater accuracy and efficiency, producing scores that ranged from average to beyond the ceiling of the WISC-R (Wechsler, 1974). The result was a gross discrepancy between his scores on the verbal and performance portions of the test (verbal I.Q. score 79, performance 129). When asked directly to distinguish between reality and fantasy, he was emphatic in calling fantasy notions "make-believe." However, his responses to the Rorschach fluctuated between a quite articulate view of reality, and reality markedly distorted by emotion laden fantasies. There was a tendency also for separate concepts to lose their distinctive boundaries and meld, forming incongruous and totally subjective conceptual categories, and an assuredness in his manner of rationalizing these that further confirmed the looseness of his grasp on reality. Mike now bore unmistakeable resemblance to an adult schizophrenic.

JOSE (AGE 5 YEARS, 5 MONTHS)

Jose, the only child of an intact Puerto Rican family, was referred by a pediatric psychiatry service to which the mother had brought him partly because she could no longer cope with his seeming refusal to respond to any means of discipline but the belt, and partly because of his continued lack of verbal behavior after two years of remedial speech training. There were no reported findings of hearing loss. The mother was observed to react to Jose in a generally punitive and extremely demanding fashion, to which he responded oppositionally and aggressively (e.g., hitting her back when she went at him with the belt). The relationship between them appeared as an ongoing power struggle. Psychological evaluation in Spanish had failed because of his inattention to tasks and queries alike, and questions of his intelligence, relatedness, and linguistic development remained open.

Jose's examination was undertaken with a Spanish-speaking psychologist present so that attempts to reach him in English could be reiterated in Spanish if they failed. Both languages were spoken in the home. Since he refused to separate from his mother, she accompanied him into the room. From the start, his behavior was extremely hyperactive, inappropriate, and at first glance, strange. He danced about in a silly manner as though showing off, made faces and laughed, and got into just about everything in the office. He seemed actually to be taunting the mother, almost as if intentionally embarrassing her, and her loud admonitions and threats with the hand failed to slow him down. He uttered no sounds other than laughter at this stage. The mother stated that he understood words and used a few, such as "milk" or "water" in Spanish to indicate his wants, and she appeared utterly distressed by the situation. She complained helplessly of his "strong-headed" refusal to respond, and noted that he had learned to use one full sentence: "I don't want to," with vexing consistency. She was equally upset about the fact that he had attended a speech clinic for two years, "and still nothing is done about helping Jose to speak."

After a full ten minutes of hyperactive behavior, Jose calmed down quickly in response to a simple form-board task which he performed with alacrity. He maintained this calm long enough to look at some animal pictures. Coaxing and cajoling by the examiners to get him to name or point to specific animals failed to produce anything until the mother, apparently unable to constrain herself any longer, pointed to a dog and said, "wow-wow." He echoed the utterance and then pointed to a dog among four other objects in another picture. Then he grew restless and began investigating objects about the room but now in a notably less active fashion. Finally, with a good deal of soft-toned reassuring, and being shown where his mother would wait, he allowed her to leave the room, repeatedly saying "bye bye" after her disappearance. At that point, his behavior changed dramatically.

Alone with the examiners, Jose began by appropriately participating in a game of catch, which he appeared to thoroughly enjoy. He waited quietly for his turn and even checked, by means of gesture, to be sure the examiner was ready to receive his throw. After this, he engaged in a number of nonverbal tasks (e.g., bead stringing, complex block building) with little, if any distraction. However, when attempts were made to initiate purely verbal activities, his distraction and restlessness started afresh. Directions were responded to with variable accuracy in both English and Spanish, but he showed no indication that he comprehended anything without demonstration and gesture. He displayed, by his appropriate use of a number of objects, that he was very aware of what things are for and made fairly subtle conceptual distinctions. Once, as the examiners were exchanging observations, he picked up a crutch and gave a well controlled and convincing impression of a person with a broken leg, showing obvious pleasure when this was met with surprised approval. He was also able to draw straight lines in imitation, copied a circle with fair accuracy, and produced a square that was nearly creditable at the five-year-old level.

The dimensions of Jose's linguistic difficulties became more evident when he was taken out into the momentarily empty children's ward and shown the murals of children, clowns, and Walt Disney characters that decorated its walls. He pointed enthusiastically but uttered nothing. Then the examiner began teaching him to label the pictures, with the following results:

E.   What is this?
J.   What is dis?
E.   It's a doggie, doggie. Say dog-gee.
J.   Goggy.
E.   Daw-ga-ee!
J.   Oggady.
E.   Daw-ga-ee!
J.   Doggy.
E.   What is this? A doggy!
J.   Doggie.
E.   What is it?
J.   Oggdy.
E.   Doggy.
J.   Doggy.

When Jose had repeated the word correctly with accurate pointing about a half-dozen times, the examiner turned to another picture and he learned to label a girl consistently as a "dirl." Returning to the dog, however, he was at a total loss, simply pointing silently or echoing when asked, "What is this?" "Doggy" was retaught in the same fashion, and he then was requested to name the girl. There was no response, and he reacted as though he had never heard "girl" before when it was uttered together with "cat" and "clown." Attempts to teach other words, in association with objects or pictures, had the same result. After he had learned to label a moon repeatedly, he ran about identifying every circular object as "moon," but a momentary distraction obliterated his recall for that word as well. Nevertheless, his enthusiasm for the activity did not abate, and he showed no concern about his mother's absence, even though she had disappeared from her seat and returned an hour late to pick him up. At the end, he made an obvious demonstration of not wanting to leave with her and tried to reengage the examiner in play and picture naming.

Jose's difficulties were quite clearly dysphasic in origin. There was more than suggestive evidence of auditory imperception, in his inability to respond to purely verbal directions and in his garbled attempts to imitate spoken words. Although he could learn to say them with some consistency after repeated, slowly enunciated exposures and associate them temporarily with referents, his inability to commit them to memory was so severe that he could no longer recognize them, much less use them moments later. On the other hand, his nonverbal behavior indicated that he was not nearly so bereft of concepts as he was of words to label and express them. For all intents and purposes, however, his lack of verbal comprehension and auditory memory undoubtedly limited his capacity for abstract conceptual learning. As for any question of basically psychotic thinking, this was negated by the remarkable shift in behavior and the uniformly appropriate relatedness and organization he showed once he no longer had to contend with the mother. The impression was that they were locked into a mutually impossible situation, with her persistent demands and helplessly desperate attempts to enforce compliance on one side, and his incomprehension, incapacity to express himself verbally and aggressive oppositionalism on the other. It appeared that the situation was equally disturbing for the child and the mother.

BELLE (AGE 6 YEARS, 4 MONTHS)

Belle was a strikingly pretty little girl, the only child of well-educated parents. She had come to a psychiatric service because of her intractably unmanageable and incongruous behavior. She was prone to sudden but short outbursts, and highly variable shifts in mood. She could be unpredictably winsome or negative and hostile in her ways, and was at times quite withdrawn. Her language was generally accurate and quite complex for a six-year-old, but occasionally interspersed with babyish or noncommunicative words. She was highly voluble in her interactions with adults and her conversational mannerisms and demeanor could be precocious, but she frequently took little account of the intent of what was spoken to her. She tended either to twist the speaker's meaning to fit her own reaction, preconception, or current preoccupation, or else continued on with her own line of discourse as if nothing had been said to her. She usually did not ask for explanations of things, simply imposing her own without hesitation. She was reported to become obsessed with particular subjects, such as boats, for days on end, which she pursued despite attempts to divert her interest. Conversely, her talk could change directions precipitously, from the immediate to the abstract and from the sensible to the fantastic, in midtopic and with little or no logical sequence. In short, Belle's communication appeared hampered predominantly in its ideational disorganization and its lack of regard for the understanding of others, to an extent that was appropriate neither to her age nor her obviously high level of conceptual ability.

From the outset of her evaluation, Belle moved in and out of contact with the examiner. At times she would smile and interact with charm, and then break into fantasy or withdraw and stare intensely at some object in the room. She might begin to respond placidly to an innocuous question, and then in midsentence impulsively refuse to continue. At other times, she spoke of her likes and dislikes with a tone of familiarity that might be reserved for an old acquaintance, yet she showed only a vague recollection of who the examiner was from one day to the next. When test materials were introduced, she would start at them methodically and with accurate comprehension of what was wanted and then, though they posed no particular difficulty for her, suddenly and angrily scatter them about the room. These outbursts quickly subsided, only to reappear inexplicably in the midst of another activity. There was no evidence of visual-motor dysfunction—in fact, she was able to grasp complex spatial relationships and draw geometric designs with an adroitness well beyond her age level. As she grew tired of the test situation, she would shout loudly about some other topic, drowning out the examiner's voice and clapping her hands over her ears.

In spite of the fact that Belle spoke with some apparent comprehension about such things as electrons and colors of the spectrum, and displayed a detailed knowledge of boats (i.e., hull, sails, keel, etc.), she could not correctly give common information such as the number of days in a week or pennies in a nickel, haughtily protesting being asked about things "I already know." That these instances represented gaps in everyday knowledge rather than lapses of recall, was evident from the fact that she did not recognize the correct responses when they were furnished. She gave substantial indication of a high degree of abstract concept formation for her age, but it was frequently embedded in answers that began peripherally and wandered off into totally subjective issues. For example, asked in what way a penny and a nickel are alike (Wechsler, 1974), she went on at length about robbery and stolen money, ending with: "If you kill, you could get killed back, right? Only if I shoot somebody, I might get killed." In response to a similar question about beer and wine, she stated, "Get high; he has to be terribly high . . . a man hammered up on a cross." Brought back to the issue of the likeness of beer and wine, she remarked: "I don't like it! I don't drink it! I get sick! I'm not old enough. Do you drink it? Why do you like it? You like it better than water?" Characteristically, she left no room for answers to her queries, and immediately moved on to something else.

Belle did accept limits to her behavior when they were imposed loudly and firmly, but maintained them for only brief periods. She showed comprehension of complex verbal directions and questions by either responding accurately, contradicting what was said, or incorporating it into her loose chain of associations. At no time did she appear to be at a loss for a word, but she sporadically did use words arbitrarily and without apparent phonemic or sematic association with words that might fit the context. Describing what she saw in a Rorschach inkblot, she pointed to a vaginalike area: "That looks like a rings, clapping rings." Although the examiner expressed puzzlement and asked for an explanation, she just continued: "A fuck it, fuck it, fuck it, fuck it, fuck it. I'm making a real paper doll." At other points, she mentioned "a glassy" and "a peeve," but likewise ignored requests for explanation. Overall, her reactions to the Rorschach were perseverative and, in most cases, had little relation to the physical properties of the inkblots. Further, she seemed to lose the distinction between the relatively amorphous blots and actual pictures, noting, "That's a—oh yuk! Get that out of here! . . . I don't want to look at these anymore! They're too terrifying!"

Belle's subjective use of her essentially well developed linguistic ability, and the erratic quality of her interchanges are exemplified in the following:

B. (Engaged in drawing detailed pictures one after another), That's a house. I like ships. No, it's not dammit! It's a teepee, a tent!

E. Who lives in it?

B. Goo-goo, Mimi, glasssy Mimi. Mimi's a real person. (Draws a human figure.) That's a goo-goo person.

E. What is a goo-goo person?

B. A person who has that kind of head—a man. (Shortly after this she begins including crosses in all of her drawings.)

E. What are those?

B. You know how many crucifixions we have with the man on the cross? Nine. Do you like them?

E. Do *you* like them?

B. There's a man I love on one. He's not there on the cross anymore (pointing to the picture), but he's still in heaven. Maybe he's still dead, but maybe he lost the cross.

E. Who is he?

B. You don't want to talk about crucified because it makes you crucified. I like to look at it. I'm brave. I'd like to talk with the river sometimes, but he's dead. I shot him. Today.

E. Who?

B. I don't tell you! It's a secret! I already know. Why don't you think I know it?

THERESA (AGE 7 YEARS, 11 MONTHS)

Theresa's referral to an outpatient children's clinic was precipitated by her parochial school, where concern was expressed about possible mental retardation or learning disability and hyperactivity, and an increasingly withdrawn attitude in the classroom. In the past, there had been complaints about fighting with her classmates, and being socially isolated by them as a result. Her mother was anxious about Theresa's problems, questioned her own possible role in them, and cooperated fully during an evaluation that extended over six sessions. The father, however, totally denied that any problem existed, and obstinately refused to come to the clinic. Both parents helped the child extensively with her schoolwork at home. The mother worried about her own lack of patience at times, while the father was described as warm and understanding in his approach to his daughter, but persistent in his demands. There were no complaints about seriously problematic behavior at home, nor about difficulty in communicating with the girl. The mother noted, however, that sometimes she "looked sad or scared" most often following a homework session with her father.

An extensive psychological evaluation was undertaken with Theresa, the results of which indicated a child of generally dull-normal intelligence with specific linguistic dysfunctioning that further lowered her performance. She was somewhat reticent and withdrawn during the initial session, but had warmed up to spontaneous conversation by the end of it. In subsequent sessions, an open and appropriately familiar relationship developed. She was always fully aware of the immediate situation, initiated interactions, and varied in mood from the serious to the playful according to the circumstances. She did grow quite frustrated, whiney and petulant, evasive, distractible, and even withdrawn, but these reactions were linked to difficulties in testing and followed a predictable pattern.

Theresa's linguistic anomalies focused around faulty immediate verbal memory, auditory incomprehension, some possible imperception, anomia, word loss in running speech, and paraphasia. Her syntactical usage was variably awkward, but it was not clear how much of this awkwardness was related to what she had learned from her environment and how much was due to her disability. Her reading was somewhat halting but fairly accurate, yet she showed an obvious discrepancy between the accuracy with which she read, and her comprehension. In the auditory-vocal realm, when she was presented with sentences of more than a half-dozen or so syllables, she was prone to both lose and distort details. Though she was usually able to get the general drift of what was said, her understanding of the message rapidly deteriorated with the length and complexity of the sentence. This response held true for reading as well as for sentences spoken to her. When the problem was described to the mother, she stated with surprise, "Oh my gosh, that's what it is—when she reads to me—by the time she gets to the end of a sentence, she can't remember what the beginning said." The problem was complicated further by the fact that Theresa grew noticeably tense and anxious as it occurred, which in turn undermined her concentration and added to the loss and confusion. An example or two from her immediate recall of spoken sentences gives the flavor of the difficulty:

E.   Say after me, "Suzie has two dolls and a brown teddy bear."
T.   Suzies has a dog-brown teddy bear.
E.   Peter would like to have new boots and a cowboy suit.
T.   Teddy wanted shoes and a cowboy suit.

She, herself, indirectly described the problem when she insisted to the examiner: "Say just one part—say it easy—not the whole thing." Repeating a sentence a number of times over with slow and emphatic enunciation helped to some degree, but still there were frequent distortions of detail. Later, when the difficulty was reported to others who were familiar with Theresa, they displayed initial disbelief, since they knew the child to have a particularly keen memory for the details of things she had seen.

The anomia and word loss were both marked, but more obvious in response to test questions than in conversation, where she used clipped phrases and changed the topic often. At times on test items, it was very apparent that she knew the required concept but was at a loss for the word that succinctly expressed it. Asked in what way a cat and a mouse are alike, she responded: "A cat is—is a mouse. The cat is a cat—meow. The mouse is a—I don't know how a mouse goes. They both—they're a—they—they are—they ain't food. They like a cat and a mouse and a dog and goat." Often, she responded accurately in verbal multiple choices, but also, quite often, she was at a loss in this testing as well. Her substitute words were both generically and phonemically related to the terms she could not retrieve, and at times she used the antonyms of intended words. Thus a knob was called a "tube," "air" was substituted for smoke, "stream" for stove, "straight" for round, "in" for on, "up" for down, and so on. Sporadically, too, she confused phonemes within words. For instance, Coney Island came out as "Clodey Island," "pakring" was given for parking, and "shict" for check. Upon occasion, particularly during a session when she was weakened by the flu, such anomalies were especially severe. When she was perkier, they were less marked and apt to be missed or passed off as the normal mistakes of a slow child with poor grammar.

The distinction between Theresa's linguistic disability and her concept formation was evidenced by her different performances on a vocal task of conceptual classification (WISC-R Similarities) and two visual tasks of essentially like conceptual functions (the Illinois Test of Psycholinguistic Abilities—Visual Reception and Visual Association [Kirk *et al.*, 1968]). The former was characterized by the sort of reaching and circumspect efforts noted above in the cat-and-mouse response, whereas the latter was marked by fairly quick and direct conceptual choices. The auditory-vocal task produced a score that was extremely below the norm for her age, yet the visual-task scores were only moderately below age expectancy. Her visual-motor functioning, looked at in a number of ways (drawing, block design, writing, etc.), were also moderately to slightly below what one could expect for an almost eight-year-old child.

ELIZABETH (AGE 8 YEARS, 3 MONTHS)

Elizabeth was the oldest of three children born to a 16-year-old mother. There was no father in the home. The child was first noticed to be different by neighbors when she was about three years old, and they asked if somehow she had learned to speak Spanish. (Neither the mother nor the people in the area were of Spanish lineage.) It was then that the mother noticed that Elizabeth did not interact with other children, but it was not until age five that she brought her to a pediatric service. From there she was referred to a psychiatric unit where she was initially seen to be suffering "possible childhood schizophrenia or possible aphasia with brain damage."

Observation in a therapeutic nursery was arranged, but Elizabeth rarely showed up. She remained at home with the mother and brother until she was eight years old, when the mother brought her back to the unit for help with school placement. Her evaluation was undertaken on an in-patient children's ward.

Elizabeth's relatedness and behavior improved a good bit over three months of hospitalization, but at the outset she simply walked around people she met and spent a large part of her time engaged in long, rambling soliloquies. She was described by staff as "sluggish" in her activities and, with the exception of occasional arm-flailing, just shuffled around like an old woman. In this state, it was difficult to tell whether the seeming neologisms she uttered were true neologisms or dysphasic distortions, or whether her circumstantial responses were totally psychotic or, perhaps partially, circumlocutions. Some evidence emerged as she began to relate directly to her peers. As her interpersonal behavior increased, so her language became clearer. Her stance toward other children, however, became that of a bossy mother rather than a playful child. It now became possible to test her, and in school her reading test yielded a 3.6 grade level score in accuracy, coupled with zero comprehension. There were still some consistent errors of word order in her speech, but she was never at a loss for words, though using them with variable semantic accuracy. Her EEG was minimally to moderately abnormal, indicating a right cerebral dysfunction, and her drawing of geometric designs was not only disorganized, but also showed gross distortions of visual-motor coordination. In fact, her overall motoric coordination was rather awkward, and she had a good bit of difficulty learning to jump in dance class.

When seen for psychological evaluation, Elizabeth was generally passive and pliant, and almost totally flat in her affective expression during the session. Her functioning with both structured cognitive tests and projective techniques was disorganized, and she only sporadically showed recognition of the examiner's intent in conversation or in testing. Even the simplest questions received tangential or disconnected answers, and she exhibited no apparent efforts to guess at or otherwise arrive at what the speaker wanted:

E.   (holding up his thumb) What do you call this finger?
E1.   (Holding up her own) It's mine. (pointing) It goes this way and that way.
E.   How many ears do you have?
E1.   I can hear you.
E.   With your ears, and how many ears do you have?
E1.   One ear, two ears.
E.   How many legs does a dog have?
E1.   See my legs? Miss P————put gopple on her legs.
E.   You have two legs. How many legs does a dog have?
E1.   A dog could bite me.
E.   What do you have to do to make water boil?
E1.   Put out the fire.
E.   But how do you make water boil?
E1.   A boil put some corn on.

When given verbal directions, she often behaved with equal inaccuracy. However, instead of performing common acts with common objects, she performed uncommon acts with common objects. For example, requested to sit at a table, she promptly climbed up and sat on top of it. As a result, Elizabeth's test scores were fairly evenly retarded across the board.

By the time she was approaching discharge, Elizabeth's communication was much more connected on the whole, and there were few linguistic anomalies in it that could be taken for dysphasic, except when she appeared to grow disorganized. As one staff member put it: "She has her off days, and she has her on days." Although she showed little trace of dysphasia during her "on" days, she was unquestionably psychotic during the "off" days.

KARL (AGE 7 YEARS, 8 MONTHS)

Karl's mother had been informed, much to her amazement and dismay, that her boy was having serious emotional difficulties in his third grade parochial school classroom. He was said to be variably withdrawn and engaged in strange and unexplainable behaviors that disrupted the class and greatly concerned his teacher and the principal. It was suggested that he might even pose a danger to other pupils. At times, he would respond to questions with a blank stare or a remark that had little to do with what the teacher had said. Bizarre mannerisms were reported—suddenly jumping up during a lesson and giving "bulletins" on irrelevant topics, gesturing as though he were writing or marking places in the air as he answered the teacher, or pacing about the room. On an occasion, he had pursued girls in the class, trying to peek under their dresses at their underwear and rear ends. Fighting, too, was noted, and recently he had menaced another boy with a pencil, as if to stab him, though he had not carried out the threat. On the other hand, his academic work was satisfactory, at grade-level in all areas, including reading and writing. By the mother's account, there was nothing very remarkable about his history, and there were no apparent problems at home. He was an only child, with a close, but far from symbiotic, relationship with the mother, and a seemingly positive one with the father. The father, busy and apparently denying the gravity of the reported problems, did not come into the clinic, and left the whole thing largely up to the mother.

When Karl was initially seen by the attending psychiatrist, he was quite reticent and anxious, but could be drawn out, and apparent dysphasic anomalies were noticed in his speech. An extensive psychological evaluation was undertaken. At the first session, Karl was prone to be quiet and somewhat withdrawn, but warmed up to the examiner's interest in the packet of comic books he was carrying with him. All were of the popular superhero or monster variety, but he was more interested in their antiquity than their contents. He proved to be a true collector of comics, and engaged the examiner in helping him find the publication date on some that did not have it printed on the cover. He began by asking: "How many years this one is?" Asked to read from one, he did so with good accuracy but exhibited difficulty in sounding out unfamiliar words aloud. There was no particularly notable comprehension problem, and he did not hesitate to ask for meanings when words stumped him. His utterances tended to be terse, and had something of a staccato quality to their flow, with frequent missequencing and awkward word usage. By contrast, the mother's language flowed smoothly and articulately, and gave the impression of no little intelligence. Karl's mood was generally positive and his affect quite appropriate, and when the demands of testing began to wear on him, he tried to avoid further involvement by making plausible excuses—"Gotta go now; my mother's gotta be some place." There were no hints of the "bizarre" qualities noted at school. (When this discrepancy was brought up later in reporting findings to the school, the contrast prompted a query about whether a child could be selectively psychotic in groups with his peers and fully normal in his interactions with certain adults.)

Karl was cooperative during testing, though usually halting and cautious in his responses. However, once he decided to open up to a particular verbal demand, he would pour out his explanations, replete with circumlocutions, gaps, word substitutions, etc. Further, he would emphatically demand that the examiner "write it down . . . everything . . . everything I say, write it," apparently to be sure that his shotgun effort at getting his ideas across could be interpreted for its gist later. This reaction fell in line with the fact that he, himself, used writing and reading as a means of ordering his linguistic activities and compensating for his defects. On a variety of tests, he showed that his level of concept formation was far above the norm for his age, and that he was basically superior in his logical abilities though his verbal test scores *per se* would indicate differently. The latter were evenly average, whereas tests using the visual modality to tap conceptual ability (ITPA Visual Reception and Visual Association) resulted in scores three to four years beyond his age. Also, purely nonverbal problem solving was markedly above average, though graphomotor behavior was only average. His verbal anomalies consisted of some apparent auditory imperception, and quite severe difficulties with word recall, missequencing, and syntax.

Karl's receptive problem, although relatively mild, did give him significant trouble. At times, he distorted key words in what was said to him in a way that changed the meaning totally and led to incongruous responses. For instance, hearing "new" as "two" in a remark about a comic book, he held it up and emphatically, but irrelevantly, contradicted: "No, no—one, only one!" Similarly, his spontaneous questions or remarks often took on strange connotations within the context of the moment because of the wording. For instance, when the examiner talked about a psychologist whom Karl would be seeing for a period of counseling about his problem, he tried to inquire about how long the examiner had known her. His query came out: "How many days did you meet her?" He could also completely perplex the listener with a single word substitution, as when he blocked on the word "put" and stated: "I'll leave out this thing there." Or he could sound as if he were expressing a twisted idea. Trying to explain the function of a nail, he said: "You hit it with a hand." The examiner remarked that that would surely hurt a lot, and he returned: "No—a ha'—a had—a hard one—(demonstrating a hammer) a stick like." One particular question, asked while Karl was responding to the Rorschach, led the examiner to momentarily doubt the soundness of his thinking:

K. (having just stated that a part of an inkblot looked like Dracula in his comics) Is the mind a tunnel?

E. A tunnel?
K. Yeah. In a catsle [sic: castle] where Dracula goes—haunted house—tunnels—haunted mind. Is the mind a tunnel?
E. (pointing to his head) You mean this mind?
K. Not this mind. (pointing to his head) A cave. It is a cave and tunnel?
E. Oh! You mean a mine, like a gold mine!
K. Yeah. Is a mine a tunnel like?

At the end of evaluation, time was taken to explain to Karl what the basis was for his problems in school, but he would have none of it. He totally denied experiencing any difficulties with language. "No, I know what words mean! I know all the words!" He did talk briefly about the fighting, singling out two boys in his class as the ones he always fought with or threatened, and noting that they made fun of him. Yet he also protested that they were his friends, that they liked what he did. He would go no further on this subject, but it appeared reasonable to conjecture that these two children might very well have instigated some of the "bizarre" behavior, with a promise of friendship to a classmate who was already singled out in the group as odd. Moreover, it appeared likely that his air-writing mannerism was related to a tendency to gesture to himself when trying to find words. It is possible that a dysphasic child, with relatively little difficulty in reading or visual memory, might try to keep answers he had read straight in his mind by visualizing them before attempting to express them. Although these conjectures could not be confirmed, they seemed more reasonable than assuming psychosis in a child who showed no trace of such behavior outside of school, in psychiatric interview, or in psychological evaluation.

FRANK (AGE 9 YEARS, 6 MONTHS)

Frank was another child referred to an outpatient psychiatric clinic for disruptive and strange behavior in school. His teacher complained of frequent fighting, periods of withdrawn behavior during which he would stare intently into space and become seemingly oblivious to everything around him, and sometimes bizarre statements. His mother had not been aware of a serious emotional difficulty, and his history was unremarkable. His academic work was satisfactory, and a partial psychological examination showed him to be capable of functioning at, at least, an above average level. There were no indications of perceptual-motor dysfunction or of linguistic problems. His response to the Rorschach, however, though not overly bizarre in content, was remarkable for the extreme concern he showed about maintaining a sharp line between what was real and what was unreal. In fact, his concern was more of an obsession that led him to classify the blots, and even small sections of blots, according to which ones were only ink blots and which ones were real pictures of real things. In the process, he confused the two and identified some articulately defined perceptions as unreal, and some ill-defined fantasy associations as "too perfect and real to be inkblots."

In interview, Frank was consistently pleasant and cooperative, responding to questioning freely, often going well beyond what was asked and gratuitously offering a good deal of information about his own thinking processes. He maintained an air of adultlike reasonableness throughout the session, even when he finally came to relate some strange concepts as fact. He was obviously a very bright child, capable of making keen conceptual distinctions on a cognitive test, but without the structure of focused questioning, his matter-of-fact logic and conceptualization could become markedly distorted. As to his confusion of reality and unreality, he was asked how one tells the difference between the two, he gave this reply: "It's like with dreams—I know by my shadow. If you have a shadow you're not dreaming."

When it came to factual material about his family, school, friends, and the like, Frank was consistently accurate and reasonable in his reports. He noted that sometimes he was "picked on" by his teacher for starting fights that he had not started, but then balanced this report by noting that sometimes he had actually been the provoker. Asked about his seeming absences, he described them as visual fixations that were self-hypnotic in quality: "I start staring at something and get fixed on it—can't move or hear anything—feel like a vegetable—lasts a couple of minutes, and you just wake yourself up." He spontaneously offered that he might have ESP, since he could sometimes foretell in his dreams particular future events of concern to him: "Like if there's gonna be a show on TV that's scarey, I dream about it so when I see it, I know what's gonna happen, and I won't be scared." He also related this to his fighting: "Like if I'm gonna have a fight, I can tell it before and be prepared." Asked if he could do this whenever he wanted, he said that it just "came on" him at certain times and only in his dreams. From this report, the following discussion ensued:

F. A dream can tell me when I die. I'm gonna know when I die.
E. Do you think a lot about dying?
F. Well, dying's not the worst thing. Like there's too much pollution and corruption. You'd be better off in heaven, if there is a heaven.
E. Do you think there's a heaven?
F. No. Why do we need a heaven, if there's pollution in a heaven? You'd be better off in the middle where there's a crucifier.
E. What's a crucifier?
F. Like if you blow your chance to go to God in heaven, there's a middle where the crucifier is and they put you on a cross and light you up with fire and you go straight to hell. Like there's sentinels. They're people who want to work for God and the devil, and you can't do both, so they go to the middle and become the crucifier. Like Cardinal Cook, he's the highest. He's a famous pope in New York, and there's this boy, Patrick Cook. He's his son—er, no— that's not right. The sentinels are next after Cardinal Cook. That's why I want to talk to him.
E. Where did you find out about all of this?
F. When I was an altar boy, I read a lot of books about that.

EMILE (AGE 6 YEARS-7 MONTHS TO 8 YEARS-7 MONTHS)

Emile presented the particularly confusing diagnostic issues involved when a child is both dysphasic and psychotic. He was first brought to the hospital by the police, in a frightened, incoherent, and obviously psychotic state. His mother had been found wandering the streets in the throes of a paranoid episode, while her child was left alone at home. The mother was a woman, 40 years of age, quite dependent and anxious, and prone to periods of despondency and poor judgment. Normally, she was not an inattentive parent, and a close bond existed between her and her child. She had a real desire to do the right things for him, in spite of her own difficulties, though her judgment was not always the best. As an example, on one occasion she had heard that alcohol baths were good for one, so she began liberally lacing her child's steamy bath with rubbing alcohol every night, and was puzzled by his headaches and grogginess each morning. Although aware of the variable incomprehensibility of her son's utterances, she understood his communications quite well and attributed his strange words to his speaking French. However, he had never really been exposed to French, his French-Canadian father having returned to Canada when Emile was an infant.

Shortly after admission, Emile was approached for examination and responded pliantly and passively, taking the examiner's hand immediately and allowing himself to be led into the office. He appeared frightened and was totally unspontaneous, responding only to direct questioning in a soft voice that grew inaudible at times. His responses were frequently only tangentially related to the questions, and invariably represented a preoccupation with negative events that had occurred very recently in his life. For instance, when asked: "Where do you live?" he responded: "Mother got sick—she say, 'Leave me alone.' " His language was disconnected and littered with seeming neologisms, much like those seen in an adultlike psychotic episode. Yet, quite often, the neologisms seemed to approximate words that would have made sense in the overall context of the inquiry or in the context of his preoccupation. The query: "Do you go to school?" elicited: "Police there—in a blalance [sic: ambulance] to the hospital." He responded to questions of general factual information, such as: "What day comes after Monday?" with: "I don't know." A few days later he was much more responsive and more variably relevant and tangential. Over the course of six weeks, his seeming neologisms disappeared for the most part and, although still uttering distorted words, they now appeared more consistently related to real words and to the context of what was said. He came to greet the examiner spontaneously on the ward, but made no moves toward interacting. Generally he remained quiet, and responsive only to direct questions during sessions, but he gradually became more at ease, to the point of smiling appropriately to the examiner's occasional joking and kidding.

During this period, Emile was seen for psychological evaluation and his performance over a number of sessions paralleled his behavior in interview. The quality, and in some cases even the scores, of his intellectual testing, indicated at least above average and more probably a basically superior cognitive capacity. There was an in-and-out aspect to his efficiency in most areas, and abstract and logical responses were interspersed with poorly focused associational ones. He could say that an apple and a banana were "fruit" and a cat and a mouse were "animals," but stated that a candle and a lamp were "big." He defined a bicycle as "riding," a nail as "bang in with a hammer," and gamble as "play cards," but a thief was a "man whistling," join was "chewy," and diamond a "domino." At times he seemed to be repeating distortions of words just spoken, misperceiving and misunderstanding questions, or substituting words for ones he could not recall, but there was usually no way to distinguish between these and tangential associations since he would not respond to further inquiry once he had given an answer. His language was clipped and one-word responses were in the majority. When he spoke in short sentences, words were elided or used in ungrammatical forms. In nonverbal areas, he performed in a similar in-and-out fashion, except in one notable instance. Presented with a task requiring both good spatial perception and analytical nonverbal thought (WISC-Block Design), he demonstrated a consistently efficient and methodical approach to the problem and attained a superior score. In his projective responses, he showed the same tendency toward reacting subjectively and relating everything to his own inner state, as he had in interview. The indication was that, although his initial perceptions of situations were objectively intact, they quickly became associated with events and feelings that were currently dominating his thinking. The result was an often irrelevant and disconnected flow of ideas which, when communicated, gave one the feeling of tuning in somewhere in the middle of two separate trains of thought that kept switching tracks. Here, too, seeming neologisms and seemingly distorted words were apparent, but it was often difficult to tell the difference. An area of a Rorschach inkblot that was frequently seen as an animal was called a "crown velson," popular human figures were called "vestors," yet an area that very much resembles a bow-tie was referred to as "blow types," and a plausible tree was identified as "a high treeps." A month later, a second Rorschach administration was still replete with confusing neologisms and/or paraphasic substitutions, but was somewhat less subjective in logic and content. Now, however, a more amorphous view of things and a proclivity for impressionistic interpretations of events began to emerge.

Emile's apparently acute psychotic state gradually subsided during his stay as an inpatient, and after three months he was discharged to the status of a daycare patient, attending the ward school and activities and going home to his now recovered mother each night. A year after admission, still a day-patient, Emile was seen for an extensive psychological evaluation in order to gain some perspective on the still debated question of whether his functioning represented an acute reactive psychosis in a dysphasic child with basically sound potential for conceptualizing and relating to the world around him, or a psychotic episode in an inherently schizophrenic child whose picture was complicated by dysphasia. During these sessions, he presented himself as generally compliant, eager to please, and very dependent upon adult support. The examiner, a particularly perspicacious intern-psychologist, described his behavior as follows:

> Emile spontaneously grasped my hand when we first met, holding it especially tightly when we were in parts of the building which were unfamiliar to him. He tended to stare directly in front of him and speak in a soft monotone voice, only when I addressed him first. His difficul-

ties with auditory-verbal comprehension were apparent throughout testing. He frequently gazed steadily at me when I asked him a question, as if I would somehow give him cues which would allow him to respond. At times, he needed several repetitions before he could attempt an answer, while at other times, he seemed reluctant to acknowledge that he did not know an answer. He was quite motivated throughout testing, and it did not appear that his unresponsiveness on verbal tests was due to a lack of attention. I often had the sense that he was immobilized by his lack of understanding, and that he needed some intervention on my part which would imply permission for him to say, "I don't know." His comprehension of directions was erratic, but in general he had the most difficulty on tasks which involved verbal stimuli only. When concrete materials were presented, he was usually able to determine what was expected of him and respond accordingly. On one occasion, in a visual-motor task, he interpreted my instructions in an overly literal way, such that he performed unnecessary movements because he thought I had said to do so.

As things progressed during the sessions, Emile gradually became more relaxed, smiling spontaneously and talking more freely. In his case, unlike many other dysphasic children, the less structured and focused the demands, the more apparent was his expressive dysfunction. This difference led to the conjecture that a lack of structure might increase his anxiety and thus undermine his ability to compensate and exacerbate his linguistic distortions. The Rorschach was the only situation in which he used words of such distortion as to occasionally resemble the incomprehensible utterances of a year earlier. Many of these clearly represented phonetic approximations of words related to what he was describing (e.g., "crasure" for creature, "liver" for river). Some, however, did not seem to have either phonetic or conceptual association with what he was trying to get across (e.g., referring to animals as "bushed"). The forms he perceived in the inkblots, though, were usually quite clearly differentiated and objective. That the variability of his linguistic defects were not simply related to the lack of structure in a situation was evident in that his expression also worsened when he began discussing his own feelings and needs, either spontaneously or in response to questions. His sentence structure tended to become garbled, and he frequently elided connecting phrases and key prepositions. However, it was usually quite obvious in the gist of his discourse that his thinking was cogent and communicable.

In spite of the fact that the weight of evidence suggested moderately severe dysphasia in a conceptually intact child, there were moments when this was questioned, as when Emile collapsed past and present in a way that was reminiscent of his state of mind upon hospitalization. Characteristically, an understandable association triggered this action. For example, one day he was identifying the different wards in the hospital when he precipitously said: "I don't know what my mother is doing on NO-6." (It was over a year now since his mother had been hospitalized on that ward during her acutely paranoid episode.) Questioned about this, Emile went on with a lengthy narrative about his mother's activities at home, describing past events as if they were occurring in the present. Similarly, while discussing his desire to be a teacher when he grows up, he related things as though he were living the fantasy in the present in a manner typical of younger children. One could not, however, rest assured in construing these instances as evidence of psychotic thinking. Emile was a child who maintained a strong proclivity for fantasy and fantasy-play, the content of which was appropriate to his age level and showed no bizarre trends. In fact, his fantasy productions showed ingenuity. At one point during his daycare, he created and engaged in an elaborate imaginary TV show centered around hospital life, in which he assumed the roles of director and narrator. At times, he involved other children in these productions, and at other times he played them out alone. Though he could become engrossed in such activities, he could easily be called from them and could describe and discuss them objectively with an adult.

Emile's responses to projective techniques were now cogent and organized, and without indication of tangential or bizarre thinking. However, his imagery and story themes were invested with a strong sense of incompetence and ineffectiveness. He seemed to perceive himself more as the recipient of fateful occurrences which might fortuitously be either good or bad, than as an agent who could have any significant effect on the course of events around him. The stories he produced for the examiner were replete with people who were described as "sad" because they were unable to do something. Yet he always introduced a hopeful note that they would eventually succeed. In one particularly pertinent story he described a little boy as "thinking about something but he can't, *can't* do it!" Pressed for what the little boy could not do, he replied: "Type." Then asked how the story ended, he said: "It's gonna be working—the typewriter." Overtly, Emile rarely showed any marked anxiety about the anomalies in his expression, using both accurate and distorted words with equal disconcern and showing little struggle to get around the defects. That he was aware of the difficulty, yet openly denied any persistent disability, was apparent in his answer to a question about why he was coming to the hospital: "Sometimes I can't talk good, because I get a sore throat."

The parameters of Emile's linguistic dysfunctioning were now relatively clear. Receptively, his performance depended partly upon the complexity of the verbal forms presented to him, partly upon what contextual cues he could glean from the situation, and partly upon his familiarity with the conceptual relationships being expressed (as distinct from the syntactical ones). He had little apparent difficulty understanding simple declarative sentences or discrete words, no matter the relative concreteness or abstractness of their meanings. Problems arose when he had to rely predominantly upon syntactical relationships associated with the positions of words in relatively long sentences in order to ascertain meaning. Thus, by altering sentence structure to express the same meaning in two different ways, one could confuse Emile. When asked: "On what do you sleep?", he responded: "Bed." "What do you bite with?" elicited, "Food," and in this case he could respond: "You bite with teeth," only after the examiner demonstrated the act of biting. The difficulty with syntactical associations also appeared to affect his function on a task requiring a yes-or-no response to questions such as: "Do logs burn?" and "Do dials yawn?" (ITPA Auditory Reception). Here he had the most trouble when the syntactical relationships were not congruent with logical conceptual relationships. Although he could demonstrate the individual meanings of "dial" and "yawn," he was confused by the question.

In the expressive area, Emile's anomalies centered around word retrieval and syntactical construction. He showed excellent recall for specific facts, such as times, dates, and events, but words that he knew and used appropriately one day, were unavailable to him another day. He could use quite advanced vocabulary at times, and in the same discourse be missing extremely simple words. Yet he rarely just left gaps in his utterance, but usually filled in with substitutes. He was prone also to simply throw in a nonsense word if a somehow related substitute were unavailable to him at the moment, showing recognition of the accurate word when given a verbal multiple choice. His syntactical problem in expression paralleled that in reception. When he had to explain himself in more than three or four words, he ran into trouble with syntactical juxtaposition and ordering. Further, he tended to learn specific formats by rote, such as noun-verb-preposition-object, and could not freely generate alternate forms to express the same thing.

Emile had a good deal going for him in the way of abilities other than linguistic. His nonverbal problem solving was superior, and he could read very well. Moreover, he was an articulate gesturer and highly adept at acting out his meaning communicatively. When last seen before leaving the hospital program, two years after admission, he still showed essentially the same linguistic defects, but they had improved significantly. He was now able to comprehend more complex verbal instructions, and his expressive anomalies were much less noticeable. He also had become a highly motivated student, attentive to detail, and capable of working with intense concentration on difficult material without growing frustrated. Although he interacted and related spontaneously and well with both peers and adults, he remained something of a reserved child whose emotional reactions were appropriate but toned down, such as those of a pleasant, but somewhat shy, adult.

Over the course of Emile's involvement with the hospital, the question of childhood schizophrenia remained for some, though no one doubted his dysphasic disability. Of course the applicability of the diagnosis depends upon the criteria by which one defines the term "schizophrenic" and applies it to children. The presence of psychosis initially could be taken as an indication of schizophrenic vulnerability, and could be combined with the child's strong fantasy orientation and generally retiring personality to justify the application of the label. However, one must also consider the vulnerability of a dysphasic child, suffering a loss of compensatory mechanisms under the tensions and compounding anxiety and confusion in the face of a severely traumatic event. Further, one must consider the habitual fantasy orientation in light of such a child's difficulties in communicating comprehensibly with others, and verbally working out the day-to-day problems of growing up. The fundamental issue for the writers lies in one's orientation to clinical diagnosis as predominantly an application of preformed, symptomatic criteria in order to arrive at a classification versus an evidential consideration of the question: "What is specifically wrong with this child's functioning?" It was this issue, exemplified by cases such as Emile's, that prompted the writing of this book.

Epilogue

Thinking and concepualization are instruments in the service of adaptation of the individual to his social and physical universe. As all other adaptive mechanisms, thinking processes are the outcome of the interplay between the organic endowment of the species and the variety of experiences available in the environment. Concepts, ideas, and thoughts have their origins in those experiences which the growing child is capable of assimilating in every stage of development, and they in turn create the new mesh through which further meaningful experiential data are captured and assimilated. Because the enfolding of the child's cognitive potentials can take place only in a social context, the relative contribution of the neurological substrate and the specific experiential data cannot be fully separated. However, the overabundance of experiences, and the randomness of their occurrence, as well as their varieties, would not have lent themselves to categorization and abstraction in the absence of an innate organizing potential. This organizing principle is the most fundamental contribution of the central nervous system to the act and the process of conceptualization. In each stage of development, a logical matrix is constructed with the help of which percepts are collected, evaluated, interpreted, and categorized, and in the process, a more adaptive matrix with a wider range and scope is created.

Out of gradual accumulation and classification of concrete percepts and situations, an awareness of relationships is born, and the abstract matrices are generated which can incorporate a larger portion of the universe. By attending to relationships among objects and ideas themselves, a more advanced instrument for adaptation is provided.

The process of conceptualization receives a boost from another fundamental organic potential which is symbolization (and language function). Reflection on relationships could not advance beyond the most primitive level if objects could not be represented by symbols. And notions and ideas could not be exchanged, modified, and enhanced without an effective way of communication and a communal code.

From the adaptive point, any situation for which a ready-made solution is not available requires thinking. Adequate adaptation is based on adequate thinking, and the first step toward such adaptive strategy is refraining from impulsive action. The following stage requires identification of the task, the investigation of the prevailing conditions, and the selection of the most appropriate method for arriving at a solution. Thus, relationships between situations and objects or ideas are conceptualized with reference to previously acquired concepts and are articulated with the help of words. The formula thus generated is then evaluated as to its appropriateness to the task at hand.

It is clear that for development of the complex and orderly processes of thinking, the organic substrate must be free of any damage and deficit, and the social context must provide the appropriate content. Defects and disturbances of the central nervous system and/or the experiential content will be reflected in disorders and inadequacies of thinking and adaptation.

Over the years, investigators and clinicians have tried to separate those deficits which are traceable to the neurological damage from those which may have their origin in experience. The task has been made difficult by the observation that form and content of thinking are parts and parcels of an interacting and interdependent whole and are inseparably present in the production of thoughts in normality and pathology. As an example, we may consider the often repeated statement that in adult schizophrenia the sensorium is clear, meaning that the patient's grasp on spatial and temporal relationships is firmly established. However, it is also noted that when the patient is in an acute stage of fright, or in confusional states, these relationships no longer hold. Conversely, patients with clearly organic psychosis may use idiosyncratic and personal frameworks to interpret their experiences and form erroneous conclusions about reality.

In children, the formation of concepts, their hierarchial ordering and the selection and evaluation of experiences required for construction of the communal reality may be affected by organic damage and deviant social content. We are, therefore, only justified in speculating about the relative contribution of organic and psychosocial factors in generating the maladaptive forms of thinking processes. Attempts to differentiate between such global entities as organic versus nonorganic psychoses, particularly during developmental period, must rest upon the knowledge that there is no *a priori* reason for assuming that children with organic pathology are exempt from maladaptive mechanisms stemming from psychosocial factors. It is a generally accepted view that in organic psychosis the formal rules of generalization and organization are impaired, whereas psychoses due to nonorganic causes result in bizarreness of ideational and symbolic content of cognitive operations. However, poor organization, whatever the cause, will result in incorporation of unrelated fragments of percepts and concepts, and faulty generalization will be reflected in distorted ideation. Conversely, disturbances of motives, indifference to communally accepted goals and the primacy of emotional discharge which characterize the nonorganic disorganization may lead to disintegration of intellectual activities.

The above considerations make it necessary to focus on characteristics of impaired functioning associated with organic and psychological factors and the interpenetration and interdependence of these elements rather than attempting to establish clearcut criteria for differential diagnosis of clinical entities.

Cognitive defects, resulting from damage to the central nervous system, are primarily reflected in the following qualities: awareness; breadth and depth of attention; operation of the memory system; analysis and synthesis of perception, reception, and production of language; control and regulation of mood and impulses; and finally, the level and variety of concepts generated and comprehended. In addition to such clear signs of disturbance of awareness as momentary losses of consciousness, fluctuating awareness may be experienced as confusion by the patient himself or as lack of responsiveness of the patient by observers. Attentional deficits are known by absence of focus in the patient's verbal and nonverbal behavior or the patient's inability to withdraw his attention from a subject and the resulting perseveration. Patients themselves may report difficulty with concentration or inability to disregard extraneous stimuli. Memory may be impaired because new informations are not retained, old ones are impossible to retrieve, or fragments of past memories intrude into the patient's awareness without any desire on his part to remember them. Analysis and synthesis of perceptions are impaired in that the patient is unable to make appropriate differentiation between various stimuli, to make adequate evaluation of their similarities, and to arrive at proper classification of present percepts in relation to the previous mental set acquired by prior experiences. Thus, practical or constructive thinking is impaired because elements of perception cannot be converted into elements of construction for problem solving. This impairment, coupled with these patients' inability to refrain from impulsive decision, result in maladaptive activities exemplifying the patient's poor judgment. Inadequate reception and production of language in developmental period contributes to defective comprehension, problematic verbal learning, memory deficits, and, finally, disturbances of discursive thinking which require verbal-logical classification and organization of concepts. Furthermore, since abstract concepts are predominantly represented in symbols, defects in language deprive the patient of the full advantages of the communal code leading to difficulties in finding extensive logical relationships or analogies. The end result of a series of inadequate intellectual activities can be seen in the paucity of new concepts and concreteness in much of the classification of perceptions and skills which are dependent on abstract notions and logical conceptualization.

Psychosocial factors impair adaptive thinking because of the overriding importance of emotions and the idiosyncratic meaning attached to percepts and concepts. Evaluation and interpretation of relationships and objects are done only in self-referential manner, and the self and its experiences come to occupy a disproportionately large space in the center of the individual's thinking. Because the symbolic quality of relationships, objects, and situations dictate the choice of cognitive operations, it is not uncommon to find examples of concrete interpretations along with overgeneralization and abstruse abstraction. Furthermore, the patient's critical judgment about his own conceptualization is inoperative in these areas and concepts. Thoughts are formed without any attention to principles of proof and standards of evidence required in the processes of thinking. Although concrete demonstration may modify the distorted notions of patients with organic defects of cognition, such reasoning does not change the disordered thinking originating from psychological factors. Instead, only those maneuvers which decrease the intensity of experienced emotions may be helpful in modification and correction of distorted conceptualization.

When psychological factors are superimposed on organic defects, or organic pathology is added to the previously maladaptive thinking associated with psychological causes, the resultant disorder becomes more pervasive and crippling. Disorders of awareness are exacerbated by the patient's tendency to affective withdrawal and inadequate scope and depth of attention suffers further from the patient's inability to free himself from the grips of overwhelming emotions. Lack of regulatory power over moods prolongs the period of dysphoric affects resulting in overabundance of anxiety, anger, and depression and the rapid changes in their intensity and expression. Because the self-referential interpretation of present percepts and concepts results in their irrelevance to the previously accumulated memories, and, conversely, because the recorded experiences are in disharmony with the patient's present conclusions, the operations of the memory system, both in terms of registration of new experiences and the retrieval of old concepts, are disrupted. The fragility of the link to the past is even more pronounced when the patient's memory function is deficient due to organic causes. When the patient misperceives a situation because of psychological factors and is unable to refrain from impulsive responses due to his organically based cognitive deficits, the resultant solution is at best maladaptive, and at worst, appears bizarre and irrational. Thus, practical thinking, as well as discursive, logical deductions, is disorganized, idiosyncratic, and unfruitful.

Psychotic behavior during developmental period, particularly in early childhood must always be examined as to the possible contribution of organic and psychological factors in its etiology and expression. The organic portion may consist of generalized limitation of intellectual ability or deficits and delays in one or several specific cognitive functionings. Psychological factors may exercise a pervasive, deleterious effect on all cognitive functions, or their harmful consequences may be felt more strongly on those activities which are impaired due to organic causes.

References and Bibliography

Chapter 1

De Sanctis, S. (1906/1973). On some varieties of dementia praecox, in S. A. Szurek and I. N. Berlin (Eds.), *Clinical Studies in Childhood Psychosis.* New York: Brunner/Mazel. (Originally published in Italian, 1906.)

Maudsley, H. (1867). *The Physiology and Pathology of the Mind.* London: Macmillan.

Orton, D. T. (1937). *Reading, Writing and Speech Problems in Children.* New York: Norton.

Worster-Drought, C., and Allen, I. M. (1930). Congenital auditory imperception. *Journal of Neurology and Psychopathology* 9:289–317.

Chapter 2

Aug, R. G. (1974). The language of the autistic child, in E. W. Straus (Ed.), *Language and Language Disturbances.* Pittsburgh: Duquesne University Press.

Bartak, L., Rutter, M., and Cox, A. (1975). A comparative study of infantile autism and specific developmental receptive language disorder. 1: The children. *British Journal of Psychiatry* 126:127–144.

Bender, L. (1942). Childhood schizophrenia. *Nervous Child* 1:138–140.

Bender, L. (1947). Childhood schizophrenia: A clinical study of one hundred schizophrenic children. *American Journal of Orthopsychiatry* 1:138–140.

Bender, L. (1956). Schizophrenia in childhood, its recognition, description and treatment. *American Journal of Orthopsychiatry* 26:449–506.

Bleuler, E. (1911/1950). *Dementia Praecox, or the Group of Schizophrenias.* New York: International University Press. (Originally published in 1911.)

Bradley, C. (1941). *Schizophrenia in Childhood.* New York: Macmillan.

Brown, R. (1973). Schizophrenia, language and reality. *American Psychologist* 28:359–403.

Churchill, D. W., and Bryson, C. Q. (1967). *Looking and Approach Behavior of Psychotic and Normal Children as a Function of Adult Presentation.* Research Report No. 1. Indianapolis: Clinical Research Center for Early Childhood Schizophrenia.

Churchill, D. W. (1970). The Effects of Success and Failure on Psychotic Children. Research Report No. 5. Indianapolis: Clinical Research Center for Early Childhood Schizophrenia.

Cohen, D. J., Caparulo, B., and Shaywitz, B. (1976). Primary childhood aphasia and childhood autism: Biological and conceptual observations. *Journal of Academy of Child Psychiatry* 15:604–645.

Creak, M. (1964). Schizophrenic syndrome in childhood. Further progress report of a working party. *Developmental Medicine and Child Neurology* 6(5):530–535.

DeMyer, M. (1975). Research in infantile autism: A strategy and its results. *Journal of Biological Psychiatry* 10:433–452.

DeMyer, M., Norton, J., Allen, J., Stelle, R. and Brown, S. (1973). Psychosis in autism. *Journal Autism and Childhood Schizophrenia* 3(3):199–201.

Despert, L. (1938). Schizophrenia in childhood. *Psychiatric Quarterly* 12:366–371.

Despert, L. (1940). A comparative study of thinking in schizophrenic children and in children of preschool age. *American Journal of Orthopsychiatry* July, 189–213.

De Sanctis, S. (1906/1973). On some varieties of dementia praecox, in S. A. Szurek and I. N. Berlin (Eds.), *Clinical Studies in Childhood Psychosis*. New York: Brunner/Mazel. (Originally published in Italian, 1906.)

Eisenberg, L. (1957). The course of childhood schizophrenia. *Archives of Neurology and Psychiatry* 78:69–83.

Fish, B. (1977). Neurobiological antecedents schizophrenia in children. *Archives of General Psychiatry* 34:1297–1313.

Fish, B., Campbell, M., and Wile, R. (1968). A classification of schizophrenic children under 5 years. *American Journal of Psychiatry* 124:1415.

Frith, U., and Hermelin, B. (1969). The role of visual and motor cues for normal, subnormal and autistic children. *Journal of Child Psychology and Psychiatry* 10:153–163.

Gittleman, M., and Birch, H. (1967). Childhood schizophrenia: Intellect, neurologic status, perinatal risk, prognosis and family pathology. *Archives of General Psychiatry* 17:16–25.

Goldfarb, W. (1974). *Growth and Change of Schizophrenic Children in Longitudinal Study*. New York: Halsted.

Goldfarb, W., Braunstein, P., and Lorge, I. (1956). A study of speech pattern in a group of schizophrenic children. *American Journal of Orthopsychiatry* 26:544–555.

Helzer, J., Robins, L., Taibleson, M., *et al.* (1977). Reliability of psychiatric diagnosis. *Archives of General Psychiatry* 34:129–133.

Hermelin, B. (1978). Images and language, in M. Rutter and E. Schopler (Eds.), *Autism: A Reappraisal of Concepts and Treatment*. New York: Plenum Press.

Hermelin, B., and O'Connor, N. (1967). Remembering of words by psychotic and subnormal children. *British Journal of Psychology* 58:213–218.

Hingtgen, J. N., and Coulter, S. K. (1967). Intensive reinforcement of imitative behavior in mute autistic children. *Archives of General Psychiatry* 17:36–43.

Hingtgen, J. N., and Bryson, C. Q. (1972). Recent development in the study of early childhood psychoses: Infantile autism, childhood schizophrenia and related disorders. *Schizophrenia Bulletin* 5:8–54.

Hutt, S. J., Hutt, C., Lee, D., and Ounsted, C. (1965). A behavioral and an electroencephalographic study of autistic children. *Journal of Psychiatric Research* 3:181–197.

Kanner, L. (1943). Autistic disturbances of affective contact. *Nervous Child* 2:217–250.

Kanner, L. (1949). Problems of nosology and psychodynamics in early infantile autism. *American Journal of Orthopsychiatry* 20:556–566.

Kanner, L. (1954). To what extent is early infantile autism determined by constitutional inadequacies? in D. Hooker and C. C. Hare (Eds.), *Genetics and Inheritance of Integrated Neurological and Psychiatric Patterns*. New York: Grune & Stratton.

Kanner, L. (1968). Early infantile autism revisited. *Psychiatry Digest* 29:17–28.

Kanner, L. (1969). Children haven't read those books. *Acta Poedopsychiatrica* 36:2–11.

Kanner, L., and Eisenberg, L. (1955). Notes on the follow-up studies of autistic children, in P. H. Hoch and J. Zubin (Eds.), *Psychopathology of Childhood.* New York: Grune & Stratton.

Kanner, L., and Lesser, L. I. (1958). Early infantile autism, in *Pediatric Clinic of North America* 5(3):711–730.

Ketty, S. S., Rosenthal, D., and Wender, P. (1968). The types and prevalence of mental illness in the biological and adoptive families of adopted schizophrenics, in D. Rosenthal and S. S. Ketty (Eds.), *The Transmission of Schizophrenia.* London: Pergamon.

Kraeplin, E. (1918). *Dementia Praecox.* London: E. and S. Livingstone.

Mahler, M. S., Ross, J. R., and DeFries, Z. (1949). Clinical studies in benign and malignant cases of childhood psychosis (schizophrenia-like). *American Journal of Orthopsychiatry* 19:295–304.

Menalascino, F. J., and Eaton, L. (1967). Psychoses of childhood: A five year follow-up of experiences in a mental retardation clinic. *American Journal of Mental Deficiency* 72:370–380.

O'Gorman, G. (1967). *The Nature of Childhood Autism.* London: Butterworth and Co.

O'Gorman, G. (1971). The Psychoses of Childhood, in J. G. Howells (Ed.), *Modern Perspectives in Child Psychiatry.* London: Oliver and Boyd.

Ottinger, D. R., Sweeny, N., and Loew, L. H. (1965). Visual discrimination learning in schizophrenics and normal children. *Journal of Clinical Psychology* 21:251–253.

Potter, H. W. (1933). Schizophrenia in children. *American Journal of Psychiatry* 89:1253–1270.

Piggot, L. R., and Simson, C. B. (1975). Changing diagnosis of childhood psychosis. *Journal of Autism and Childhood Schizophrenia* 5:239–245.

Rutter, M. (1964). Intelligence and childhood psychiatric disorder. *British Journal of Social and Clinical Psychology* 3:120–129.

Rutter, M. (1974). The development of infantile autism. *Psychological Medicine* 4:147–163.

Rutter, M., Greenfield, D., and Lockyer, L. (1967). A five to fifteen year follow-up study of infantile psychosis: 11, social and behavioral outcome. *British Journal of Psychiatry* 113:1183–1199.

Rutter, M., Lebovici, S., Eisenberg, L. (1969). A tri-axial classification of mental disorders in childhood: an international study. *Journal of Child Psychology and Psychiatry* 10:41–61.

Ruttenberg, B. A., and Wolf, E. G. (1967). Evaluating the communication of the autistic child. *Journal of Speech and Hearing Disorders* 32:314–324.

Sahlman, J. (1969). *Pathological and Normal Language.* New York: Atherton Press.

Schilder, P. (1954). The psychology of the development of language and the symbol, in L. Bender (Ed.), *A Dynamic Psychopathology of Childhood.* Springfield, Ill.: Charles C Thomas.

Shapiro, T., Roberts, A., and Fish, B. (1970). Imitation and echoing in young schizophrenic children. *Journal of the American Academy of Child Psychiatry* 9:548–567.

Szurek, S. A. (1956). Psychotic episodes and psychotic maldevelopment. *American Journal of Orthopsychiatry* 26:519–543.

Ward, C. H., Beck, A. T., Mendelson, M., *et al.* (1962). The psychiatric nomenclature. *Archives of General Psychiatry* 7:198–205.

Weitzel, W., Morgan, D., Guyden, T., and Robinson, J. (1973). Toward a more efficient mental status examination. *Archives of General Psychiatry* 28:125–129.

Wing, L. (1978). Autism, social, behavioral and cognitive characteristics. An epidemological approach. in M. Rutter, and E. Schopler (Eds.), *Autism: A Reappraisal of Concepts and Treatment.* New York: Plenum Press.

Wing, J. K. (1966). Diagnosis, epidemiology, aetiology, in Wing, J. K. (Ed.), *Early Childhood Autism: Clinical, Educational and Social Aspects.* London: Pergamon Press.

Wolff, S., and Chess, S. (1964). A behavioral study of schizophrenic children. *Acta Psychiatrica Scandinavica* 40:438–466.

Chapter 3

Alajouanine, T., and Lhermitte, F. (1965). Acquired aphasia in children. *Brain* 88:653–662.

Benton, A. L. (1964). Developmental aphasia and brain damage. *Cortex* 5:40–52.

Benton, A. L. (1965). Contributions to aphasia before Broca. *Cortex* 6:314–327.

Benton, A. L., and Joynt, R. J. (1960). Early descriptions of aphasia. *Archives of Neurology* 3:205–222.

Berg, I. S. (1961). A case study of developmental auditory imperception: some theoretical implications. *Journal of Child Psychiatry and Psychology* 2:86–93.

Bloom, L., and Lahey, M. (1978). *Language Development and Language Disorders.* New York: John Wiley & Sons.

Burr, C. W. (1912). Congenital aphasia. *Pediatrics* 24:137–145.

Cantwell, D. P., and Baker, L. (1977). Psychiatric disorder in children with speech and language retardation. *Archives of General Psychiatry* 34:583–591.

Cohen, D. J., Caparulo, B., and Shaywitz, B. (1976). Primary childhood aphasia and childhood autism. *Journal of the American Academy of Child Psychiatry* 15:604–645.

Critchley, M. (1970). *Aphasiology and Other Aspects of Language.* London: Arnold.

de Ajuriaguerra, J., Jaeggi, A., Guignard, F., Kocher, F., Maquard, M., Roth, S., and Schmid, E. (1976). The development and prognosis of dysphasia in children, in D. M. Morehead and A. E. Morehead (Eds.), *Normal and Deficient Child Language.* Baltimore: University Park Press.

de Hirsch, K. (1973). Early language development and minimal brain dysfunction. *Annals of the New York Academy of Sciences* 205:158–163.

Dutty, R. J., and Ulrich, S. R. (1976). A comparison of impairments in verbal comprehension, speech, reading and writing in adult aphasics. *Journal of Speech and Hearing Disorders* 41:110–119.

Eisenson, J. (1963). Disorders of language in children. *Journal of Pediatrics* 62:20–24.

Eisenson, J. (1966). Perceptual disturbances in children with central nervous system dysfunctions and implications for language development. *British Journal of Disorders of Communication* 1:21–32.

Eisenson, J. (1968). Developmental aphasia: A speculative view with therapeutic implications. *Journal of Speech and Hearing Disorders* 33:3–13.

Eisenson, J. (1972). *Aphasia in Children.* New York: Harper & Row.

Ewing, A. (1930). *Aphasia in Children.* London: Oxford University Press.

Goldstein, K. (1948). *Language and Language Disturbances.* New York: Grune & Stratton.

Goodglass, H., and Kaplan, E. (1972). *The Assessment of Aphasia and Related Disorders.* Philadelphia: Lea & Febiger.

Gordon, N. (1966). The child who does not talk. *British Journal of Disorders of Communication* 1:78–84.

Guttmann, E. (1942). Aphasia in children. *Brain* 65:205–219.

Hardy, W. G. (1965). On language disorders in young children: A reorganization of thinking. *Journal of Speech and Hearing Disorders* 30:3–16.

Head, H. (1926). *Aphasia and Kindred Disorders of Speech*. New York: Macmillan.

Hecaen, H. (1976). Acquired aphasia in children and the ontogenesis of hemispheric functional specialization. *Brain and Language* 3:114–134.

Inhelder, B. (1976). Observations on the operational and figurative aspects of thought in dysphasic children, in D. M. Morehead and A. E. Morehead (Eds.), *Normal and Deficient Child Language*. Baltimore: University Park Press.

Jenkins, J. J., Jiminez-Pablon, E., Shaw, R. E., and Sefer, J. W. (1975). *Scheull's Aphasia in Adults*. Hagerstown: Harper & Row.

Lenneberg, E. H. (1962). Understanding language without ability to speak. *Journal of Abnormal and Social Psychology* 65:419–425.

Lenneberg, E. H. (1967). *Biological Foundations of Language*. New York: John Wiley & Sons.

Lowe, A. D., and Campbell, R. A. (1965). Temporal discrimination in aphasoid and normal children. *Journal of Speech and Hearing Research* 8:313–314.

Mark, I., and Hardy, W. (1958). *Language Acquisition*. Stanford: Stanford University Press.

Masland, M. W., and Case, L. W. (1968). Limitation of auditory memory as a factor in delayed language development. *British Journal of Disorders of Communication* 3:139–142.

McCready, E. B. (1926). Defects in the zone of language (word-deafness and word-blindness) and their influence in education and behavior. *American Journal of Psychiatry* 6:267–277.

McReynolds, L. V. (1966). Operant conditioning for investigating speech and sound discrimination in aphasic children. *Journal of Speech and Hearing Research* 9:519–528.

Meyer, A. (1974). The frontal lobe syndrome, the aphasias and related conditions. *Brain* 97:565–600.

Morely, M. E. (1972). *The Development and Disorders of Speech in Childhood*. Baltimore: Williams & Wilkins.

Myklebust, H. R. (1952). Aphasia in children. *Exceptional Child* 19:9–14.

Myklebust, H. R. (1954). *Auditory Disorders in Children*. New York: Grune & Stratton.

Myklebust, H. R. (1956). Rh child. Deaf or aphasic? Some psychological considerations of the Rh child. *Journal of Speech and Hearing Disorders* 21:423–425.

Orton, S. T. (1937). *Reading, Writing and Speech Problems in Children*. New York: Norton.

Scheull, H. (1969). Aphasia in adults, in *Human Communication and Its Disorders: An Overview*. Bethesda: NINDS, U.S. Department of Health, Education and Welfare.

Shoumaker, R. D., Bennett, D. R., Bray, P. F., and Curless, R. G. (1974). Clinical and EEG manifestations of an unusual aphasic syndrome in children. *Neurology* 24:10–16.

Silver, A. A., and Hagin, R. A. (1965). Developmental language disability simulating mental retardation. *Journal of the Academy of Child Psychiatry* 4:485–494.

Smith, A. (1972). *Diagnosis, Intelligence and Rehabilitation of Chronic Aphasics*. Final Report, SRS Grant 14-P-55198/5-01. Ann Arbor: University of Michigan Press, Department of Physical Medicine and Rehabilitation.

Tallal, P., and Piercy, M. (1973a). Defects of nonverbal auditory perception in children with developmental aphasia. *Nature* 241:468–469. (a)

Tallal, P., and Piercy, M. (1973b). Developmental dysphasia: Impaired rate of nonverbal processing as a function of sensory modality. *Neuropsychologia* 11:389–398. (b)

Tallal, P., and Piercy, M. (1974). Developmental aphasia: Rate of auditory processing and selective impairment of consonant perception. *Neuropsychologia* 12:83–93.

Tallal, P., and Piercy, M. (1975). Developmental aphasia: The perception of brief vowels and extend stop consonants. *Neuropsychologia* 13:69–74.

Weiner, P. S. (1974). A language-delayed child at adolescence. *Journal of Speech and Hearing Disorders* 39:202–212.

Weisenberg, T. H., and McBride, K. E. (1935). *Aphasia*. New York: Commonwealth Fund of New York.

Wepman, J. M., and Jones, L. V. (1961). *The Language Modalities Test for Aphasia*. Chicago: Industrial Relations Center, University of Chicago Press.

Worster-Drought, C. (1968). Speech disorders in children. *Developmental Medicine and Child Neurology* 10:427–440.

Worster-Drought, C. (1971). An unusual form of acquired aphasia in children. *Developmental Medicine and Child Neurology* 13:563–571.

Worster-Drought, C., and Allen, I. M. (1929a). Congenital auditory imperception (congenital word-deafness): With report of a case. *Journal of Neurology and Psychopathology* 9:193–208. (a)

Worster-Drought, C., and Allen, I. M. (1929b). Congenital auditory imperception (congenital word-deafness): Investigation of a case by Head's method. *Journal of Neurology and Psychopathology* 9:289–317. (b)

Worster-Drought, C., and Allen, I. M. (1930). Congenital auditory imperception (congenital word-deafness): And its relation to idioglossia and other speech defects. *Journal of Neurology and Psychopathology* 10:193–236.

Chapter 4

Blank, M. (1964). The mother's role in infant development. *Journal of the American Academy of Child Psychiatry* 3:89–105.

Call, J. D. and Marschak, M. (1966). Styles and games in infancy. *Journal of the American Academy of Child Psychiatry* 5:193–210.

Dunn, J. (1977). *Distress and Comfort*. Cambridge: Harvard University Press.

Emde, R. N., Katz, E. and Thorpe, E. (1978) Emotional expression in infancy: Early deviations in Down's Syndrome, in M. Lewis and L. A. Rosenblum (Eds.), *The Development of Affect*. New York: Plenum Press.

Escalona, S. (1962). The study of individual differences and the problem of state. *Journal of the American Academy of Child Psychiatry* 1:11–37.

Fantz, R. L., and Nevis, S. (1967). Pattern preferences and perceptual-cognitive development in early infancy. *Merrill-Palmer Quarterly* 6:77–108.

Fish, B. (1968). The maturation of arousal and attention in the first month of life. A study of variations in ego development. *Journal of the American Academy of Child Psychiatry* 2:253–270.

Kagan, J. (1976). Emergent themes in human development. *American Scientist* 64:186–196.

Safrin, R. K. (1964). Differences in visual perception and in visual–motor functioning between psychotic and nonpsychotic children. *Journal of Consulting Psychology* 28:41–45.

Sameroff, A. J. and Chandler, M. J. (1975). Reproductive risk and the continuum of caretaking casualty, in F. D. Horowitz, E. M. Hetherington, S. Scarr-Salapateck, and J. Siegel (Eds.), *Review of Child Development Research, Vol. 4. Chicago: Chicago University Press.*

Wolff, P. H. (1966). The causes, controls and organization of behavior in the neonate. *Psychological Issues.* Mong. 17. New York: International University Press.

Wynne, L. (1978). From symptoms to vulnerability and beyond: An overview, in L. Wynne, R. H. Cromwell, and S. Matthysse (Eds.), *The Nature of Schizophrenia: New Approaches to Research and Treatment.* New York: John Wiley and Sons.

Chapter 5

Anders, T. F. (1978). State and rhythmic processes. *Journal of the American Academy of Child Psychiatry* 12(3):401–420.

Bennett, S. L. (1971). Infant caretaker interactions. *Journal of the American Academy of Child Psychiatry* 10:321–335.

Bretheron, I. (1978). Making friends with one year olds. *Merrill-Palmer Quarterly* 24(1):29–51.

Campos, J. J., Hiatt, S., Ramsay, D., Henderson, C., and Swedja, M. (1978). The emergence of fear on the visual cliff, in M. Lewis and L. A. Rosenblum (Eds.), *The Development of Affect.* New York: Plenum Press.

Emde, R. N., Kligman, D. H., Reich, J. and Wade, T. D. (1978). Emotional expression in infancy: Initial studies of social signaling and an emergent model, in M. Lewis and L. A. Rosenblum (Eds.), *The Development of Affect.* New York: Plenum Press.

Izard, C. (1978). On the ontogenesis of emotions and emotion-cognitive relationships in infancy, in M. Lewis and L. A. Rosenblum (Eds.), *The Development of Affect.* New York: Plenum Press.

Lamb, M. E. (1978). Influence of the child on maternal quality and family interaction during the prenatal, perinatal and infancy period, in R. M. Lerner and G. B. Spanier (Eds.), *Child Influences on Marital and Family Interaction.* New York: Academic Press.

Lenneberg, E. H. (1967). *The Biological Foundations of Language.* New York: John Wiley & Sons.

Lewis, M., Brooks, J., and Haviland, J. (1978). Self-knowledge and emotional development. in M. Lewis and L. A. Rosenblum (Eds.), *The Development of Affect.* New York: Plenum Press.

MacFarlane, A. (1975). The first hours and the smile, in R. Lewin (Ed.), *Child Alive.* London: Temple Smith.

Mayo, C., and La France, M. (1978). On the acquisition of nonverbal communication: A review. *Merrill-Palmer Quarterly of Behavior and Development* 24(4):213–228.

Piaget, J. (1926). *The Language and Thought of the Child.* London: Routledge and Kagan Paul.

Piaget, J. (1937). *The Construction of Reality in the Child.* New York: Basic Books, 1959.

Sander, L. G. (1962). Issues in early mother–child interaction. *The Journal of the American Academy of Child Psychiatry* 1:141–166.

Schaffer, H. R. (1974). Cognitive components of the infant's response to strangeness, in M. Lewis and L. A. Rosenblum (Eds.), *The Origin of Fear.* New York: John Wiley & Sons.

Schaffer, R. (1977). *Mothering.* Cambridge: Harvard University Press.

Sroufe, L. A. and Waters, E. (1976). The ontogenesis of smiling and laughter: A perspective on the organization of development in infancy. *Psychological Review* 83:173–179.

Stern, D. N. (1974). Mother and infant at play: The dyadic interaction involving facial, vocal and gaze behavior, in M. Lewis and L. A. Rosenblum (Eds.), *The Effects of Infants on its Caregivers*. New York: John Wiley & Sons.

Chapter 6

Bates, E. (1976). Pragmatics and sociolinguistics in child language, in D. M. Morehead and A. E. Morehead (Eds.), *Normal and Deficient Child Language*. Baltimore: University Park Press.

Bloom, L. (1973). *One Word at a Time: The Use of Single-Word Utterances Before Syntax*. The Hague: Mouton.

Bloom, L., Hood, L., and Lightbown, P. (1974). Imitation in language development: If, when and why. *Cognitive Psychology* 6:380–420.

Bloom, L., and Lahey, M. (1978). *Language Development and Language Disorders*. New York: John Wiley & Sons.

Bowerman, M. (1976). Semantic factors in the acquisition of rules for word use and sentence construction, in D. M. Morehead and A. E. Morehead (Eds.), *Normal and Deficient Child Language*. Baltimore: University Park Press.

Boyd, E. F. (1975). Visual fixation and voice discrimination in 2-month-old infants, in F. D. Horowitz (Ed.), *Visual attention, auditory stimulation, and language discrimination in young infants*. Monographs of the Society for Research in Child Development, 39 (Nos. 5 and 6, Serial No. 158).

Brown, R. (1956). The original word game, Appendix in J. Bruner, J. Goodnow, and G. Austin (Eds.), *A Study in Thinking*. New York: John Wiley & Sons.

Brown, R. (1973). *A First Language: The Early Stages*. Cambridge: Harvard University Press.

Bruner, J. S. (1974–1975). From cognition to language: a psychological perspective. *Cognition* 3:225–287.

Bruner, J. S. (1975). The ontogenesis of speech acts. *Journal of Child Language* 2:1–19.

Culp, R. E., and Boyd, E. F. (1975). Visual fixation and the effect of voice quality and content differences in 2-month-old infants, in F. E. Horowitz (Ed.), *Visual attention, auditory stimulation, and language discrimination in young infants*. Monograph of the Society for Research in Child Development, 39 (Nos. 5 and 6, Serial No. 158).

de Ajuriaguerra, J., Jaeggi, A., Guignard, F., Kocher, F., Maguard, M., Roth, S., and Schmid, E. (1976). The development and prognosis of dysphasia in children, in D. M. Morehead and A. E. Morehead (Eds.), *Normal and Deficient Child Language*. Baltimore: University Park Press.

de Hirsch, K. (1973). Early language development and minimal brain dysfunction. *Annals of the New York Academy of Science* 205:158–163.

Eimas, P. D., Sigueland, E. P., Jusczyk, P., and Vigorito, J. (1971). Speech perception in infants. *Science* 171:303–306.

Eisenberg, L. (1964). Behavioral manifestations of cerebral damage in childhood, in H. G. Birch (Ed.), Brain Damage in Children, Baltimore: Williams & Wilkins.

Eisenberg, R. B. (1967). Stimulus significance as a determinant of newborn responses to sound. Paper presented at the Biennial Meeting of the Society for Research in Child Development, March 1967, New York.

Eisenson, J. (1972). *Aphasia in Children*. New York: Harper and Row.

Gordon, N. (1966). The child who does not talk. *British Journal of Disorders of Communication* 1:78–84.

Inhelder, B. (1976). Observations on the operational and figurative aspects of thought in dysphasic children, in D. M. Morehead and A. E. Morehead (Eds.), *Normal and Deficient Child Language*. Baltimore: University Park Press.

Lenneberg, E. H. (1962). Understanding language without ability to speak. *Journal of Abnormal and Social Psychology* 65:419–425.

Lenneberg, E. H. (1967). *Biological Foundations of Language*. New York: John Wiley & Sons.

Lieberman, P. (1967). *Intonation, Perception, and Language*. Cambridge: The MIT Press, 1967.

Meynuk, P., and Looney, P. L. (1976). A problem of language disorder: Length versus structure, in D. M. Morehead and A. E. Morehead (Eds.), *Normal and Deficient Child Language*. Baltimore: University Park Press.

Moerk, E. L. (1977). *Pragmatic and Semantic Aspects of Early Language Development*. Baltimore: University Park Press.

Morehead, D. M., and Morehead, A. E. (Eds.). (1976). *Normal and Deficient Child Language*. Baltimore: University Park Press.

Myklebust, N. R. (1952). Aphasis in children. *Exceptional Child* 19:9–14.

Penfield, W. (1965). Conditioning the uncommitted cortex for language learning. *Brain* 88:787–798.

Schlesinger, I. (1974). Relational concepts underlying language, in R. L. Schiefelbusch and L. Loyd (Eds.), *Language Perspectives—Acquisition Retardation and Intervention*. Baltimore: University Park Press.

Whitehurst, G. J. (1973). Laboratory studies of imitation and language acquisition: Is there an interface with the normal environment? Paper presented at the Biennial Meeting of the Society for Research in Child Development, March 1973, Philadelphia.

Wittgenstein, L. (1958). *The Blue and Brown Books*. New York: Harper & Row.

Wolff, P. H. (1966). The causes, controls and organization of behavior in the neonate, in *Psychological Issues*, Vol. 5, No. 1, Monograph 17. New York: International Universities Press.

Wood, N. E. (1975). Assessment of auditory processing dysfunction. *Acta Symbolica* 6:113–124.

Worster-Drought, C. and Allen, I. M. (1930). Congenital auditory imperception (congenital word-deafness) and its relation to idioglossia and other speech defects. *Journal of Neurology and Psychopathology* 10:193–236.

Chapter 7

Bleuler, E. (1911/1950). *Dementia Praecox or the Group of Schizophrenia*. New York: International University Press, 1950. (Originally published in 1911.)

Brown, R. (1973). Schizophrenia, language and reality. *American Psychologist* 28:359–403.

Campos, J. J., Hiatt, S., Ramsay, D., Henderson, C., and Swedja, M. (1978). The emergence of fear on the visual cliff. In M. Lewis and L. A. Rosenblum (Eds.), *The Development of Affect*. New York: Plenum Press.

Fromkin, V. A. (1975). A linguist looks at schizophrenic language. *Brain and Language* 2(4):498–503.

Kasanin, J. A. (1940). *Language and Thought in Schizophrenia*. Berkley: University of California Press.

Lewis, M., and Brooks, J. (1978). Self knowledge and emotional development, in M.

Lewis and L. A. Rosenblum (Eds.), *The Development of Affect*. New York: Plenum Press.

Maher, B. (1972). The language of schizophrenia. *British Journal of Psychiatry* 120:3–17.

Menyuk, P. (1975). The language impaired child: Linguistic or cognitive impairment. *Annals of the New York Academy of Science* 263:59–69.

Piaget, J. (1926). *The Language and Thought of the Child*. New York: Harcourt-Brace.

Potter, H. W. (1933). Schizophrenia in children. *American Journal of Psychiatry* 89:1253–1270.

Rapoport, D. (Ed.) (1951). *Organization and Pathology of Thought*. New York: Columbia University Press.

Rochester, S. R. (1977). Thought process disorder in schizophrenia. *Brain and Language* 4:95–114.

Shapiro, T. (1976). Language behavior in schizophrenic children as a prognostic indicator in schizophrenic children under 42 months, in E. N. Rexford, L. W. Sanders, and T. Shapiro (Eds.), *Infant Psychiatry: A New Synthesis*. New Haven, London: Yale University Press.

Tubbs, V. K. (1966). Types of linguistic disability in psychotic children. *Journal of Mental Deficiency Research* 10:230–240.

Werner, H. (1965). *Comparative Psychology of Mental Development*. New York: John Wiley & Sons.

Wynne, L. E. and Singer, M. T. (1963). Thought disorder and family relations of schizophrenics. *Archives of General Psychiatry* 9:199–206.

Chapter 9

Kirk, S. A., McCarthy, J. J., and Kirk, W. D. (1968). *Illinois Test of Psycholinguistic Abilities* (revised edition). Urbana: University of Illinois Press.

Rorschach, H. (1921). *Psychodiagnostics* (Plates). Bern: Hans Huber. (Distributed in U.S.A. by Grune & Stratton, New York.)

Terman, L. M., and Merrill, M. A. (1960). *Stanford–Binet Intelligence Scale* (3rd revision). Boston: Houghton Mifflin.

Wechsler, D. (1963). *Wechsler Preschool and Primary Scale of Intelligence*. New York: Psychological Corporation.

Wechsler, D. (1974). *Wechsler Intelligence Scale for Children-Revised*. New York: Psychological Corporation.

Index

Abstraction. *See* Symbolization
Acalculia, 36
Affect, distortions and deviations of, 18–20, 133–135
Agraphia, 34, 36
American Psychiatric Association, 7, 10
Anomia, 31, 33, 36, 110–111, 146–147, 153, 156, 176, 177
Anxiety, chronic, 19
Aphasia, 26, 28–38, 54, 56–58, 114
    acquired in adulthood, 30–32
    acquired in childhood, 32–38, 56–57, 115, 141
        prognosis, 37–38
    congenital, 29
    developmental, 29–30
    See also Dysphasia
Apraxia, 41, 44, 45, 48, 55, 151
Autism, 9, 11, 12, 13, 15–16, 17–18, 19, 21, 23, 24, 25, 29, 63, 166
    diagnosing, 26–27

Bender Gestalt Test, 130
Bleuler, Eugen, on schizophrenia, 9–10, 118, 120
Body intelligence, 127
Broca, 30–31

Cognition and emotions, 80
Cognitive organization, 96, 97–98, 189–193
Cognitive processes. *See* Thinking
Communication, 71–73, 81–85, 86, 88–89, 130–136, 141. *See also* Dysphasia; Psycholinguistic development

Comprehension of speech, 104–106
Conceptualization, 82–85, 189–190, 192. *See also* Thinking

Dementia, premature, 4
Dementia praecox, 9, 12
Diagnosis, difficulties of, 3, 5–6, 7–9, 10, 13–15, 17, 26–27, 138
Disability, psychological, 1, 7
Disease, definition of, 1
Disordered thinking. *See* Thinking
Down Syndrome, 61
Dysarthria, 35, 36
Dyslexia, 34, 35, 36, 44, 55, 152
Dysphasia, developmental, 29, 39–58, 108–117, 137–157
    and anomia, 110–111, 146–147, 153, 156
    and auditory perception, 144–145, 152
    behavioral characteristics, 142–157
    behavioral problems, 52–53
    and characteristics of language, 52
    characteristics of the syndrome, 40
    and deafness, 46–48, 57, 111, 115
    definition and origination, 137
    diagnosing and evaluating, 57–58, 138–142, 143, 155
    in early years, 142–151
    and emotional difficulties, 157
    and intelligence, 50, 57
    and linguistic development, 108–117
    prognosis, 54–56, 117
    in school years, 151–157
    and self-awareness, 155–156
    See also Testing

Echolalia, echoing, 21, 22, 42, 45,
131–132, 145–146, 151, 158
Emotional development, 79–81
Emotional reactions, distortions and
deviations of, 18–20, 68–71, 72,
157, 179–182, 192–193
Emotions, importance of, 192

Gall, 39
Generalization, 95, 96–97

Hippocrates, 30
Human relatedness, disturbances of,
16–18

Idioglossia, 45, 108, 146, 148, 167
Imagery, 88, 97, 114
Imitative behavior, 99–100
Intelligence
and childhood schizophrenia, 23–25,
183–184, 193
and dysphasia, 50, 57, 116, 153
and emotions, 68–69
and self-awareness, 66

Johnson, Samuel, 30

Language, 86, 88–89, 91, 95, 108, 142
classification, 56–58
and communication, 81–82, 83, 93
comprehension, 71–72, 83, 84–85
development. *See* Psycholinguistic
development
disorders, 20–23, 28–30, 34–35,
131–136, 137, 151
See also Aphasia; Dysphasia
Logical thinking, 84–85, 97, 126
Logorrhea, 35, 36

Maturation, 1–2, 4, 20
Meaning
conventional, 99–100, 104, 139
idiosyncratic, 192
Memory and comprehension, 105–106,
146, 193
Mental age, 7–8, 24, 139
Motivation, 84
"Mute" children, 20–21, 22, 26, 33, 34,
36, 45, 48, 158

Paragrammia, 33–34
Paraphasia, 31, 33, 35, 111, 117, 153,
176
Psycholinguistic development, 86–95,
142–143
auditory attention, 102–104, 108–109,
142–143
characteristics, process, course,
95–101
dysfunctioning, 108–111
dysphasic development, 112–117
expression, direction, reference, 93
functioning, 101–107
holophrases, 99
imitation, 99–100
nature and nurture, 87–88
and psychotic children, 131–136, 137,
157–162
reception, cognition, expression, 102,
107, 113
role of adults, 100–101
Psychosis
definition, 7, 121, 140
diagnosis, 136
Psychotic children, 137, 139–142, 155,
183–188, 190–191, 193
and language development, 131–136,
137, 157–162
See also Schizophrenia; Testing

Regression, 11, 14–15

Schizophrenia, 9, 17–23, 29, 118–120,
168, 187–188, 190
course and outcome, 25–26
differential diagnosis, 26–27
"hereditary taint," 12
and intelligence, 23–25
summary of literature, 9–16
Self-awareness, 65–68, 77–81, 124, 128,
132–134, 155–156, 161, 192–193
Socialization and social development,
56–60, 76
disturbed, 61–75
communication, 71–73
emotions, 68–71
factors, 61–65
self-awareness, 65–68
normal, 76–86
arousal and alertness, 76–77
communication, 81–82, 83

Socialization and social development
  (*cont.*)
  normal (*cont.*)
    concepts and symbols, 82–85
    self- and social awareness, 77–81
    visual behavior, 77
Stanford University Institute for
    Childhood Aphasia, 47
Stereotyped behavior, 127, 151, 158,
    166
Symbolization, 82–85, 87, 89, 96–97,
    122, 132, 189–190, 191, 192. *See
    also* Psycholinguistic
    development
Synergism, 4

Testing, psychological, 138–139,
    163–188
  boys, particular cases
    3 years 10 months, 165–168
    3 years 8 months to 9 years 3
      months (boy given girl's name),
      168–171
    5 years 5 months, 171–173
    7 years 8 months, 179–181
    9 years 6 months, 181–182
    6 years 7 months to 8 years 7
      months, 183–188
  girls, particular cases
    6 years 4 months, 173–175
    7 years 11 months, 175–177

Testing, psychological (*cont.*)
  girls particular cases (*cont.*)
    8 years 3 months, 177–179
    special difficulties, 163–165
"Things-of-action," 83
Thinking
  development, 122–126, 189–190
  disordered, 20–23, 72, 73–75, 109,
    118–136, 137, 142, 189–193
    categorization, 119–120
    and development, 122–126
    and manipulatory activities,
      128–130
    and physical activities, 126–128
    and verbal communication,
      130–136
  logical, 84–85, 97, 126, 189, 192

Values and psychiatric diagnoses, 1, 2, 6
Verbal restraint and unrestraint, 51–52
Verbalization, 82, 94, 98, 101–103, 113,
    121–122, 125–126, 130–136, 139
  and dysphasics, 149–151

Werner, H., 83
Wernicke, 31, 35
Word-deafness, 40–41, 43, 46, 55, 109
Word loss. *See* Anomia
Words, 89, 91, 97–100, 105–107,
    108–111, 122, 190. *See also*
    Aphasia